Country Life Guides

COUNTRYSIDE
of Britain
and Northern Europe

COUNTRYSIDE
of Britain
and Northern Europe

Editor Pat Morris

COUNTRY LIFE BOOKS

COUNTRY · LIFE
NEWNES·BOOKS

Published by Country Life Books an imprint of
The Hamlyn Publishing Group Limited,
Bridge House, 69 London Road, Twickenham, Middlesex,
England and distributed for them by
Hamlyn Distribution Services Limited,
Sanders Lodge Estate, Rushden, Northants, England
Created by Midsummer Books Ltd.
10 Barley Mow Passage, London W4 4PH

© Midsummer Books Limited and
The Hamlyn Publishing Group Limited, 1982
Artwork of British Birds
© Royal Society for the Protection of Birds
Fourth impression 1986

ISBN 0 600 35606 X (softcover)
     0 600 35607 8 (hardcover)

Printed in Italy

Contents

Useful addresses

Addresses of countryside-related organisations you can join or from whom information may be obtained.

Fauna and Flora Preservation Society
Zoological Gardens
Regent's Park
London NW1 4RY

National Trust for Places of Historic Interest or Natural Beauty
42 Queen Anne's Gate
London SW1H 9AS

Scottish Wildlife Trust
6 Dublin Street
Edinburgh EH1 3PP

Royal Society for Nature Conservation
The Green
Nettleham
Lincoln LN2 2NR
(umbrella organisation looking after all the local County Naturalists' Trusts)

World Wildlife Fund UK (has local groups too)
11–13 Ockford Road
Godalming
Surrey

British Trust for Nature Conservation Volunteers
10–14 Duke Street
Reading
Berkshire RG1 3RU
(organises practical conservation working parties)

Royal Society for Protection of Birds
The Lodge
Sandy
Beds SG19 2DL

Botanical Society of the British Isles
c/o Department of Botany
British Museum (Natural History)
Cromwell Road
London SW7 5BD

The Mammal Society
Harvest House
62 London Road
Reading
Berkshire RG1 5AS

Introduction

The British Isles, over 400 of them in all, face an ocean on one side and a continent on the other. From the ocean they receive a flow of warm water (in the form of the Gulf Stream) which serves to ameliorate climatic extremes, especially in the west. Winds tend also to come from the ocean more often than from elsewhere, having become moisture-laden, so the country is generally wet, especially in Ireland and western counties.

The continental influences are most obvious in the eastern regions, where winters can be bitterly cold due to the proximity of a large land mass (which cools much more in winter than does the sea) and to the winds that blow from it. Such winds bear little moisture, and prevailing westerlies have lost much of their rain before reaching eastern counties. The eastern regions are thus characterised by a drier climate with colder winters and warmer summers than are found in the equable west, where extremes are buffered by the effects of the ocean.

Climatic diversity is enhanced because Britain is long and thin. It spans 9° of latitude: a tenth of the distance separating the North Pole from the Equator. So Scotland has a generally cooler climate than the south, but also has longer days in summer (and thus more growing and feeding time per day).

Altitude, which is in turn governed by geological factors, also influences the climate and wildlife of an area. Temperatures and sunshine decrease markedly with increased altitude, so that the growing season at 600 metres is perhaps half as long as that at sea level. Moreover, moist air rising to cross high grounds gets cooler and deposits its water as rain. Uplands are thus wet, leaving drier areas in the "rain shadow" beyond the high ground.

Geology

The formation of Britain's fabric has taken over 2,600 million years to fashion. The oldest rocks are found in the north west of Scotland; the youngest in the south east of England. In between lies a diversity of rock and soil types, greater than anywhere else of comparable area in the world. The geological background is important because older rocks tend to be harder and thus resist erosion and remain protruding as mountains and high ground. High ground traps moisture, is cooler, and less grows

there. Younger rocks are smoothed by erosive forces and provide flatter landscapes and low rolling hills. Softer rocks erode more rapidly and contribute more of their chemical constituents to the soils derived from the rocks. Thus lowland soils are usually richer in nutrients. Certain rock types (particularly chalk and limestone) have a profound effect on soil acidity and calcium content; major factors in determining the distribution of many plants and animals.

Hard, old rocks provide jagged scenery and coastlines, steep rushing rivers and a generally more austere and open landscape. Younger rocks and the rich soils generated from them support a much greater diversity of species and a more varied landscape. They also are more fertile for agricultural use and provide flat land for towns, roads, airports and other major human modifications to the countryside. Today, man's is the greatest single influence in shaping the land and what lives on it, but in the past it was ice.

Britain's Ice Ages

During the last two million years there have been at least four major "Ice Ages" when masses of solid ice spread over Britain. In places it may have been several kilometres thick at times, and its tremendous weight gouged away rock, moulding and scraping the land, pushing soil and boulders to form new hills, and digging out valleys and basins which today contain major lakes and rivers.

In between the glacial epochs were long periods when the climate was often warmer than it is today. This alternation, over thousands of years, between a cold and warm environment, together with the direct effects of the ice, played a profound part in determining the flora and fauna of Britain today.

The effect of the Ice Ages on the British flora and fauna

At its maximum, the ice must have virtually covered Ireland, Wales and Scotland, and reached as far south as London. The last glaciation was less severe, but the ice did reach south Wales and the Wash, only about 20,000 years ago. South of the ice, open tundra vegetation covered the country, just as it does in northern Scandinavia today, and reindeer, lemmings and mammoths roamed the Home Counties. Very few of our present animals could have lived and bred here then –

mountain hare, stoat and perhaps pigmy shrew among the mammals; ptarmigan and dunlin among the birds. Otherwise the ice wiped the slate clean, so to speak. With so much water locked up in the ice, the sea level was about 100 metres lower than it is now, so that these animals would have been able to wander across the floor of what is now the English Channel and the North Sea.

About 12,000 years ago, the climate started to improve, and plants and animals spread north in the wake of the retreating ice. First birch, then pine, and then deciduous trees such as oak and alder spread back into England, and with them came associated animals; black grouse with the pine, wild boar with the oak.

Man adds to the land

Whilst he has destroyed some habitats, man has also created others. Similarly, having exterminated some species, he has introduced new ones. The pheasant, for example, must have been introduced, perhaps by the Romans or the Normans, and the fallow deer was probably introduced very early on.

The rabbit was also introduced; it was far too valuable as a source of food to be turned loose, and the Normans used to keep them carefully tended in enclosures termed warrens. The right to have a warren was a considerable privilege, a contrast to the modern attitude of farmers. The carp is another animal which was introduced in Norman times as a source of food; monasteries frequently had "stew ponds", used for rearing the carp needed for Friday's meat.

More recently, a number of animals have been imported for fur farms. The coypu, a large rodent from South America, and the American mink, have escaped and established themselves in the wild.

Many more foreign species have been imported simply for their aesthetic appeal. The muntjac and Chinese water deer were brought to Britain by the Duke of Bedford, but escaped and are now widespread. The edible dormouse and little owl were also introduced from southern Europe. The vogue for managing large estates in the nineteenth century resulted in the introduction of Sika deer from the Far East, and the red-legged partridge from the Mediterranean; both are now well established here. Canada geese, mandarin duck and, of course, the grey squirrel, also owe their original introduction to various park owners who thought they would look attractive in the grounds. This activity continues and many other exotic animals are locally established in the wild and may become more widespread (e.g. the golden pheasant, Egyptian goose, ruddy shelduck and even the ring-necked parakeet).

Thus the fauna of modern Britain comprises a legacy from the Ice Age, substantially modified by more recent human additions and deletions.

Habitats of Britain

Britain possesses a wide variety of habitat types, containing an astonishing diversity of plants and animals, but these are not randomly distributed. Generally the wildlife is found in "sets" of associated plants and animals; the same (or similar) species occur wherever the same physical conditions exist, to form a distinctive living community in each habitat.

And so recognition of a general habitat, and the "sub-habitats" within it, is an interesting and useful exercise when investigating our countryside and its wildlife.

The major habitat types found in Britain are described on the following few pages, though it must be borne in mind that habitats are rarely so clearly delineated: muddy shores grade into sandy ones; farmland, heathland and woodland are often a continuum, not discrete separate entities. Also, habitats evolve; a pond may gradually fill with weed and become a wetland habitat, followed later by the invasion of trees, ultimately to become woodland. Recognising habitat development and its causes can be very revealing, since it often indicates the changing regime of man's land management and introduces aspects of local history into the picture.

We hope that this book will be a useful guide to readers and that it will enhance their visits to the countryside. But we especially hope that their awareness will help strengthen the nation's will to give our wonderful countryside the care and protection it so desperately needs.

Inshore waters

Surrounding the coasts of Britain is a zone of shallow seas. Beyond lies the edge of the Continental Shelf where the sea bed plunges to great depths and the open ocean begins. Our shallow coastal waters are very productive, and the numbers and diversity of fish in coastal waters is considerable. Some species remain in large shoals well offshore, but others move in with the tide to feed in the shore area which has been exposed at low tide. These are the species most likely to be caught by line fishermen from the shore. Many sea birds, seals and other animals use these fish as a source of food. Inshore waters are also rich in plankton, much of which comprises the immature stages of the life cycle of intertidal animals such as barnacles, starfish and crabs.

The sea warms and cools only slowly, so maintaining an equable climate in coastal areas. However, it also provides an endless source of water vapour which descends on coastal regions in the form of rain, mist and sea fog. Coastal habitats thus tend to be moister than inland, especially in the west of Britain where prevailing winds come off the sea.

The region between high and low water marks is called the **'intertidal zone'**. The organisms that live here have to tolerate alternating conditions of exposure to the atmosphere and inundation by the sea.

Below the low water mark the sea bed is sandy and slopes gently. Wave action is

almost imperceptible here and organisms are never exposed to the air. Usually we only see these creatures when severe storms have stirred up the sea to an unusual depth and dislodged animals from their normally undisturbed habitat. They may then be washed up on the strandline in great numbers (e.g. starfish and sea mouse).

Offshore waters. Many species of offshore fish live in large shoals for 'safety in numbers'. In the open sea there is nowhere to hide except among large numbers of your own species! Fish living in open water are called 'pelagic'.

The offshore waters of Britain used to support enough fish to sustain large and specialised fishery operations. However, overfishing has now reduced many fish populations to such low numbers that catching them is no longer an economic proposition.

The sea bed is an open habitat offering few places to hide. Consequently many species burrow into the sand, though some (e.g. fan worms) construct a shelter of their own in the form of a tube made of sand grains cemented together. In places the sea bed may be covered by 'forests' of these worm tubes (which can sometimes also be seen in the intertidal zone). Sea bed creatures are called 'benthic' organisms.

The surface waters of the sea are well-lit and support high densities of sun-loving planktonic marine algae. These in turn are food for animal plankton, itself the food of fish, invertebrates and birds.

9

Sandy shores

Sandy shores tend to be flat or gently sloping. The tide goes out a long way, exposing extensive areas to the sun and atmosphere for many hours a day. Anything living on the surface would be very vulnerable to desiccation or predation, so most sandy shore animals are burrowing creatures. They are only likely to be seen if they are dug up with a spade or washed up dead on the strandline. At low tide, the sand dries out and surface grains may be blown up the shore by the wind. There they accumulate in mounds to form dune systems. Unfortunately these are very popular with holidaymakers, the sheer numbers of which threaten to dislodge the dunes and all that lives in them. Few British dune systems now escape this destructive disturbance.

Sandy spits and sandbank islands exposed temporarily by the tide are excellent places for shore birds to feed and rest. Not only is there plenty of food in the form of worms and other burrowing shore animals, but the open nature of the exposed sand means that nothing can approach the birds without being seen.

The strandline of sandy shores is often a particularly good place to find washed up the remains of animals that normally live out of sight below low water mark. Piles of seaweed and other jetsam form a damp refuge for sand-hoppers and other shore creatures that could not survive exposure out on the open sand surface.

Sandy beaches slope gently, so often the tide goes out it exposes a very large intertidal area. When it comes in, the sea is shallow and wave action therefore only gentle. **Shingle beaches** have steeper

slopes, less area exposed at low tide and suffer severe churning and stirring up as the waves break on the shore.

Windblown sand accumulate as dunes. The sand retains little moisture, is contaminated with salt and is constantly being moved by the wind. Only two or three plants can tolerate these conditions (notably marram grass) and these dominate the dunes.

Dunes or sandbanks often cut off **shallow lagoons** from connection with the sea. Their water becomes diluted by rain and they are not subject to disturbance by waves. They provide a tranquil haven for many invertebrates and the birds that feed on them.

Valleys between the dunes may become quite wet through the accumulation of rainwater. These **'dune slacks'** support willow scrub and the water is home for insect larvae. The shelter provided by surrounding dunes enables quite tall, specialised dune system flowers to grow (e.g. spurge and sea holly) and offers a quiet place for birds to nest (e.g. ringed plover and oyster catcher).

Dunes continue to form at their seaward face, while at their rear the sand has been stabilised by vegetation growth. Here the rain washes out sea salt and dissolves away the remains of sea shells, leaving a clean, rather acidic sand. On this a typical heather-dominated heathland habitat develops eventually to be succeeded by scrub woodland.

Rocky shores and cliffs

Where the coast consists of hard rocks, erosion by the sea leads to the formation of cliffs. The harder the rock the steeper the cliff face. Softer rocks (e.g. chalk, marls) tend to erode continuously in small pieces, so the cliff face is smooth and unstable. It offers few secure sites for birds to nest or plants to establish themselves. Hard rocks fracture in chunks, forming clefts and ledges ideal for sea birds. Where water oozes from cracks in the cliff face, rich plant communities become established.

Cliff tops are exposed and frequently doused with salty spray. Many land plants cannot tolerate these conditions, so the vegetation consists of specialised, adapted cliff top species.

Rocks falling from the cliff face accumulate on the shore below. A plateau of jumbled boulders, washed by the sea at high tide, is characteristic; but on some coasts the water is deep enough to cover the rocks at all states of the tide.

Higher up the shore the boulders may only be washed by the highest tides. Further down shore, the rocks are exposed for long periods at low tide. Only a few species of seaweeds and marine animals can tolerate this combination of conditions; zonation of plants and animals results from their different levels of tolerance of submergence and exposure.

At low tide, water is trapped in rock pools. Here can survive animals and plants that would otherwise be killed by drying out at low tide. Rock pools are excellent places to search for intertidal animals.

Rocky shore seaweeds and animals have to withstand wave battering as the tide comes in, so most are firmly attached to the rocks to prevent being washed away. Some animals seek shelter in crevices, under rocks and among seaweed fronds and need to be carefully searched out.

Below the low water mark, the coast slopes gently, usually with fewer rocks, but this zone can only be explored using diving apparatus.

Muddy shores and estuaries

Mud consists of very fine particles which only settle out from suspension in water when the latter is almost stationary. Such conditions are found where slow flowing rivers meet the seat. Then sediment is deposited as flat mud banks which are easily reshaped or washed away in storms or if there is any change in tidal movements. The mud is rich in nutrients and so is the water. Consequently the animal life is dominated by worms and filter feeding molluscs (which are adapted to take maximum advantage of these conditions) and the birds which feed on them.

Mud flats are a very soft and open habitat unsuited to large creatures. Small ones seek protection and shelter by burrowing: an easy task in the soft mud. Burrowers are the dominant types of invertebrates.

Where the mud is exposed at low tide, salt tolerant plants grow. These trap more mud and stabilise it. The firmer land thus created is washed by rain, allowing a wider variety of plants to grow, which in turn are shelter for birds.

Tidal mudflats often have extensive growths of 'eelgrass' and algae, attracting

large flocks of geese and ducks to feed on them.

Soft mud is easily probed by long-billed birds seeking burrowing invertebrates for food. In winter, the mudflats do not freeze (being salty and also covered by sea twice a day), so they are important as a winter feeding area for large congregations of birds. These are mainly waders which nest in the uplands but cannot easily find sufficient food there in the cold winter months.

As the tide goes out, water drains off the mud banks, cutting complex runnels into the soft mud. Some of these may retain water while the tide is out.

Worms and bivalve molluscs are well adapted to burrowing into the soft mud and they dominate the invertebrate species of this habitat.

Fixed objects such as logs, posts or sunken boats soon become partially buried by the mud that accumulates around them. Meanwhile, in a soft and unstable habitat, they represent welcome and attractive stable objects for the attachment of seaweeds, sessile invertebrates (e.g. barnacles) and a useful perch for birds.

Rivers

The range of species which can inhabit a river is governed mainly by the speed of water flow. Fast flowing rivers tend to occur in rocky and stony areas. The rapid movement of water creates turbulence that carries away any animals not adapted to holding tight to fixed objects or able to swim against the current; but turbulence also ensures that the water stays cool and well oxygenated. Conversely, slow flowing water tends to be less well oxygenated, excluding many invertebrates and fish. Slow flowing rivers are features of the lowlands, where they often become contaminated by agricultural chemicals draining from adjacent farmland. Industrial pollutants may also be added by the factories and towns past which the rivers carries flow.

Splashing turbulent water picks up plenty of oxygen from the air, but dislodges most aquatic plants. Fast flowing streams therefore have little fringing vegetation. Most animals of fast flowing water shelter from the current and need to be sought out by looking under stones.

Splash zone spray from turbulent water keeps rocks and soil permanently wet, encouraging growth especially of mosses and liverworts.

On flat land in the valleys rivers flow more slowly and tend to meander. Water draining down from a large catchment area tends to build up rapidly in the lower parts of a river system (especially after storms). The river then may become overfilled and glood the surrounding land.

Lowland rivers often flow through clays and gravels deposited by the river in earlier times. Such deposits occur as flat layers, so the riverside land is typically flat and liable to flood. The wet ground provides rich farmland, but where flooding is frequent crops cannot be grown and the land is grazed. Wet grassland is a particularly good habitat for many birds and the invertebrates on which they feed.

Slow flowing waters permit the growth of fringing vegetation, though river authorities frequently clear this away because it impedes water flow.

Conifer plantations are established in many upland areas and act like a huge sponge, absorbing rainfall which would otherwise run off the steep hillsides in torrents and cause erosion.

Still waters and wetlands

The wet margins of lakes and ponds provide some of the richest and most interesting habitats in Britain, but they are transient by nature. The continuous cycle of growth and death of waterside vegetation gradually causes the accumulation of peat, displacing water plants and permitting their succession by land plants.

The plant and animal life within the water itself is greatly influenced by the chemical content of the water. This in turn is governed by soil type and the incidence of agricultural chemicals and other pollutants washed from the surrounding land.

The fringe of emergent plants (e.g. reeds) provides nest sites for birds and a sheltered microclimate for many aquatic invertebrates.

In deeper water, plants such as lilies may be rooted in the mud at the bottom of the pond, but have leaves floating at the surface. These die back each autumn. However, in muddy or eutrophic waters sunlight cannot penetrate far, and such plants are unable to begin their growth in the spring and will no longer be found in the pond.

High levels of organic pollutants or agricultural fertilisers washed from nearby farmland may cause a massive growth of algae in the pond. This enrichment of the water and excessive algal 'bloom' is referred to as 'eutrophication' and is frequent in lowland areas. It results in diminution of the diversity of animal species able to survive.

Water depth greatly affects what plants can grow and which water birds (especially ducks) are able to feed. Natural lowland ponds and lakes usually have gently shelving shores, providing 'beaches' and a fringe of shallow water where plants and animals flourish. Many artificial water bodies (e.g. reservoirs and gravel pits) have banks which slope steeply into deep water. Their shores support less wildlife.

Freshwater animals are best obtained using a pond net swept through the water, over the bottom and among the aquatic vegetation. Many of them need a magnifying glass to be seen properly and are best examined in a white dish or clear jar with a piece of white paper held behind it to reflect the light.

Water meadows bordering rivers often flood periodically and nutrients from the river are deposited producing a very fertile soil and consequent rich flora. Flooding prevents arable farming and many water meadows have been grazed or cut for hay in the same way for many container producing a stable, specialised community of great interest.

Waterside trees are restricted to a few specialised types that can tolerate waterlogged roots and occasional flooding. Even so those trees that are so adapted form a major contribution to the wetland environment especially providing nesting sites for many birds.

Wetlands and fenlands are areas that are permanently waterlogged and they support a lightly specialised wildlife. Once large areas of England were fenland but this has been much reduced by agricultural drainage.

19

Deciduous woodland

Although Britain is one of the least-wooded countries in Europe, our deciduous forests are of great interest and diversity. This is mot simply due to the variety of trees present, but also because the trees are themselves an environment for animals. Some creatures can live at ground level, while others live over their heads in the treetops. Some trees may support over 200 different species among their leaves and branches.

The tree canopy provides food for mammals, birds and insect larvae (e.g. the 'defoliating' caterpillars, which eat leaves). The branches also offer a protective and relatively inaccessible support for nests. Once the trees are in leaf, the canopy shades the ground, limiting the types of plants that can grow, so tree tops and ground level are not totally independent.

Coppice. Some tree species will grow vigorously from cut stumps, sending up a mass of young leafy stalks. In the past, ash, hazel and sweet chestnut were deliberately cut back to encourage such growth ('coppicing') because the thin poles were useful for fencing and other purposes. Coppiced woodland has plenty of new growth and consequently high populations of insects and birds. Regular cutting allows light to reach the forest floor, stimulating growth of a rich diversity of herbs.

Dead trees and their stumps are decomposed by the action of fungi, bacteria and soil animals. Stumps and logs also provide a vantage point for squirrels when

they are feeding. The debris left after a squirrel's meal can often be found on top. Decaying trees support a wide range of invertebrates, especially wood-boring beetles.

Wheel ruts, ditches and other wet spots often provide a home for midge larvae (which can also live in water trapped in tree trunk crevices and branch forks).

Deciduous woodland is characterised by autumnal leaf fall. The dead leaves are decomposed by soil organisms and their nutrient content returned to the soil. The leaves are shelter for many small mammals and invertebrates, and may also be used as nesting material. Different species of leaves take different lengths of time to decay, thus different types of woodland have a characteristic ground carpet; extensive bare layers of decay-resistant leaves are a distinctive feature of beech woods, whereas oak and birch leaves decay rapidly and are soon overgrown by herbs and shrubs.

Pollarding. Certain trees have a mass of thick branches arising at once from the trunk, about three metres off the ground. This is usually a sign of 'pollarding', where the tree has been deliberately cut in the past. Few trees grow like this naturally.

Woodland rides and open spaces provide a break in the canopy through which sunlight can reach the ground and stimulate growth of herbs providing food for insects, especially butterflies.

Many wild flowers grow on the sheltered woodland floor, enjoying early growth and flowering before the tree canopy shades out their environment in early summer.

Conifer woodland

Today Britain has more woodland than at any time in the last 200 years. However, most of it is recently-planted conifer forest: conifers grow quickly, so yield an earlier economic return than native hardwood species. In general, these conifer woodlands are less interesting than deciduous forests, but they are far from being wildlife deserts. They harbour many specialised and notable plants and animals not normally found elsewhere.

The dense canopy of conifer trees casts a deep shade over the ground. Moreover, because conifers do not shed their leaves for the winter the shade persists all year round. The darkness of conifer woods is very characteristic, as is the consequent lack of ground flora.

The Scots pine is Britain's only native conifer. It has a fairly open, diffuse canopy and under natural conditions (especially in Scotland) the trees grow well spaced apart. There is thus ample scope for a herb and shrub layer to develop below them.

Conifers are planted in dense stands but in their early stages of growth, these plantations are often rich in wildlife owing to the thick growth of long grasses, herbs and other vegetation among the trees.

At the edge of the plantation, and along forest rides, sunlight can penetrate to ground level and support a variety of herbs, grasses and shrubs.

Conifers grow well on poor soils and in bleak conditions where deciduous trees do not thrive. Consequently the poor soils of the uplands are frequently planted out with conifers to gain a return from otherwise unproductive land.

Where conifer plantations are more than a few years old the spreading tree canopies shade out the underlayer of grasses and shrubs, excluding many species of animals. But the dense canopy also provides year-round shelter from wind and rain and is the preferred home of many birds and a few special mammals.

Alien species. Most of the conifers growing today are alien species and support far fewer dependent insects and other animals than our native species of trees.

Heathland

Heathlands occur on poor sandy soils in the lowlands. Such soils tend to be well drained, well aerated and warm up quickly in the sun. These are features that favour many insects and reptiles, and the low nutrient content of the soil ensures that only a few plant species thrive. Heathlands tend to be dominated by heathers, but if fires and grazing are completely prevented gorse, scots pine or birch may take over large areas. In places, waterlogging can occur due to accumulation of iron salts just below the ground surface. Heathland pools are often inhabited by insectivorous plants and also harbour a rich assortment of dragonflies.

Rain soaking into the porous sandy ground leaches out nutrients, leaving a very poor soil. This is often covered by a very thin layer of peat and plant debris at the surface. These conditions are clearly visible in cuttings and erosion gulleys.

Dry heathland is dominated by heathers which grow to form large twiggy clumps. These provide shelter for many insects, spiders and also lizards. Woody heather burns well and heath fires are frequent.

Burnt areas are soon recolonised, provided that the fire was only superficial and did not ignite the peat. Bracken shoots up from its protected underground rhizomes; heathers and gorse regrow from heat-resistant seeds. Most other plants are kept at bay by regular fires.

Scots pines frequently invade heathland, being able to tolerate poor soils.

Water accumulates in low lying areas and supports a range of bog plants dominated by sphagnum mosses.

Water draining off the sandy heaths runs into small streams. This ground water tends to be acidic and stained with peaty compounds that make it look like cold tea. Such water contains few aquatic organisms.

Valley bottoms often develop narrow strips of sphagnum bog fringing small streams.

25

Grassland scrub and farmland

In most parts of lowland Britain, if nothing were done to manage the land it would be gradually taken over by scrub. This in time would grow into woodland. In fact, most of our land is not forest simply because some kind of human intervention prevents the growth of scrub. Over large areas the intervention is in the form of farming, where the land is ploughed regularly and treated to ensure that only crops can grow. Other areas are maintained as grassland by grazing animals (mostly sheep and cattle, but also rabbits). Part of this land management entails the erection of fences or maintenance of hedgerows, the whole providing a mosaic of interesting open habitats.

Grass grazed short by sheep and rabbits allows tiny plants to grow that would otherwise be swamped by larger species.

Scrub. If grazing or mowing ceases, perennial woody plants are not kept at bay and they gradually take over. Scrub develops as a new habitat with its own insects and birds.

Roadsides are often mown to prevent scrub encroachment. Mowing has the same effect as grazing, but for economy reasons takes place infrequently. Roadsides thus develop a different flora of tall plants compared to grazed areas.

Fields may be cut for hay or grazed by cattle. Either way they remain as grassland, with their own typical complement of species.

Hedges are artificial habitats in that they are planted and maintained by man. They do nevertheless shelter a great variety of plants and animals. Some hedges are very old and may be comprised of four or more shrub species (on average, one extra woody species for every 100 years the hedge has existed).

Ancient downland. Some of our downlands date back to man's first colonisation of these islands. Constantly grazed since those times, they now support a wide range of plants, insects and other animals (up to 30 species of plant can be found in a single square metre of downland turf). Despite their apparent fertility, the chalk substrate is usually low in nutrients and provides meagre results if ploughed up for arable use.

Ant colonies and anthills are a common component of grassland and can be of considerable age (100 years or more). The anthills provide an unstable substrate on which only specialised plants can exist.

Slugs and snails are often the major grazers in an area of chalk grassland and can consume far more vegetation than sheep. Sometimes several hundred can be found within a square metre of downland.

Uplands

Britain's uplands are areas of old hard rock that yields poor soil. Moreover, the higher ground is both colder and wetter. Consequently the diversity of vegetation able to survive is considerably reduced. The habitats tend to be dominated by a few, suitably adapted species which then cover extensive areas of the landscape.

Average temperatures decrease 1°C for every 150 metres gained above sea level. At higher altitudes winds are stronger too, so plant growth is stunted. On the highest peaks only a few species can survive.

Steep slopes of unstable scree, lacking soil, can support very little plant or animal life.

Gentler slopes develop thick peaty soil and become dominated by heathers.

Poor upland soils are unsuitable for farming, so large areas are often planted with conifers to obtain an economic return from the land. This afforestation greatly changes the species present in an area and also profoundly alters the landscape.

Blanket bogs. The hard rocks of the

uplands do not absorb water, so boggy areas develop in valleys and in patches on the hillsides. These then become dominated by sphagnum mosses and cotton grass: characteristic indicators of wet, mineral-deficient conditions.

Hard rocks do not erode away very fast, so upland scenery is often angular and jagged. The rocks themselves support encrusting growths of lichens.

Lakes in upland areas are usually deficient in nutrients and so have little emergent vegetation and reduced algal content. Their coldness also serves to restrict plant diversity. Their water is usually very clear.

Grazing. Many upland areas are extensively grazed by sheep, resulting in dominance of the landscape by coarse grasses. Elsewhere, smaller numbers of sheep may be kept, allowing dominance by heather. Heathers may be further encouraged by burning, usually so that young heather shoots are available as food for red grouse. Grouse production and shooting is an important traditional form of land use in the uplands (especially in Scotland) and results in vast areas of characteristic heather-dominated landscape.

29

Town and garden

We tend to imagine that the spread of urban areas obliterates wildlife: in fact, suburban areas probably have the highest species diversity of any British habitat. Many of the species are garden plants, and gardeners do their best to reduce the number of animals that feed upon them. Nevertheless, many birds and mammals find gardens very suitable for their needs and urban areas often contain 'wild' areas (e.g. railway banks, derelict sites, old cemeteries etc) where the dominant vegetation is naturally-seeded wild plants. In such places, the scarcity of big predators and the lack of interference by farmers and agricultural chemicals often ensures survival of at least as many plants and animals as in the countryside.

House attics are dark, warm and undisturbed. These are ideal conditions for birds (e.g. starlings and swifts) and wasps to build their nests, for spiders to live and breed and for bats to raise their young. In fact attics are so important to the survival of our declining bat populations that it is now illegal to disturb attic colonies of bats, even in your own house. House martins will build their nests on the walls outside.

Cellars offer a cool, dark, damp environment suitable for a range of invertebrates that shun the light. Urban foxes also utilise cellars and underfloor spaces, as do rats and mice.

Garden sheds are cool and dry sites for butterflies (e.g. peacock and small tortoiseshell) to hibernate. The space under the shed is a favourite site for hedgehogs and foxes to raise their young. Piles of garden refuse also form important nest sites for mammals, and compost heaps

provide grass snakes with a warm environment in which to lay their eggs.

Town parks act as refuges for larger birds and they are also an important stopover site for migrant species. Park trees are home for squirrels and bats, and many wild plants occur which are the food plants of insects (especially moth caterpillars).

Derelict buildings and old walls are important calcareous habitats for mosses and lichens. Their cracks also provide shelter for spiders and other invertebrates, most of which do not venture out except under cover of darkness.

Old graveyards are often dominated by wild plants. The gravestones themselves are important substrates for lichens because they are undisturbed and often formed of calcareous or very hard rocks which lichens find particularly favourable. Dates on the tombstones tell the maximum possible age of the lichens, a useful way of ageing these slow growing plants.

Urban areas generate waste and the disposal sites are often a rich source of food for a great variety of wildlife. Sewage farms are a favoured site for birds.

Factories and households generate smoke from boilers and heating systems. The smoke often contains gases such as sulphur dioxide which, added to the poisonous gases in vehicle exhausts, make urban air deadly to many of the more delicate forms of plant life. Soot, ash and dust, the particulate air pollutants, smother everything and again make conditions intolerable for many plants. Fortunately, modern pollution control mechanisms mean that this problem is less severe than it used to be, allowing more plants to thrive. More plants means more insects, which in turn means that more insectivorous birds (e.g. house martins) can live in our towns.

Non-flowering plants

We tend to think that plants and flowers are synonymous, but in fact there are major groups of plants which do not have flowers. Generally they are representatives of groups which evolved hundreds of millions of years ago, long before flowers. In fact, the main purpose of flowers is to encourage pollination by insects or other animals; but several groups of plants reproduce by quite different means.

Fungi

Fungi differ from all other plants in that they do not have any of the green chlorophyll pigment necessary for photosynthesis. Therefore, instead of being able to synthesise their own food from carbon dioxide and water, they absorb ready-made biological food molecules. It is for this reason that they normally grow as saprophytes (digesting the bodies of dead plants and animals) or parasites. However, because they do not depend upon photosynthesis, they do not need sunlight and can therefore grow in dense shade or even complete darkness.

The main part of a fungus plant consists of masses of hair-like hyphae: fungal threads which penetrate the substrate to absorb food. The familiar mushrooms and toadstools are merely the reproductive part of this fungal mass which sprout above ground to distribute spores. Many fungi never produce this type of 'fruiting bodies' and we recognise them as 'moulds'. These

and other small and inconspicuous fungi, though very numerous, are not normally noticed by the non-specialist (nor easily identified) so are omitted from this book.

The umbrella-like cap fungi and the bracket fungi are important and conspicuous plants. There are hundreds of species; only the most evident ones are described here. Their caps, brackets and billowing bag-like structures produce immense quantities of spores (millions every day in some species). Spores differ from seeds in having no food store and are thus very tiny: literally like specks of dust. Huge numbers are therefore able to drift about on the wind and achieve wide distribution.

Ecology

Most fungi are not well adapted to dry conditions, so they are most numerous in moist shady places. Some form a special association with the roots of trees, so that particular species are characteristic of certain types of woodland (e.g. fly agaric and the birch tree). Many are distinctly seasonal in their appearance, with autumn the best time to see the greatest variety. Though generally inconspicuous, fungi are of vital importance in ecosystems. Their

The Puff-ball fungus disperses its spores to be distributed by wind. Such fungi can produce around a million spores per day, and they can be carried high up into the upper atmosphere.

The bracket fungus *Trametes versicolor* attacks an old tree. Most trees die from fungal attack, and bracket fungus are the commonest forms on large living trees.

digestive activities serve to break down dead wood, animal dung, fallen leaves and all manner of biological detritus which would otherwise continue to accumulate. Unfortunately some fungi perform the same function, but in the wrong place, causing house timbers and fences to rot away. Similarly, some of the parasitic species (not described here) are serious agricultural and horticultural pests as they attack crop plants. Many fungi provide food (of low nutritive value) for animals including insects, slugs and squirrels; and some are regarded as delicacies for human consumption. Three British species are deadly poisonous to humans (though not to animals) and many more cause sickness and diarrhoea. To be on the safe side, never eat any fungi unless a competent expert is certain of their identifications and safety.

Algae

The algae include two very dissimilar types of plant: tiny, single-celled organisms and also the comparatively massive seaweeds. The former are a very important source of food for fish and planktonic animals in the sea and in freshwater. They are extraordinarily numerous and diverse, but are not included in this field guide because their identification is normally only carried out by specialists armed with microscopes and other technical equipment. Some simple freshwater algae occur as long filamentous chains of cells ('blanket weed'). Those and the unicellular types often increase massively when ponds are enriched by fertiliser run-off or sewage, causing major disruption of the aquatic ecosystem.

Seaweeds

The seaweeds share with the uni-cellular algae the characteristic of being very simple in structure. They do not have the complex water- and sap-transporting cells inside their 'stems', nor do they have leaves or roots (their 'holdfast' merely anchors them to the substrate; it does not absorb water or nutrients as proper roots do). They have no wood, bark, or any other specialised structure, and are thus unable to support themselves on dry land or withstand long periods out of water. They do possess chlorophyll, the green pigment that helps convert water and carbon dioxide to plant food, but often this is masked by brown and red pigments. Seaweeds have no flowers or pollen. Fertilisation is achieved by the male cells swimming to the female parts of the plant. This can only take place in water, another reason why seaweeds do not live on dry land.

Lichens, Mosses and Liverworts

Lichens, mosses and liverworts are all small, simple plants which are easily overlooked. To the casual observer they are

Though often large and complex in shape, seaweed are in fact algae. Essential attributes for a seaweed are the ability to withstand drying out at low tide and the provision of a 'hold fast' with which to attach themselves to rocks.

only really noticeable en masse, as a green or grey textured covering to the ground or tree bark. We are conscious of a mossy carpet in shady places or crusty patches on trees and rocks; it requires a conscious effort (and a magnifying glass) to become aware of the delicate details of these plants and their specific recognition features.

Lichens

Lichens are in fact a composite construction, made up of a fungus and an alga living in partnership as if they were a single plant. There are an enormous number of species ranging in colour from black, through various greens and greys to white. Some are bright orange. They grow very slowly and so only reach a reasonable size on stable substrates such as rock and tree bark. In fact the substrate is a helpful guide to identification; those that grow on rocks (and their equivalents such as roofs, walls and tombstones) normally do not grow on trees. Tree bark lichens can have a foliose, crusty growth form or they can be hair-like tufts or appear as just a grey-green dusty powder on the surface. Lichens gain their inorganic chemical nutrients from dust in the atmosphere, but they are very sensitive to atmospheric pollution. Soot, oil and similar materials quickly smother lichens, preventing photosynthesis by their algal component. Lichens are unusually sensitive to sulphur dioxide (from burning coal and oil) and the number of species

The natural habitat for many lichens is limestone cliffs and outcrops. A close approximation to this (for a lichen) is a tombstone in a country graveyard.

present, especially on trees, is an indication of relative atmospheric purity. Thus in the west of Britain, comparatively unpolluted damp air coming off the Atlantic encourages prolific and diverse lichen growths; whereas areas downwind of major industrial centres such as London or the Midlands are often almost devoid of lichens.

Mosses

Mosses are the simplest types of terrestrial green plants. They are mostly

Epiphytic lichens growing on an oak tree in the west of England. Such luxuriant growth is found only in areas of clean air free from pollution. For Britain, this means the west and north, for anywhere downwind of the cities is usually too polluted.

Non-flowering plants

very small, and because of their primitive method of reproduction they depend upon living in damp places (or at least somewhere that they can periodically be thoroughly wetted). Despite this ecological limitation, some mosses (e.g. those that grow on stone walls) can survive long periods of drought better than more highly evolved plants. This is because their cell structure is such that they can lose almost all their internal water and shrivel up, only to recover completely when it rains. This ability also helps them withstand high temperatures.

Generally speaking, mosses are of little ecological importance except in boggy areas. Here, some of the largest mosses (20 cm long) such as *Sphagnum* and *Polytrichum* may dominate the other vegetation. Indeed, *Sphagnum* is very efficient at competing with other plants in wet places, though it is comparatively unsuccessful in drier areas. Mosses have no economic importance, though *Sphagnum* is again the exception. Over the centuries, this moss only partially rots away, accumulating as a mass of peat. This is valuable for horticultural purposes and may also be dried to use as fuel. In the wetter parts of Ireland moss peat is so abundant that it is used instead of coal to fuel power stations.

Liverworts

Liverworts grow only in wet, shady places, again, like mosses, partly because of their primitive method of reproduction which requires the presence of a thin film of water on the plant. Stream and ditch banks, tree roots, bridge abutments are the places to look for liverworts – and unless you look you are unlikely to notice them. All are small and grow as a soft, dark green lobed mass, pressed flat against the substrate. In many ways they resemble green terrestrial seaweeds. Their plate-like structure is anchored by roots and they do photosynthesise (unlike fungi, which also thrive in similar dark and damp places), but they do not produce flowers or any other distinctive structures.

Ferns

Ferns are predominantly a tropical group of plants; comparatively few live in the cool temperate regions. The European types are usually less than a metre high. Most have their leaves (called 'fronds') deeply divided to form delicate and characteristic shapes, though in some (e.g. the hart's-tongue) the leaves are simple and strap-like. The undersides of the leaves bear small capsules, called 'sporangia', which contain large numbers of minute spores. When ripe, these are shed and dispersed by the wind. They later grow in damp places to form an inconspicuous prothallus. This bears sexual cells which achieve fertilisation and later give rise to new fern plants. Ferns thus have an alternation of generations, the sporophyte being the large plant that bears asexual spores and the prothallus being the tiny sexual stage of the life cycle. This is a feature shared with the mosses and is characteristic of very primitive plants. Ferns can also spread

Liverworts prosper in cool, damp areas. Here the reproductive organs of the species *Marchantia polymorpha* rise above the normal plant.

Ferns, unlike higher plants, produce alternate generations. This photograph shows the inconspicuous prothallus which arises in damp places from the shed spores of the larger sporophyte stage.

rapidly by vegetative growth of their underground part (the rhizome).

Unlike mosses, ferns have a complex system of water-transporting cells inside their stem (a feature they share with flowering plants), but their leaves are usually poorly resistant to drying out, so ferns tend to live in cool moist places. However, some species, like some mosses, can tolerate a remarkable degree of shrivelling and drying out with being killed.

Ferns are classified according to their frond shape and subdivision. The pattern of sporangia underneath is also an important recognition feature to note.

Ecology

Most ferns are ecologically of little significance, but one (bracken, *Pteridium*) is of major consequence. Not only does this grow well in open situations, but it spreads rapidly by extension of its underground rhizomes and once its dense fronds form a canopy above the ground they shade other plants, suppressing their growth. Bracken can then quickly become dominant over large areas. This is a particular nuisance on grazing land where the unpalatable bracken replaces useful grass. It is also a problem on heathland where bracken quickly grows again after fires and, once established, prevents other more interesting and diverse plants from growing up in its shadow.

Horsetails

Ferns are a very ancient group of plants which evolved over 300 million years ago. Somewhat similar to them are the horsetails, plants which used to form the dense swamp forests whose fossil remains now comprise our coal deposits. Horsetails have a peculiar jointed appearance and simpe rod-like leaves. Superficially they do not look much like ferns (though they share important, less obvious characteristics) but they do not look much like anything else either, so they should be easily recognised. They normally only grow in damp shady places.

Woodlands provide the main habitat for ferns where they prosper on the cool, damp and shaded woodland floor. Ferns are amongst the oldest of plants and pre-date the evolution of flowers.

Non-flowering Plants

Hart's Tongue Fern
Aspleniaceae *Phyllitis scolopendrium*. **Habitat:** Woodland, hedgerows, walls, rock ledges throughout British Isles, but rare in central and N. Scotland. **Notes:** Common on calcareous soils.

Black Spleenwort
Aspleniaceae *Asplenium adiantum-nigrum*. **Habitat:** Woodland, rocks and walls throughout British Isles. **Notes:** Prefers rocky, alkaline soils. Tolerates some exposure.

Hard Fern Blechnaceae *Blechnum spicant*. **Habitat:** Local in woodland, heaths and rock ledges throughout most of British Isles up to 1300m; absent or rare in the Midlands and E. Anglia. **Notes:** On acid soils.

Common Horsetail
Equisetaceae *Equisetum arvense*. **Habitat:** Locally abundant in hedgerows, waste ground and dunes throughout British Isles, up to 950m. **Notes:** Grows on inorganic soils; absent from peat-covered areas.

Wall-rue Aspleniaceae *Asplenium ruta-muraria*. **Habitat:** Common on rock ledges and walls throughout British Isles. **Notes:** On basic substrates.

Bracken Hypolepidaceae
Pteridium aquilinum. **Habitat:**
Very common on lowland
heaths, woodland rides and
clearings throughout British
Isles. **Notes:** On acid, well-
drained soils; often replaces
heather on burnt areas; partially
fire-resistant.

Rusty back Fern Aspleniaceae
Ceterach officinarum. **Habitat:**
Rock crevices in limestone hills
and on walls in W. and S.W.
British Isles, up to 450m,
becoming rare in N.

Male Fern Aspidiaceae
Dryopteris filix-mas. **Habitat:**
Common in woodland,
hedgerows and by road sides,
thoughout British Isles; often on
walls. **Notes:** Has wide
ecological tolerance. Often
planted in gardens.

Lady Fern Athyriaceae
Athyrium filix-femina. **Habitat:**
Common in damp woodland,
shady hedgerows, damp places
in mountains, especially along
spring lines throughout British
Isles.

Non-flowering Plants

Hard Shield Fern Aspidiaceae
Polystichum aculeatum.
Habitat: Woodland,
hedgerows, rocky mountain
ledges, by polluted water,
throughout British Isles, but
rarer in N. **Notes:** Requires
base-rich soil.

Broad Buckler Fern
Aspidiaceae *Dryopteris dilatata.*
Habitat: Woodland, hedgerows
and shady rock ledges
throughout British Isles. **Notes:**
Variable, often confused with
similar fern *D. carthusiana* but
differs in having dark scales with
pale margins.

Marsh Fern Thelypteridaceae
Thelypteris palustris. **Habitat:**
Very local in wetland (fens) and
alder woodland throughout
British Isles, but rare in N.
England and Scotland. **Notes:**
Fertile parts of fronds have
inrolled edges. Fronds usually
solitary.

Soft Shield Fern Aspidiaceae
Polystichum setiferum.
Habitat: Woodland and
hedgerows throughout British
Isles, but rare in N. and in
Scotland. **Notes:** Requires
base-rich soil. Prefers wet,
warm winters.

Adder's Tongue
Ophioglossaceae
Ophioglossum vulgatum.
Habitat: Fairly common in
wetland, old meadows, coastal
dune slacks throughout much of
British Isles, but rare in Scotland
and S. Ireland. **Notes:** Prefers
deep, loamy soils. Often
overlooked.

Moonwort Ophioglossaceae
Botrychium lunaria. **Habitat:**
Dry grassland, rock ledges and
fixed dunes throughout British
Isles, up to 1000m, but more
common in N. England and
Scotland. **Notes:** On well-
drained soils.

Polypody Polypodiaceae
Polypodium vulgare. **Habitat:**
Common in woodland, on rocks
and walls throughout British
Isles. **Notes:** Variable.
Sometimes epiphytic.

Non-flowering Plants

Devil's Boletus Boletineae *Boletus satanus*. **Habitat:** Open deciduous woodland on calcareous soils in S. England. **Notes:** Pores blood-red. Poisonous. (Diameter 6-30cm)

Destroying Angel Agaricineae *Amanita virosa*. **Habitat:** Uncommon in coniferous and mixed woodland in British Isles. **Notes:** Usually pure white but occasionally cream or brown-tinged in centre of cap. Poisonous. (Diameter 5-10cm)

The Panther Agaricineae *Amanita pantherina*. **Habitat:** Uncommon in all types of woodland, throughout British Isles. **Notes:** Especially under beech. Poisonous. (Diameter 5-12cm)

Death Cap Agaricineae *Amanita phalloides*. **Habitat:** Woodland, meadows, parks and gardens throughout British Isles. **Notes:** Solitary or in groups. One of the most poisonous mushrooms. (Diameter 4-12cm)

Fungi

Horn of Plenty, Black Trumpet
Cantharellaceae *Craterellus
cornucopioides*. **Habitat:**
Deciduous and (occasionally)
coniferous woodland
throughout British Isles. **Notes:**
In large numbers among rotting
leaves. Found summer and
autumn. (Diameter 3-10cm)

Common Blewit, Blue-leg
Agaricineae *Lepista personata*.
Habitat: Grassland,
hedgerows, parks and gardens
throughout British Isles. **Notes:**
In colonies, often forming rings.
Found in autumn. (Diameter
6-12cm)

Fairy ring Champignon
Agaricineae *Marasmius
oreades*. **Habitat:** Grassland
and gardens throughout British
Isles. **Notes:** Forms extensive
rings. Cap distinctly raised in
centre. Found spring to autumn.
(Diameter 2-6cm)

Saffron Milk Cap Russulineae
Lactarius deliciosus. **Habitat:**
Pine woods and moors in N.
British Isles. **Notes:** Concentric
colour rings on cap; cap and
stem orange-red becoming
green. Found summer and
autumn. (Diameter 3-10cm)

Non-flowering Plants

Bare-edged Russula
Russulineae *Russula vesca*.
Habitat: Deciduous and (occasionally) coniferous woodland throughout British Isles. **Notes:** Especially under oak and beech. Mature cap has central depression. Found summer and autumn. (Diameter 5-10cm)

Karsten, Buff Meadow Cap
Agaricineae *Camarophyllus pratensis*. **Habitat:** Grassland, grassy woodland rides and margins, hedgerows, throughout British Isles. **Notes:** Found summer to late autumn. (Diameter 2-8cm)

Anise Cap Agaricineae *Clitocybe odora*. **Habitat:** Deciduous and (rarely) coniferous woodland throughout British Isles. **Notes:** Usually in groups among decaying leaves and often near roads. Found summer and autumn. (Diameter 3-9cm)

Common Morel Pezizales *Morchella esculenta*. **Habitat:** Locally common in hedgerows, grassland, woodland, parks and gardens in most of British Isles. **Notes:** Usually on rich calcareous, often disturbed, soils. Found spring and early summer. (Height 16-20cm)

Fungi

Oyster Mushroom Agaricineae *Pleurotus ostreatus*. **Habitat:** On tree trunks in deciduous woodland and parks throughout British Isles. **Notes:** Large, dense clusters, often on beech and poplar. Found autumn to spring. (Diameter 7-13cm)

Common Puff-ball Gasteromycetales *Lycoperdon perlatum*. **Habitat:** Woodland and grassland on sandy soils throughout British Isles. **Notes:** Often in groups; white-grey when young, becoming yellow-brown. Found summer and autumn. (Diameter 4-7cm)

Sponge Cap Boletineae *Leccinum versipelle*. **Habitat:** Associated with birch trees throughout British Isles. **Notes:** Often in large groups. Found summer and autumn. (Diameter 7-15cm)

Boletus erythropus Boletineae. **Habitat:** Coniferous woodland on acid soils throughout British Isles. **Notes:** Solitary or in groups. Pores brownish, maroon or orange with yellow edge. Found in autumn. (Diameter 5-16cm)

Non-flowering plants

Bay-capped Bolete Boletineae *Boletus badius*. **Habitat:** Woodland throughout British Isles. **Notes:** Cap sticky when mature; brown or ochre-coloured. Found summer and autumn. (Diameter 3-15cm)

Penny Bun, Ceps Boletineae *Boletus edulis*. **Habitat:** Woodland throughout British Isles. **Notes:** Pores white at first, turning yellow. Found summer and autumn. (Diameter 5-20cm)

Lawyer's Wig, Shaggy Ink Cap Agaricineae *Coprinus comatus*. **Habitat:** Grassland, parks, gardens, roadsides, rubbish tips, throughout British Isles. **Notes:** Usually in small groups; short-lived. Gills white at first, later pink, then black and finally dissolving into ink-like substance. Found spring to early winter. (Diameter 3-5cm)

Field Mushroom Agaricineae *Agaricus campestris*. **Habitat:** Grassland and gardens throughout British Isles. **Notes:** Usually appears in large numbers after rain in warm weather. Gills pinkish at first, later dark brown. Found summer and autumn. (Diameter 4-12cm)

Fungi

Horse Mushroom Agaricineae *Agaricus arvensis*. **Habitat:** Grassland, coniferous woodland edges and hedgerows throughout British Isles. **Notes:** Gills white at first, turning through red to dark brown. Found summer and autumn. (Diameter 5-17cm)

Parasol Mushroom Agaricineae *Macrolepiota procera*. **Habitat:** Common in woodland rides and edges, grassland, gardens, parks and hedgerows all over British Isles. **Notes:** Often near ant-hills; usually in large groups; sometimes forms rings. Found summer and autumn. (Diameter 8-25cm)

Wood Hedgehog Cantharellaceae *Hydnum repandum*. **Habitat:** Common in woodland throughout British Isles. **Notes:** Usually in groups or forming rings. Gills absent; lower surface covered with short "spines". Found summer and autumn. (Diameter 3-12cm)

Chantarelle Cantharellaceae *Cantharellus cibarius*. **Habitat:** Woodland and under pines in moorland. **Notes:** Often along roads and under birches; usually in large groups; always with trees. Smells faintly of apricots. (Diameter 2-10cm)

Codium tomentosum
Chlorophyceae. **Habitat:** Fairly common on middle shore and in deep pools, to depth of 20m, on all British coasts. **Notes:** Has texture of felt.

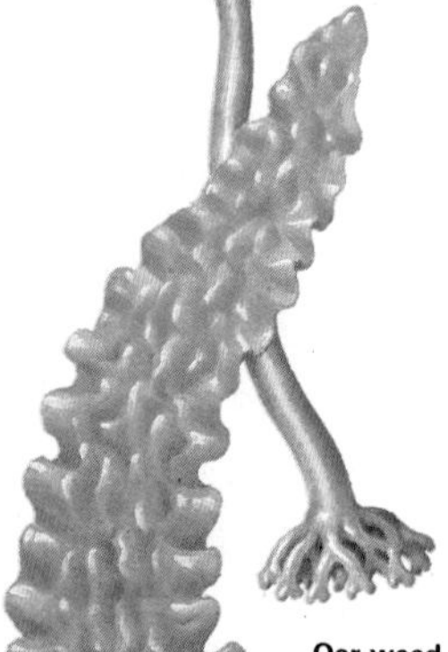

Oar-weed, Tangle
Phaeophyceae *Laminaria digitata*. **Habitat:** Common on rocks at low-water level and to depths of 30m, on all British coasts. **Notes:** Stalk oval in cross-section and usually free from epiphytic species.

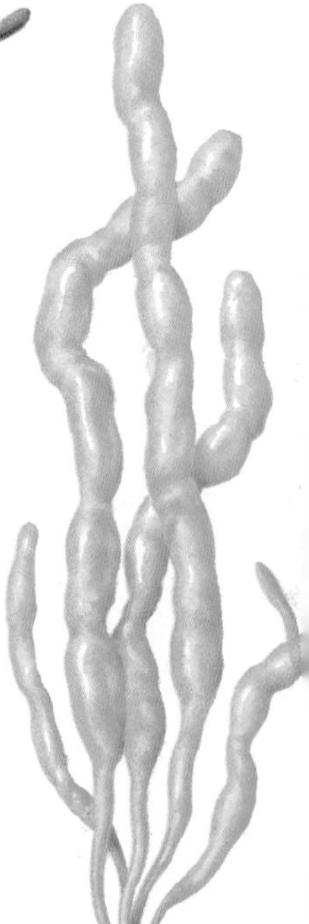

Sea Belt Phaeophyceae *Laminaria saccharina*. **Habitat:** From low-tide level to depth of 20m. **Notes:** Ribbon-like. Holdfast appears two-tiered. Easily distinguished by wrinkled surface. (Up to 2.5m long)

Sea Lettuce Chlorophyceae *Ulva lactura*. **Habitat:** On all but most exposed rocky shores in British Isles, from intertidal zone to depth of 20m. **Notes:** Green when young, becoming brown, then black, with age. Somewhat pollution tolerant.

Enteromorpha intestinalis
Chlorophyceae. **Habitat:** Very common on all British coasts and in estuaries and ditches where water is almost fresh. **Notes:** Especially in upper shore rock-pools.

Sea Thong Phaeophyceae *Himanthalia elongata.* **Habitat:** Common on lower shore, in pools and to depth of 10m, on rocky British coasts. **Notes:** Often forms dense colonies. Basal "button" often exists without rest of frond. (Up to 2.5m long)

Knotted Wrack Phaeophyceae *Ascophyllum nodosum.* **Habitat:** Rocky shores from high- to mid-tidal zones around British Isles. **Notes:** Under sheltered conditions can blanket entire beach and plants can be very large. No midrib. The red seaweed *Polysiphonia lanosa* frequently grows on it as an epiphyte.

Cuvie Phaeophyceae *Laminaria hyperborea.* **Habitat:** Attached to rocks and stones and in pools on all British coasts. **Notes:** Forms a brown belt at low-tide level, below *L. digitata.* Stalk round in cross-section, rough and usually covered with zoophytes.

Furbelows Phaeophyceae *Saccorhiza polyschides.* **Habitat:** Common on rocks at low tide level and to depth of 30m, on all British coasts. **Notes:** Plants occur in isolation. (Up to 5m long and 3m wide)

Channelled Wrack Phaeophyceae *Pelvetia canaliculata.* **Habitat:** Common, often abundant, on rocks of upper shore, on all British coasts. **Notes:** Forms a distinctive zone.

Spiral Wrack Phaeophyceae
Fucus spiralis. **Habitat:**
Abundant in upper zone of all but
most exposed rocky shores
around British Isles. **Notes:** Not
always spirally twisted. Never
has air bladders.

Toothed Wrack Phaeophyceae
Fucus serratus. **Habitat:**
Common on all but most
exposed rocky shores, around
British Isles. **Notes:** Often
forms distinctive zone low on
middle shore. Frequently
covered with zoophytes.

Bladder Wrack Phaeophyceae
Fucus vesiculosus. **Habitat:**
Common on middle shore rocks
on all British coasts. **Notes:**
Forms distinct zone. Very
variable. Bladders usually in
groups of two or three.

Gigartina stellata
Rhodophyceae. **Habitat:**
Common on rocks near low-tide
level on all British coasts.
Notes: Fronds channelled,
variable. Older plants covered
with fleshy pimples.

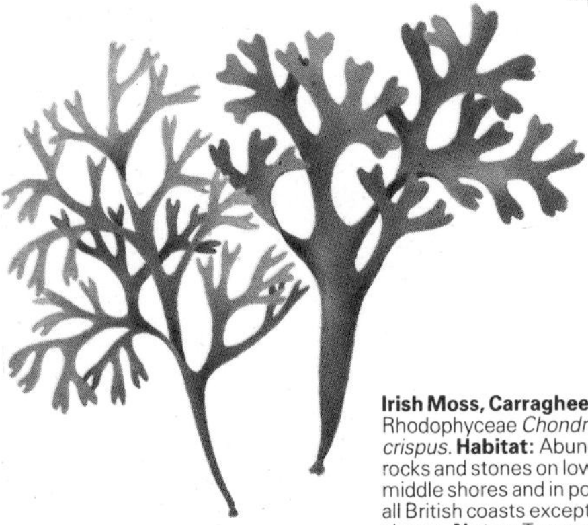

Irish Moss, Carragheen
Rhodophyceae *Chondrus
crispus.* **Habitat:** Abundant on
rocks and stones on lower and
middle shores and in pools, on
all British coasts except muddy
shores. **Notes:** Turns green in
strong light.

50

Lithophyllum incrustans
Rhodophyceae. **Habitat:**
Common in pools, especially on
exposed coasts, all around
British Isles. **Notes:** Forms
irregular crust up to 4cm thick;
adheres strongly to substrate.

Corallina officinalis
Rhodophyceae. **Habitat:**
Common throughout intertidal
zone, especially in middle shore
rock pools, on all British coasts.
Notes: Colour varies from
purple to red, pink, yellow or
white.

Polysiphonia lanosa
Rhodophyceae. **Habitat:** On
other seaweeds around all
British coasts. **Notes:** Usually
epiphytic on *Ascophyllum
nodosum*.

Ceramium rubrum
Rhodophyceae. **Habitat:** On
rocks and in pools on upper,
middle and lower shore down to
10m, on all British coasts.
Notes: Colour varies from deep
red to brown or yellow. A
variable species.

Dilsea carnosa Rhodophyceae.
Habitat: Common on middle
and lower shores on all British
coasts; on rocks, stones, sand
flats down to 10m and deeper.

Laver Rhodophyceae *Porphyra
umbilicalis*. **Habitat:** Rocks on
most levels of shore, on all
British coasts. **Notes:** Shape
irregular and very variable;
margin wavy, entire or unevenly
toothed.

Flowering plants

The flowering plants are enormously diverse in form and habitat. There are over 1500 species in Britain, large and small, inhabiting most places from the inner cities to the mountain tops. Some are long-lived perennial plants, others ('annuals') grow and die in a single season, leaving their seeds to overwinter and grow the following year.

The most significant feature of all these plants is that they possess true flowers. These are composed of four basic elements: the *sepals*, which are usually green and serve to protect the thin *petals* which lie concentrically within them. The petals form a ring (or series of rings) and make up the corolla, which is often brightly coloured. Within these are the *stamens* and *carpels,* respectively the male and female parts of the flower containing the ovules. The stamens shed pollen which is carried by insects or the wind to fertilise the female parts of another flower. Fertilised ovules later develop into seeds, which are often furnished with elaborate devices to ensure their dispersal. Flowers are frequently highly complex in form, brightly coloured and often furnished with quantities of attractive scent and nectar, all to ensure that they are visited by insects which then carry pollen away to other flowers. Further complexity is often built in to ensure that a flower is not fertilised by its own pollen and

The Pyramid Orchid, a spectacular plant of calcareous grassland. Like most species of orchid, they are particularly dependent on the maintainence of their habitat, in this case the regular grazing of animals to keep down competing species.

to ensure that it can only be visited by a limited range of insect types.

This complexity and colour of flowers makes them conspicuous and very interesting. Careful examination of both flowers and leaves is necessary in order that correct identifications may be made.

Habitat

Many species are of considerable ecological importance, particularly those which form the only food plant acceptable to certain insects. Some flowering plants, the legume family (peas, gorse etc) have special root nodules in which bacteria create nutrients for the soil, improving its quality for other plants. some distinctive flowers (e.g. most orchids) will grow only on calcareous soils, others (e.g. heathers) only in acid conditions. They thus constitute helpful and easily identifiable indications of soil type. Most flowering plant species grow in places where specific combinations of soil type, wetness,

A honey bee visits a flower in order to exploit the food source of nectar. By so doing the bee 'incidentally' carries pollen from one flower to the next, so benefitting the plant. Flowers are a highly adapted mechanism solely to achieve this distribution of pollen.

Flowering Plants

sunlight or shade exist. Thus certain habitats (e.g. woodland, moorland, fenland, sand dunes) all have their own characteristic 'sets' of species, most of which are unlikely to be found elsewhere. Thus habitat type is a helpful guide to the identification of species. A few flower types are almost cosmopolitan, but even they will not occur in some of the more challenging habitats where only the specialy adapted types can grow.

Flowering season

The majority of species have their flowers open in summer, but some species bloom very early in the year (e.g. snowdrops) before they are overshadowed by the growth of taller plants around them. Other species flower late; some continue to do so for several months while others bloom only for a short time. This season is another helpful guide to identification.

Many flowers are so attractive that people are tempted to pick them and take them home. For some very rare species this is now illegal, but even common ones suffer from thoughtless over-collecting and from people digging up whole plants to transfer to their garden (often with negative results due to incorrect soil type). To prevent this harmful and selfish behaviour, it is now illegal to uproot *any* wild plant without the permission of the land-owner.

Grasses

Grasses comprise a single family of flowering plants, the Graminae. Their flowers, though very tiny, dull coloured and inconspicuous, are nevertheless very complex. They produce pollen which is carried on the wind in great quantity to fertilise other flowers (and incidentally cause hay fever!) The grasses are one of the most recently evolved families of plants and one of the most highly developed. Characteristically they grow from the leaf base and at nodes along the stem, not the tips. Consequently they can be trampled, grazed or mown (cutting off their tips) yet can still grow again to their previous size. Cutting the tips off most plants stunts growth or even kills them. So resilient are grasses that we take them for granted and drive, run, play football and even land aeroplanes on them as though they were inert and non-living like concrete.

The Sundew makes its living by eating visiting insects after capturing them on its sticky leaves. This method of feeding enables the plant to exploit a bogland environment devoid of soil nutrients.

Flowering Plants

Ecology
Grasses are ecologically of major significance. They dominate certain habitats and provide food for a host of insects, mammals, birds and other creatures, most of which require special adaptations to cope with eating the tough and gritty cells. In fact, grassland habitats are a form of partnership between eaters and the eaten. Grazing animals eat the plants, but only the grasses can easily tolerate this and regrow continuously, thus the habitat becomes dominated by the grasses (which continue to feed the grazers) while other groups of plants are squeezed out. Grass as fodder for grazing animals is economically important, but the cereal crops (e.g. wheat, oats, barley, maize) which dominate many agricultural landscapes are also grasses. So the importance of this group of plants in economic and ecological terms cannot be overstated.

Structure
Whereas most flowering plants are dicotyledons and (among other characteristics) have branching veins in their broad leaves, grasses are monocotyledons. These plants characteristically have long, narrow leaves in which the veins lie parallel. Grasses also do not normally branch except at ground level to form rosettes or tussocks. Below ground they have a fibruous and extensive root system that forms a dense mat and helps to hold soil particles together, preventing erosion. The roots, and also underground stems (called 'rhizomes') can grow rapidly and quickly extend the plant to cover more ground or colonise newly exposed habitat such as freshly dug soil.

Identification
Identification of grasses relies upon careful observation of the leaf structure and its associated sheath. The shape and structure of the flower head is important (though often missing because of grazing or mowing). Some grasses are hairy, some are woody; certain species form tussocks, others do not. Again, soil type and moisture content often dictate which species will or will not be present.

Grasses are often taken for granted or even thought of as a single species, 'grass'. But there are many fascinating species showing a wide range of adaptations; moreover, they often provide the basis for a whole complex ecosystem.

Flowering Plants

Kingcup, Marsh Marigold
Ranunculaceae *Caltha palustris.*
Habitat: Common in marsh,
damp meadows, wet woodland
and ditches throughout British
Isles up to 1200m, but less
common in S. Ireland. **Notes:**
Grows well in partial shade.
Rare on acid peat. Very variable,
can be creeping or erect.

Globe Flower Ranunculaceae
Trollius europaeus. **Habitat:**
Locally common in wet
meadows, marsh and damp
woodland in upland areas of
Wales, N. England, Scotland and
N.W. Ireland. **Notes:** In damp
situations.

Green Hellebore
Ranunculaceae *Helleborus
viridis.* **Habitat:** Locally
common in woodland on
calcareous and base-rich soils in
England and Wales; more
common in S. **Notes:** Flowers
early in year (March).

Monkshood Ranunculaceae
Aconitum napellus. **Habitat:**
Rare by streams and in
woodland in S.W. England and
Wales. **Notes:** Leaves more
deeply cut than garden variety
which occasionally escapes.

Wood Anemone
Ranunculaceae *Anemone
nemorosa*. **Habitat:** Woodland
throughout British Isles, but rare
in N. Scotland and central and S.
Ireland. **Notes:** Often abundant,
forming large carpets on all but
most acid, water-logged soils.
Flowers usually white or pink;
rarely red-purple or blue.

Pasque Flower Ranunculaceae
Pulsatilla vulgaris. **Habitat:** Very
local and decreasing in
calcareous grassland in central
and E. England. **Notes:** Colour
varies from purple to red, violet
or white.

Flowering Plants

Old Man's Beard, Traveller's Joy Ranunculaceae *Clematis vitalba*. **Habitat:** Hedgerows, scrub and woodland margins on calcareous and base-rich soils in England and Wales, north to the Humber. **Notes:** Climbs up to 30m.

Meadow Buttercup Ranunculaceae *Ranunculus acris*. **Habitat:** Very common in damp lowland grassland and on mountains throughout British Isles. **Notes:** Flowers usually yellow but may be cream or white. Very variable.

Creeping Buttercup
Ranunculaceae *Ranunculus repens*. **Habitat:** Very common on farmland, meadows and wet woodland throughout British Isles, up to 1000m. **Notes:** Especially on heavy soils.

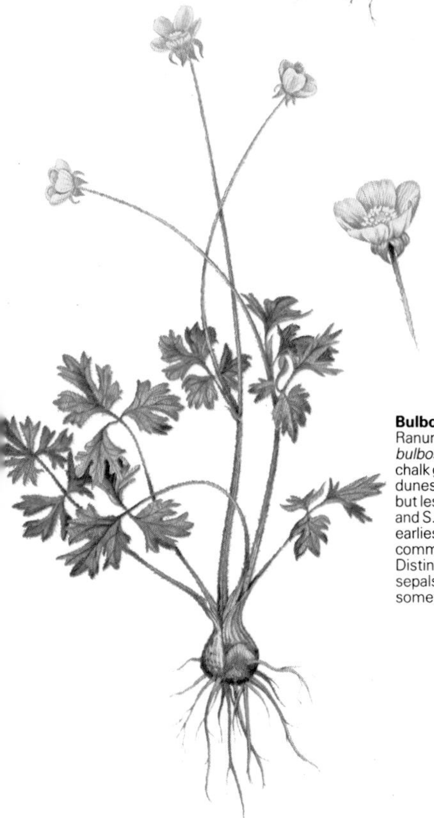

Bulbous Buttercup
Ranunculaceae *Ranunculus bulbosus*. **Habitat:** Abundant in chalk grassland, also on sand dunes, throughout British Isles, but less common in Scotland and S. Ireland. **Notes:** The earliest flowering of the common buttercups. Distinguished by reflexed sepals. Usually yellow but sometimes cream or white.

Flowering Plants

Pheasant's Eye Ranunculaceae *Adonis annua.* **Habitat:** Rare weed of arable farmland and occasionally pasture on calcareous soils in S. England. **Notes:** Seeds wrinkled.

Lesser Spearwort Ranunculaceae *Ranunculus flammula.* **Habitat:** Common in wet places throughout the British Isles. **Notes:** Variable, divided into three subspecies.

Lesser Celandine Ranunculaceae *Ranuncula ficaria.* **Habitat:** Locally common in woodland, meadows, hedgerows and streamsides throughout British Isles, but scattered in N. Scotland and central and S. Ireland. **Notes:** Grows in shade or in open. Variable.

Columbine Ranunculaceae
Aquilegia vulgaris. **Habitat:**
Local in damp woodland and
wetlands throughout British
Isles, up to 950m, becoming
rarer in N., and absent from N.
Scotland. **Notes:** Usually on
calcareous soils or fen peat.

Common Meadow Rue
Ranunculaceae *Thalictrum
flavum*. **Habitat:** Locally
common in meadows and by
rivers in England, especially in
E.; scattered in Ireland, Wales
and S. Scotland; up to 300m.
Notes: Very variable.

61

Flowering Plants

Common Red Poppy
Papaveraceae *Papaver rhoeas*.
Habitat: Common on farmland
in England; local in Wales,
Scotland, N. and W. Ireland.
Notes: Variable in shape and
hairiness of leaves, colour of
petals and capsule shape.

Yellow Horned Poppy
Papaveraceae *Glaucium flavum*.
Habitat: Shingle beaches in
England, Wales, E. and W.
Ireland, S. Scotland. **Notes:**
Yellow latex.

Greater Celandine
Papaveraceae *Chelidonium
majus*. **Habitat:** Locally
common in hedgerows,
hedgebanks and on walls
throughout British Isles,
especially in S.; usually near
buildings. **Notes:** Orange latex.
Poisonous.

Fumitory Fumariaceae *Fumaria officinalis*. **Habitat:** Very common on farmland, waste ground and dunes throughout British Isles, but rarer in W. **Notes:** Especially on calcareous and sandy soils.

Black Mustard Cruciferae *Brassica nigra*. **Habitat:** Locally common on waste ground, cliffs and river banks in England and Wales; rare in Scotland and Ireland. **Notes:** Seed pods beaded with slender beak.

Charlock Cruciferae *Sinapis arvensis*. **Habitat:** Very common on farmland and waste ground throughout British Isles. **Notes:** Lower leaves toothed and bristly.

Wall Rocket Cruciferae *Diplotaxis tenuifolia*. **Habitat:** Locally common on waste ground, especially on calcareous soils, and old walls in S. England; casual further north. **Notes:** Hairless, woody stem.

Flowering Plants

Common Winter-cress
Cruciferae *Barbarea vulgaris*.
Habitat: Very common by
streams, in hedgerows and on
damp waste ground throughout
British Isles.

Hedge Mustard Cruciferae
Sisymbrium officinale. **Habitat:**
Abundant in hedgerows, by
roadsides and on waste ground
throughout British Isles.

Creeping Yellow Cress
Cruciferae *Rorippa sylvestris*.
Habitat: Frequent but not
common on moist ground, by
streams and in gardens in
England, S. Scotland, Wales,
and Ireland except for N. and W.

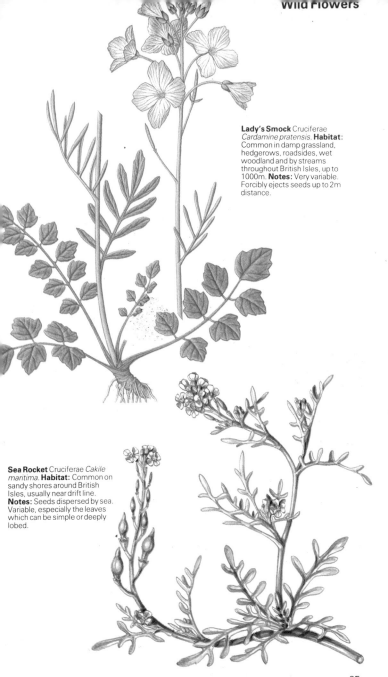

Lady's Smock Cruciferae
Cardamine pratensis. **Habitat:**
Common in damp grassland,
hedgerows, roadsides, wet
woodland and by streams
throughout British Isles, up to
1000m. **Notes:** Very variable.
Forcibly ejects seeds up to 2m
distance.

Sea Rocket Cruciferae *Cakile
maritima*. **Habitat:** Common on
sandy shores around British
Isles, usually near drift line.
Notes: Seeds dispersed by sea.
Variable, especially the leaves
which can be simple or deeply
lobed.

Flowering Plants

Sea Kale Cruciferae *Crambe maritima*. **Habitat:** Scattered on shingle beaches around British coasts, most common in S. England; occasionally on sand or cliffs. **Notes:** Sprouts readily after being buried under shingle. Fruits dispersed in sea-water where remain viable for several days.

Field Penny-cress Cruciferae *Thlaspi arvense*. **Habitat:** Common on farmland and waste ground throughout British Isles. **Notes:** Fruits large, almost circular with very broad wings, 12-22mm across.

Shepherd's Purse Cruciferae *Capsella bursa-pastoris*. **Habitat:** Very common on farmland, roadsides, waste ground and gardens throughout British Isles. **Notes:** Variable, often forms distinct local populations.

Common Scurvy Grass
Cruciferae *Cochlearia officinalis.*
Habitat: Coasts, near fresh
water in mountains throughout
most of British Isles but rare in
S. England. **Notes:** Recently
becoming common on motor-
way verges. Very variable.
Visited by flies and beetles.

Hairy Bitter Cress Cruciferae
Cardamine hirsuta. **Habitat:**
Very common on farmland, bare
ground, rocks and walls
throughout British Isles, up to
1300m. **Notes:** Seed-pods
erect; usually self-pollinated.

Whitlow Grass Cruciferae
Erophila verna. **Habitat:** Locally
common in dry open grassland,
on rocks and walls throughout
much of British Isles, but less
common in W. Britain, N. and S.
Ireland. **Notes:** Size and shape
of seedpod varies.

Flowering Plants

Watercress Cruciferae *Rorippa nasturtium-aquaticum.* **Habitat:** Very common in slow-flowing, clear water throughout British Isles. **Notes:** Evergreen.

Wild Mignonette Resedaceae *Reseda lutea.* **Habitat:** Common on grassland and waste ground in England; local in Wales, Ireland and E. Scotland. **Notes:** Especially on chalk.

Common Milkwort Polygalaceae *Polygala vulgaris.* **Habitat:** Common on dry grassland throughout British Isles. **Notes:** On basic soils. Flower colour varies.

Chalk Milkwort Polygalaceae *Polygala calcarea.* **Habitat:** Local on chalk grassland in central, S. and S.E. England; occasional in Midlands. **Notes:** Flower colour varies from intense blue to bluish-white.

Common Rockrose Cistaceae *Helianthemum chamaecistus.* **Habitat:** Common on calcareous grassland and scrub throughout British Isles up to 680m, except S.W. England and N.W. Scotland. **Notes:** When touched stamens move back against petals within a few seconds.

Purging Flax Linaceae *Linum cartharticum.* **Habitat:** Common on calcareous grassland, heaths, moors, rock ledges and dunes throughout British Isles, up to 950m. **Notes:** Stems usually, but not always, solitary.

Touch-me-not Balsaminaceae *Impatiens noli-tangere.* **Habitat:** Very local by streams and in wet woodland in England, Wales and S. Scotland. **Notes:** Two flower types occur on same plant – either normal opening or remaining closed (cleistogamous). Seeds are forcibly ejected by explosive capsule.

Common St John's Wort Hypericaceae *Hypericum perforatum.* **Habitat:** Very common in scrub, hedgerows and rough, dry grassland throughout British Isles. **Notes:** Especially on chalk and sand. Black dots on edges of petals; small translucent spots on leaves.

Flowering Plants

Imperforate St John's Wort
Hypericaceae *Hypericum
maculatum*. **Habitat:** Locally
common in woodland edges
and rides, hedgerows and
roadsides in British Isles.
Notes: Usually on damp, heavy
soils.

Common Dog Violet Violaceae
Viola riviniana. **Habitat:** Very
common in woodland,
hedgerows, grassland and on
rocks throughout British Isles.
Notes: Often flowers in both
spring and autumn. Flower
colour variable.

Hairy St John's Wort
Hypericaceae *Hypericum
hirsutum.* **Habitat:** Damp
woodland and grassland
throughout England, S. and E.
Scotland, E. Wales; scattered in
E. Ireland. **Notes:** Mainly on
basic soils. Hairy.

Wood Dog Violet Violaceae
Viola reichenbachiana. **Habitat:**
Locally common in woodland
and hedgerows in S. central and
E. England; local in Wales and
Ireland; rare in S. Scotland.
Notes: Usually on calcareous
soils. Flowers usually lilac, rarely
pink or white. Flowers earlier
than *V. riviniana.*

Hairy Violet Violaceae *Viola hirta*. **Habitat:** Locally common in calcareous grassland, woodland and scrub in England, but rare in S.W. and N.; scattered in S. Scotland and Wales; very local in Ireland; up to 650m.

Field Pansy Violaceae *Viola arvensis*. **Habitat:** Farmland and grassland throughout Britain; less common in W.; scattered in Ireland. **Notes:** Usually on calcareous or neutral soil. Very variable.

Wild Pansy Violaceae *Viola tricolor*. **Habitat:** Locally common on grassland, dunes, waste ground and farmland throughout British Isles. **Notes:** Very variable; annual and perennial forms exist.

Maiden Pink Caryophyllaceae *Dianthus deltoides*. **Habitat:** Local on dry grassland in Britain; one locality in S.E. Ireland. **Notes:** Lowland species.

71

Flowering Plants

Ragged Robin Caryophyllaceae *Lychnis flos-cuculi.* **Habitat:** Meadows, marsh, damp woodland throughout most of British Isles up to 650m, but less common in N. Scotland and S.E. Ireland. **Notes:** Flowers usually red, occasionally white.

White Campion Caryophyllaceae *Silene alba.* **Habitat:** Common on farmland, waste ground and in hedgerows throughout British Isles. **Notes:** Hybridizes with *S. dioica.*

Red Campion Caryophyllaceae *Silene dioica.* **Habitat:** Very common in hedgerows and woodland throughout British Isles, but very rare in Cambs. **Notes:** On base-rich soils.

Sea Campion Caryophyllaceae
Silene maritima. **Habitat:**
Locally abundant on cliffs and
shingle shores around most of
British Isles; less common in E.
Also on mountains, by gravelly
lake shores and alpine streams
in N. Britain.
Bladder Campion *S. vulgaris* is
similar but taller with less fleshy
leaves. It is common on chalk
grassland, in hedgerows and
farmland in S. Britain, but rarer in
the north

Spanish Catchfly
Caryophyllaceae *Silene otites*.
Habitat: Confined to the
Breckland heaths of Norfolk,
W. Suffolk and Cambs. **Notes:**
Evening scented.

Common Chickweed
Caryophyllaceae *Stellaria
media*. **Habitat:** Very common
almost everywhere in British
Isles, especially luxuriant around
sea-bird colonies. **Notes:**
Stamens red-violet.

Flowering Plants

Field Mouse-ear Chickweed
Caryophyllaceae *Cerastium arvense.* **Habitat:** Locally common on dry grassland and roadsides in E. England; rare in rest of Britain; scattered in Ireland especially in central E. and W. **Notes:** On calcareous and slightly acid soils. Variable.

Greater Stitchwort
Caryophyllaceae *Stellaria holostea.* **Habitat:** Very common in woodland and hedgerows throughout British Isles. **Notes:** Absent from very acid soils.
Lesser Stitchwort *S. graminea* is smaller but very similar. It is common on acid soils in grassland, heaths and open woodland.

Sea Sandwort
Caryophyllaceae *Honkenya peploides.* **Habitat:** Common on mobile sand and sandy shingle on all British coasts. **Notes:** Often with Sand Couch Grass. Tolerates short periods of immersion in salt water.

Wild Flowers

Perennial Sea Spurrey
Caryophyllaceae *Spergularia. media.* **Habitat:** Common in salt marsh around all British coasts. **Notes:** Petals white or pink. Only inflorescence hairy.

Perennial Knawel
Caryophyllaceae *Scleranthus perennis.* **Habitat:** Very rare in sandy fields in E. Anglia and Radnor in Wales. **Notes:** Visited by flies.

Annual Knawel *S. annuus* is similar but sepals are pointed and white-edged. It is locally frequent on dry, sandy waste ground, grassland and farmland.

Corn Spurrey Caryophyllaceae *Spergula arvensis.* **Habitat:** Locally abundant on farmland throughout British Isles, up to 500m. **Notes:** Never on calcareous soils. A troublesome weed. Variable.

Flowering Plants

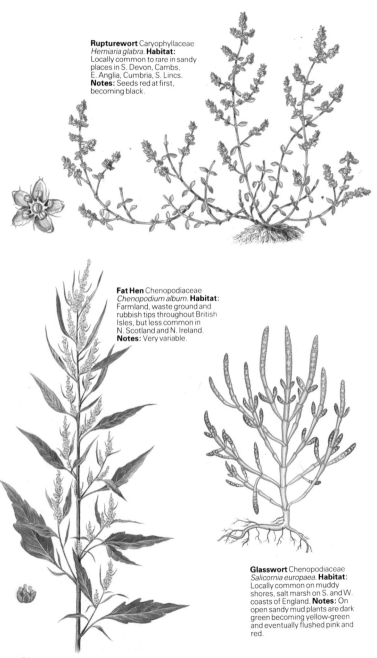

Rupturewort Caryophyllaceae *Herniaria glabra*. **Habitat:** Locally common to rare in sandy places in S. Devon, Cambs, E. Anglia, Cumbria, S. Lincs. **Notes:** Seeds red at first, becoming black.

Fat Hen Chenopodiaceae *Chenopodium album*. **Habitat:** Farmland, waste ground and rubbish tips throughout British Isles, but less common in N. Scotland and N. Ireland. **Notes:** Very variable.

Glasswort Chenopodiaceae *Salicornia europaea*. **Habitat:** Locally common on muddy shores, salt marsh on S. and W. coasts of England. **Notes:** On open sandy mud plants are dark green becoming yellow-green and eventually flushed pink and red.

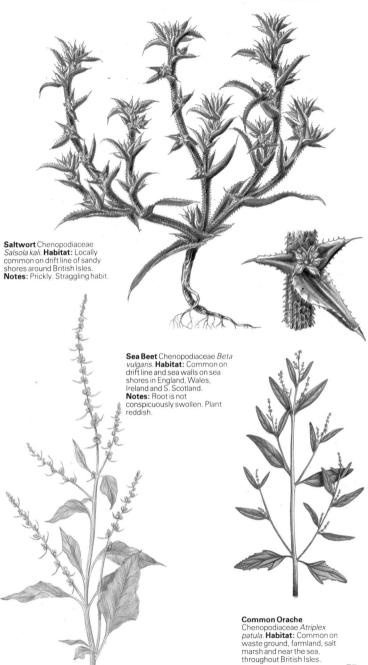

Saltwort Chenopodiaceae *Salsola kali*. **Habitat:** Locally common on drift line of sandy shores around British Isles. **Notes:** Prickly. Straggling habit.

Sea Beet Chenopodiaceae *Beta vulgaris*. **Habitat:** Common on drift line and sea walls on sea shores in England, Wales, Ireland and S. Scotland. **Notes:** Root is not conspicuously swollen. Plant reddish.

Common Orache Chenopodiaceae *Atriplex patula*. **Habitat:** Common on waste ground, farmland, salt marsh and near the sea, throughout British Isles.

77

Flowering Plants

Sea Purslane Chenopodiaceae
Halimione portulacoides.
Habitat: Salt marsh around
English, Welsh, S. Scottish, S.
and E. Irish coasts; on upper
parts of salt marsh and along
margins of pools and channels
flooded at high tide. **Notes:**
Grey-white, mealy in
appearance.

Common Mallow Malvaceae
Malva sylvestris. **Habitat:**
Common on waste ground, in
hedgerows and roadsides in S.
British Isles; rarer in N. **Notes:**
Variable, erect or spreading.

Tree Mallow Malvaceae
Lavatera arborea. **Habitat:**
Rocky coasts and waste ground
near sea in S., S.E., W. and S.W.
England, Wales and Ireland.
Notes: Seeds sometimes hairy.
(up to 3m)

Herb Robert Geraniaceae
Geranium robertianum.
Habitat: Common in woodland
and hedgerows throughout
British Isles up to 750m. **Notes:**
A dwarf form grows on shingle
beaches.

Dovesfoot Cranesbill
Geraniaceae *Geranium molle.*
Habitat: Common on dry
grassland, farmland, waste
ground and dunes in England;
less common in Wales,
Scotland and Ireland; up to
550m. **Notes:** Covered with
long, soft, white hairs.

Wood Cranesbill Geraniaceae
Geranium sylvaticum. **Habitat:**
Locally common in damp
woodland, meadows and
hedgerows in N. England and
Scotland; very rare in Ireland;
absent from Wales and S.
England. **Notes:** Flowers red or
pink-violet.

79

Wood Sorrel Oxalidaceae
Oxalis acetosella. **Habitat:**
Common, often abundant, in
woodland, hedgerows, on rocks
throughout British Isles up to
1300m. **Notes:** Very shade
tolerant. Often common in
beech and oak woods.
Sometimes epiphytic.

Common Storksbill
Geraniaceae *Erodium
cicutarium.* **Habitat:** Common
on dunes, sea-cliffs and inland
on sandy waste ground
throughout British Isles. **Notes:**
Flowers rose-purple to white.

Dyer's Greenweed
Papilionaceae *Genista tinctoria.*
Habitat: Locally common on
rough grassland, old pastures
and commons in Britain, except
N. Scotland; absent from
Ireland. **Notes:** On heavy soils.

Broom Papilionaceae
Sarothamnus scoparius.
Habitat: Common on heaths,
cliffs, waste ground, in
woodland throughout most of
British Isles, but less common in
central Ireland. **Notes:** Prefers
sandy soils.

Common Gorse, Furze
Papilionaceae *Ulex europaeus.*
Habitat: Common on heaths
and rough grassland throughout
British Isles. **Notes:** Prefers
light, non-calcareous soils. Seed
pods dehisce explosively.
Dwarf Gorse *U. minor* is much
smaller and confined to heaths
in S. and S.E. England.
Western Gorse *U. gallii* is
similar but is common in W.
Britain.

Restharrow Papilionaceae
Ononis repens. **Habitat:** Locally
common in rough grassland in
England, Wales and E. Scotland;
occasional in Western Isles;
scattered in Ireland, especially
S.E. **Notes:** Prefers calcareous
soils.

Red Clover Papilionaceae
Trifolium pratense. **Habitat:**
Abundant in grassland
throughout British Isles. **Notes:**
Very variable – flowers usually
pink-purple, but sometimes
white. Often cultivated for hay.

White Clover Papilionaceae
Trifolium repens. **Habitat:**
Abundant in grassland
throughout British Isles, on
most soil types. **Notes:** Flowers
usually white or pink, but
occasionally purple.

Flowering Plants

Tufted Vetch Papilionaceae *Vicia cracca*. **Habitat:** Common in hedgerows, woodland edges and rides and scrub, throughout British Isles. **Notes:** Climbing. Tendrils branched. Flowers fade to red-violet.

Bush Vetch Papilionaceae *Vicia sepium*. **Habitat:** Very common in woodland, hedgerows and scrub throughout British Isles. **Notes:** Climbing, with branched tendrils.

Common Vetch Papilionaceae *Vicia sativa*. **Habitat:** Very common in hedgerows, grassland and scrub throughout British Isles. **Notes:** Very variable. A cultivated form occurs with paler flowers.

Hairy Tare Papilionaceae *Vicia hirsuta*. **Habitat:** Generally common in hedgerows and rough grassland throughout British Isles, but rarer in N.W. Scotland and Ireland. **Notes:** Not on very acid soils. Trailing

Slender Tare Papilionaceae *Vicia tenuissima*. **Habitat:** Locally common in grassy places in central and S.E. England. **Notes:** Tendrils usually simple.

Bitter Vetch Papilionaceae *Lathyrus montanus*. **Habitat:** Locally common in woodland, hedgerows, scrub and heaths throughout British Isles, except E. Anglia and central Ireland. **Notes:** On acid soils. Flowers turn from crimson to blue or green.

Sea Pea Papilionaceae *Lathyrus japonicus*. **Habitat:** Very local on shingle beaches in S. and S.E. England. **Notes:** Flowers purple to blue. Creeping or ascending; tendrils simple, branched or absent.

Black Medick Papilionaceae *Medicago lupulina*. **Habitat:** Very common in grassland and on roadsides throughout much of British Isles up to 350m; less common in N. and W. Scotland, Wales, N. and S.W. Ireland.

Bird's-foot Trefoil Papilionaceae *Lotus corniculatus*. **Habitat:** Very common in grassy places throughout British Isles. **Notes:** Very variable.

Kidney Vetch Papilionaceae *Anthyllis vulneraria*. **Habitat:** Locally common in grassland and by the sea throughout British Isles. **Notes:** Most abundant on calcareous soils; prefers dry places with shallow soils. Variable; flowers yellow or red.

Greater Bird's-foot Trefoil Papilionaceae *Lotus pedunculatus*. **Habitat:** Locally abundant in damp meadows and marsh throughout most of British Isles, but rare in N. Scotland and central Ireland. **Notes:** Stem hollow. Hairy or hairless.

Flowering Plants

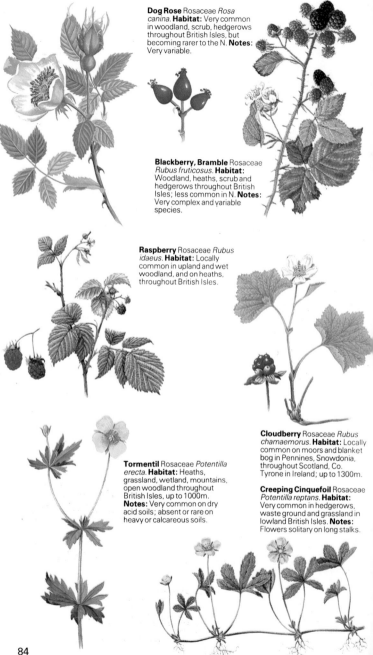

Dog Rose Rosaceae *Rosa canina.* **Habitat:** Very common in woodland, scrub, hedgerows throughout British Isles, but becoming rarer to the N. **Notes:** Very variable.

Blackberry, Bramble Rosaceae *Rubus fruticosus.* **Habitat:** Woodland, heaths, scrub and hedgerows throughout British Isles; less common in N. **Notes:** Very complex and variable species.

Raspberry Rosaceae *Rubus idaeus.* **Habitat:** Locally common in upland and wet woodland, and on heaths, throughout British Isles.

Cloudberry Rosaceae *Rubus chamaemorus.* **Habitat:** Locally common on moors and blanket bog in Pennines, Snowdonia, throughout Scotland, Co. Tyrone in Ireland; up to 1300m.

Creeping Cinquefoil Rosaceae *Potentilla reptans.* **Habitat:** Very common in hedgerows, waste ground and grassland in lowland British Isles. **Notes:** Flowers solitary on long stalks.

Tormentil Rosaceae *Potentilla erecta.* **Habitat:** Heaths, grassland, wetland, mountains, open woodland throughout British Isles, up to 1000m. **Notes:** Very common on dry acid soils; absent or rare on heavy or calcareous soils.

Spring Cinquefoil Rosaceae *Potentilla tabernaemontani*. **Habitat:** Very local on dry grassland throughout Britain. **Notes:** Prefers sunny slopes on basic soils.

Silverweed Rosaceae *Potentilla anserina*. **Habitat:** Very common on waste ground, roadsides, pathways, meadows and dunes throughout British Isles. **Notes:** Creeping. Foliage silver with fine hairs.

Agrimony Rosaceae *Agrimonia eupatoria*. **Habitat:** Common in grassland, hedgerows, roadsides and scrub throughout British Isles, except N. Scotland. **Notes:** Especially on calcareous soils. Stem reddish.

Salad Burnet Rosaceae *Poterium sanguisorba*. **Habitat:** Locally common in calcareous grassland throughout England; occasional in S. Scotland and Ireland; common in N. and S. Wales but absent from centre; up to 550m. **Notes:** Smells of cucumber when crushed.

Wild Strawberry Rosaceae *Fragaria vesca*. **Habitat:** Woodland, scrub, hedgerows and grassland on calcareous soils throughout British Isles up to 750m, but less common in N. Scotland. **Notes:** Fruit edible.

Flowering Plants

Marsh Cinquefoil Rosaceae
Potentilla palustris. **Habitat:**
Locally abundant in marsh, wet
heaths and moors throughout
most of British Isles up to 950m,
but less common in N. Scotland,
Midlands and S.W. England.
Notes: All parts of flower
purple.

Meadow Sweet Rosaceae
Filipendula ulmaria. **Habitat:**
Common in wet meadows,
marsh, ditches and by rivers
throughout British Isles up to
950m. **Notes:** Sometimes
locally dominant. Absent from
acid peat.

Dropwort Rosaceae *Filipendula
vulgaris*. **Habitat:** Locally
common, often abundant, in
dry, usually calcareous
grassland in England, especially
in E.; scattered in Wales,
S. Scotland and W. Ireland; up to
400m. **Notes:** Roots have egg-
shaped tubers.

Herb Bennet, Wood Avens
Rosaceae *Geum urbanum*.
Habitat: Woodland, scrub,
hedgerows throughout British
Isles up to 550m, but rare in
N. Scotland. **Notes:** Prefers
shade and rich, damp soils.

Sundew Droseraceae *Drosera rotundifolia*. **Habitat:** Locally common in bogs and wet, peaty heaths and moors, often in *Sphagnum* moss, throughout the British Isles; most common in N. and W. **Notes:** Can form floating fringe to small pools. Reddish, covered with long, glistening, sticky hairs that ensnare and digest insects.

Water Avens Rosaceae *Geum rivale*. **Habitat:** Locally common in meadows, marsh, damp woodland, moist mountain ledges throughout British Isles up to 1000m, except S. England and Ireland. **Notes:** Shade tolerant. Prefers base-rich soil.

Starry Saxifrage Saxifragaceae *Saxifraga stellaris*. **Habitat:** Locally common in wet places on mountains in Snowdonia, N. England and Scotland; scattered throughout Ireland. **Notes:** Found at highest British altitudes.

Meadow Saxifrage Saxifragaceae *Saxifraga granulata*. **Habitat:** Locally common on dry, sandy grassland in lowland Britain; absent from N.W. Scotland, S.W. England and Sussex; very rare in E. Ireland. **Notes:** Not on very acid soils or mountains.

Opposite-leaved Golden Saxifrage Saxifragaceae *Chrysosplenium oppositifolium*. **Habitat:** Common by streams in woodland and on mountain ledges throughout British Isles, except E. England. **Notes:** Creeping; mat-forming.

Flowering Plants

Grass of Parnassus
Parnassiaceae *Parnassia palustris*. **Habitat:** Locally frequent in wet grassland, marsh, and dune slacks in British Isles, but common only in Scotland; absent from extreme S. Englan '. **Notes:** On basic soils.

Biting Stonecrop Crassulaceae *Sedum acre*. **Habitat:** Common on dry grassland, dunes, by the sea and on walls throughout British Isles. **Notes:** Has peppery taste.

English Stonecrop
Crassulaceae *Sedum anglicum*. **Habitat:** Cliffs, sand-dunes, shingle around all British coasts; rocks and grassland inland up to 1100m; very common in W. England and Ireland. **Notes:** Not on strongly basic soils.

Great Willowherb Onagraceae *Epilobium hirsutum*. **Habitat:** Very common in marsh, ditches, and by streams throughout British Isles except N.W. Scotland; up to 400m.

Rosebay Willowherb
Onagraceae *Epilobium angustifolium*. **Habitat:** Very common in woodland margins and clearings, waste ground and rocky places in Britain except N. Scotland, up to 1000m; scattered in Ireland, especially in E. **Notes:** Very variable.

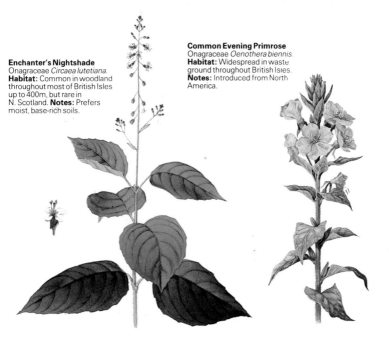

Enchanter's Nightshade
Onagraceae *Circaea lutetiana*.
Habitat: Common in woodland
throughout most of British Isles
up to 400m, but rare in
N. Scotland. **Notes:** Prefers
moist, base-rich soils.

Common Evening Primrose
Onagraceae *Oenothera biennis*.
Habitat: Widespread in waste
ground throughout British Isles.
Notes: Introduced from North
America.

Purple Loosestrife Lythraceae
Lythrum salicaria. **Habitat:**
Locally abundant in marsh, by
lakes and slow-flowing rivers
throughout much of British
Isles, but rare in N.E. England,
E. Scotland; absent from
N. Scotland. **Notes:** Often
forms large stands.

Sea Spurge Euphorbiaceae
Euphorbia paralias. **Habitat:**
Locally common on sand
and mobile dunes on coasts in
W., S. and S.E. England, Wales,
and Ireland except for W.
Notes: Milky latex.

Dog's Mercury Euphorbiaceae
Mercurialis perennis. **Habitat:**
Common in woodland, on shady
rocks, throughout England,
Wales, central and S. Scotland
up to 1200m; local in N.
Scotland and Ireland. **Notes:**
Often dominant in beech woods
on chalk.

Flowering Plants

Sun Spurge Euphorbiaceae
Euphorbia helioscopia. **Habitat:**
Very common on farmland and
waste ground throughout
British Isles.

Stinging Nettle Urticaceae
Urtica dioica. **Habitat:**
Abundant on cultivated land,
hedgerows, woodland and river
banks throughout British Isles
up to 900m. **Notes:** On fertile
soils. Covered with stinging
hairs.
Small Nettle *U. urens* is smaller
with more deeply toothed
leaves and shorter
inflorescence borne on leafy
sidebranch.

Petty Spurge Euphorbiaceae
Euphorbia peplus. **Habitat:**
Farmland and gardens
throughout British Isles up to
450m, but less common in
N. Ireland and Scotland.

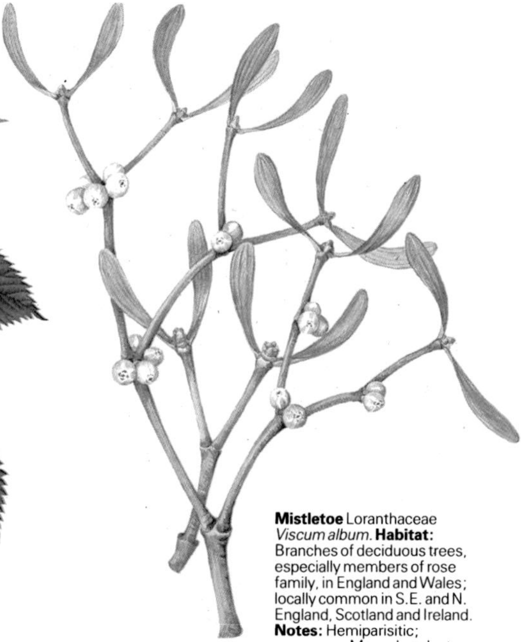

Mistletoe Loranthaceae
Viscum album. **Habitat:**
Branches of deciduous trees,
especially members of rose
family, in England and Wales;
locally common in S.E. and N.
England, Scotland and Ireland.
Notes: Hemiparisitic;
evergreen. More abundant on
calcareous soils.

Ivy Araliaceae *Hedera helix*.
Habitat: Woodland,
hedgerows, walls, rocks
throughout British Isles up to
650m; less common in extreme
N. **Notes:** Climbs up to 30m;
occurs on all but very acid, dry or
water-logged soils; very shade
tolerant. Flowers only in sunny
position. Has two distinct leaf
forms.

Sea Buckthorn Elaeagnaceae
Hippophae rhamnoides.
Habitat: Locally common, and
often dominant, on fixed sand
dunes and rarely sea cliffs on all
British coasts; rare in W. Ireland.
Notes: A shrub; often planted.

Heart Willow Salicaceae *Salix
herbacea*. **Habitat:** Locally
abundant on mountain ledges
from 95-1400m in Scotland and
Lake District; scattered in
Wales and Ireland.

Marsh Pennywort
Hydrocotylaceae *Hydrocotyle
vulgaris*. **Habitat:** Locally
common in marsh, wet
woodland and bog throughout
British Isles to 550m, but less
common in Midlands, E.
Scotland and central E. Ireland.
Notes: A creeping plant.

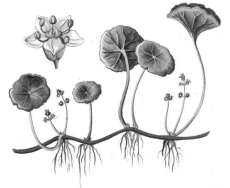

91

Flowering Plants

Sanicle Umbelliferae *Sanicula europaea*. **Habitat:** Very common in woodland throughout most of British Isles especially in beech and oak woods on calcareous soils; less common in E. Scotland and Ireland. **Notes:** Flowers pink or white.

Hemlock Umbelliferae *Conium maculatum*. **Habitat:** Common by freshwater in meadows and open woodland in S. and E. Britain; rare in Scotland, especially in W.; scattered in Wales and Ireland. **Notes:** Very poisonous.

Cow Parsley Umbelliferae *Anthriscus sylvestris*. **Habitat:** Abundant in meadows, hedgerows, by roadsides and woodland edges throughout most of British Isles, but rare in N.W. Scotland and S.E. Ireland. **Notes:** Begins flowering in April.

Sea Holly Umbelliferae *Eryngium maritimum*. **Habitat:** Coastal sand dunes of England, Wales, Ireland and S.W. Scotland. **Notes:** Distinctive blue-green; flowers and bracts blue to purple. Fruit covered with hooks.

Wild Flowers

Fool's Watercress
Umbelliferae *Apium nodiflorum*.
Habitat: Common in ditches,
streams and ponds in lowland
England, Wales and Ireland; rare
in Scotland. **Notes:** Foliage can
be mistaken for Watercress.

Burnet Saxifrage Umbelliferae
Pimpinella saxifraga. **Habitat:**
Dry grassland throughout British
Isles, but rare in N. Scotland and
N. Ireland. **Notes:** Prefers basic
soils. Usually hairy.

Ground Elder Umbelliferae
Aegopodium podagraria.
Habitat: Gardens, waste
ground, near buildings
throughout British Isles, but less
common in N. Scotland. **Notes:**
Persistent garden weed.

Lesser Water Parsnip
Umbelliferae *Berula erecta*.
Habitat: Locally common in
ditches, slow streams and
ponds in England; rare in
N. England, Scotland, Wales and
Ireland.
Greater Water Parsnip *Sium
latifolium* is larger, erect, with
thick hollow stem and longer
less-toothed leaves. It is locally
common in wetland in E. Anglia;
rare elsewhere.

Fool's Parsley Umbelliferae
Aethina cynapium. **Habitat:**
Common on farmland and
waste ground throughout
British Isles, except N.W.
Scotland. **Notes:** Drooping
bracts conspicuous.

93

Flowering Plants

Wild Angelica Umbelliferae
Angelica sylvestris. **Habitat:**
Common in damp meadows,
woodland and wetland,
throughout British Isles. **Notes:**
Flowers white or pink.

Milk Parsley Umbelliferae
Peucedanum palustre. **Habitat:**
Local in fen peat in E. Anglia;
rare in damp places in S. and E.
England. **Notes:** All parts of
plant have watery, milky sap
when young.

Wild Parsnip Umbelliferae
Pastinaca sativa. **Habitat:**
Locally abundant in grassland,
waste ground, roadsides in
England, Wales and Ireland;
common in central, S. and E.
England; rare in Scotland.
Notes: Especially on basic soils.
Strong smelling.

Wild Carrot Umbelliferae
Daucus carota. **Habitat:**
Common on grassland,
roadsides, hedgerows and
coastal cliffs throughout British
Isles, but not on mountains or
moors. **Notes:** Especially on
calcareous soils and near sea.

Cow Parsnip, Hogweed
Umbelliferae *Heracleum sphondylium*. **Habitat:** Common in meadows, woodland margins, hedgerows and by roadsides throughout British Isles up to 1000m. **Notes:** Leaf shape variable. Foliage edible. Flowers white or pink.

Giant Hogweed
H. mantegazzianum is similar but up to 5m tall with red-spotted stem. It is locally abundant by freshwater.

Broad-leaved Dock
Polygonaceae *Rumex obtusifolius*. **Habitat:** Field margins, hedgerows, waste ground throughout British Isles, but less frequent in N. **Notes:** Especially on disturbed ground.

Curled Dock Polygonaceae *Rumex crispus*. **Habitat:** Common on rough grassland, waste ground, farmland, sand dunes and shingle throughout most of British Isles, but rarer in N.

Flowering Plants

Water Dock Polygonaceae *Rumex hydrolapathum.* **Habitat:** Frequent but not common in wet soils and shallow water throughout central and S. England; scattered in Wales, S. and central Scotland, Ireland and S.W. England. **Notes:** Leaf margin flat or undulating.

Common Sorrel Polygonaceae *Rumex acetosa.* **Habitat:** Very common in rough grassland and by roadsides throughout British Isles.
Sheep's Sorrel *R. acetosella* is smaller with narrower, stalked leaves. It is very common on dry, acid grassland, heaths and shingle.

Bilberry, Whortleberry Edricaceae *Vaccinium myrtillus.* **Habitat:** Woodland and heaths throughout British Isles up to 1300m; rarer in Midlands and E. Anglia. **Notes:** Often dominant at higher altitudes.

Japanese Knotweed Polygonaceae *Polygonum cuspidatum.* **Habitat:** A common garden escape throughout most of British Isles, but rare in extreme N. Scotland.

Cowberry Ericaceae *Vaccinium vitis-idaea.* **Habitat:** Locally common on upland moors and in woodland in N. England, Ireland and Scotland. **Notes:** On acid soils. Evergreen. Occasionally dominant.

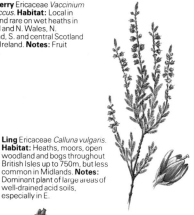

Cranberry Ericaceae *Vaccinium oxycoccus*. **Habitat:** Local in bogs and rare on wet heaths in central and N. Wales, N. England, S. and central Scotland and E. Ireland. **Notes:** Fruit edible.

Ling Ericaceae *Calluna vulgaris*. **Habitat:** Heaths, moors, open woodland and bogs throughout British Isles up to 750m, but less common in Midlands. **Notes:** Dominant plant of large areas of well-drained acid soils, especially in E.

Bog Rosemary Ericaceae *Andromeda polifolia*. **Habitat:** Common in bogs and on wet heaths in central Ireland; local in central W. Wales, N.W. England and S.W. Scotland up to 550m. **Notes:** Evergreen.

Bell Heather Ericaceae *Erica cinerea*. **Habitat:** Heaths throughout British Isles up to 700m, but rare in Midlands and central Ireland. **Notes:** Usually in dry places.

Common Wintergreen Pyrolaceae *Pyrola minor*. **Habitat:** Locally common in pine woods, on moors, damp rocks and dunes in N. and S. England; occasional to rare in Scotland and Ireland.

Crowberry Empetraceae *Empetrum nigrum*. **Habitat:** Common on moors, mountain tops and drier parts of blanket bogs in Scotland, N. England, Wales and Ireland; occasional in S.W. England. **Notes:** Sometimes dominant.

Flowering Plants

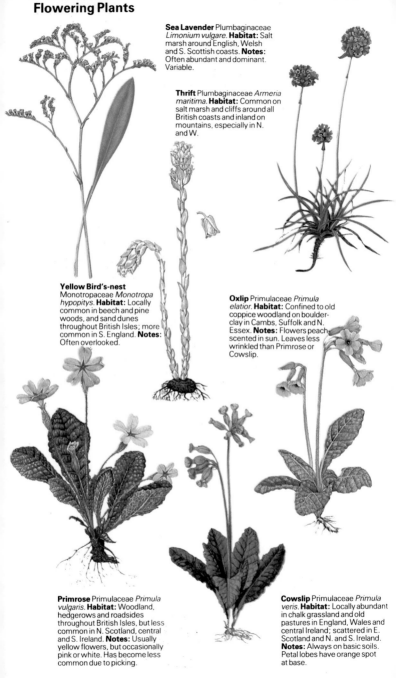

Sea Lavender Plumbaginaceae *Limonium vulgare*. **Habitat:** Salt marsh around English, Welsh and S. Scottish coasts. **Notes:** Often abundant and dominant. Variable.

Thrift Plumbaginaceae *Armeria maritima*. **Habitat:** Common on salt marsh and cliffs around all British coasts and inland on mountains, especially in N. and W.

Yellow Bird's-nest Monotropaceae *Monotropa hypopitys*. **Habitat:** Locally common in beech and pine woods, and sand dunes throughout British Isles; more common in S. England. **Notes:** Often overlooked.

Oxlip Primulaceae *Primula elatior*. **Habitat:** Confined to old coppice woodland on boulder-clay in Cambs, Suffolk and N. Essex. **Notes:** Flowers peach scented in sun. Leaves less wrinkled than Primrose or Cowslip.

Primrose Primulaceae *Primula vulgaris*. **Habitat:** Woodland, hedgerows and roadsides throughout British Isles, but less common in N. Scotland, central and S. Ireland. **Notes:** Usually yellow flowers, but occasionally pink or white. Has become less common due to picking.

Cowslip Primulaceae *Primula veris*. **Habitat:** Locally abundant in chalk grassland and old pastures in England, Wales and central Ireland; scattered in E. Scotland and N. and S. Ireland. **Notes:** Always on basic soils. Petal lobes have orange spot at base.

Yellow Loosestrife Primulaceae *Lysimachia vulgaris*. **Habitat:** Locally common in marsh, by lakes and rivers in England, Wales, Ireland and S. Scotland; absent from extreme N. **Notes:** Leaves dotted with orange or black glands.

Scarlet Pimpernel Primulaceae *Anagallis arvensis*. **Habitat:** Common on farmland, by roadsides and sand dunes in England, becoming rarer in N. and in Scotland; less common in N. Ireland. **Notes:** Stems and lower surfaces of leaves have black dots.

Field Gentian Gentianaceae *Gentianella campestris*. **Habitat:** Frequent on neutral grassland and dunes in N. England, Scotland and Ireland; rare in S. England and Wales.

Chickweed Wintergreen Primulaceae *Trientalis europaea*. **Habitat:** Rare to locally common in pine woods in Scotland and N. England; very rare in Suffolk.

Common Centaury Gentianaceae *Centaurium erythraea*. **Habitat:** Common in dry grassland, dunes, wood margins in England, especially in S., Wales and Ireland; rare in Scotland. **Notes:** Very variable.

Flowering Plants

Field Bindweed
Convolvulaceae *Convolvulus arvensis*. **Habitat:** Very common on cultivated ground and short turf by sea in S. Britain; rarer in N. **Notes:** Prefers light, basic soils. A persistent weed.

Yellow-wort Gentianaceae *Blackstonia perfoliata*. **Habitat:** Frequent in calcareous grassland and on dunes in England, Ireland and extreme N. and S. Wales. **Notes:** Stems pass through the centre of the leaves.

Common Dodder
Convolvulaceae *Cuscuta epithymum*. **Habitat:** Locally common on heaths throughout British Isles; more common in S., rare in N. and Ireland, absent from central and N. Scotland. **Notes:** Parasitic, especially on Gorse and Ling. Flowers pink and scented. Twines counter-clockwise.

Great Bindweed
Convolvulaceae *Calystegia sepium*. **Habitat:** Common in hedgerows and waste ground in England and Wales; scattered in Ireland and Scotland. **Notes:** Variable.

Black Nightshade *S. nigrum* is similar but smaller with white flowers and black berries. It is common in England and Wales, as a weed of arable and waste ground; very rare in Scotland and Ireland.

Woody Nightshade
Solanaceae *Solanum dulcamara*. **Habitat:** Common in woodland, waste ground, hedgerows, shingle beaches in England; local in Scotland, especially in S; rare in central Wales; scattered in Ireland. **Notes:** Flowers occasionally white.

Great Mullein
Scrophulariaceae *Verbascum thapsus*. **Habitat:** Common in open woodland, hedgerows and waste ground in Britain, but rare in N. and W. Scotland; occasional in Ireland. **Notes:** On base-rich soils. Covered with dense white hairs.

Common Figwort
Scrophulariaceae *Scrophularia nodosa*. **Habitat:** Common in woodland and hedgerows throughout British Isles, but rare in N. Scotland. **Notes:** Sticky hairs on inflorescence.

Water Figwort
Scrophulariaceae *Scrophularia aquatica*. **Habitat:** Common in damp meadows, wet woodland, by pond and stream sides in England; less common in N.; scattered in Wales, Ireland and S.E. Scotland. **Notes:** Petioles and stems winged. Usually visited by wasps.

Foxglove Scrophulariaceae *Digitalis purpurea*. **Habitat:** Woodland, heaths, mountains throughout British Isles up to 950m; less common in central Ireland and E. Midlands. **Notes:** Prefers light, dry acid soils in open woods; often the dominant species in clearings and burnt areas.

101

Flowering Plants

Common Toadflax
Scrophulariaceae *Linaria vulgaris*. **Habitat:** Common on grassland, farmland, waste ground and in hedgerows in Britain, but rare in N.W. Scotland; occasional in Ireland.

Germander Speedwell
Scrophulariaceae *Veronica chamaedrys*. **Habitat:** Very common in woodland, grassland, hedgerows, gardens throughout British Isles. **Notes:** Four rows of long, white hairs on stem.

Marsh Speedwell
Scrophulariaceae *Veronica scutellata*. **Habitat:** Locally common in bogs, water meadows and ponds throughout British Isles. **Notes:** Flowers white or pale blue.

Brooklime Scrophulariaceae *Veronica beccabunga*. **Habitat:** Streams, ponds, marsh and water meadows throughout British Isles; less common in N. and W. Scotland.

Water Speedwell
Scrophulariaceae *Veronica anagallis-aquatica*. **Habitat:** Common in ponds, streams, water meadows and mud in central and S. England; scattered in rest of England and Ireland; very local in Scotland and Wales. **Notes:** Usually hairless, but inflorescence sometimes glandular.

Heath Speedwell
Scrophulariaceae *Veronica officinalis*. Creeping, like Germander Speedwell, but with shallowly toothed leaves and dense inflorescence. Very common on heaths, acid grassland and woodland.

Common Field Speedwell
V. persica has triangular, coarsely toothed leaves and single flowers on long stalks. Very common on arable farmland and waste ground.

Spring Speedwell
Scrophulariaceae *Veronica verna*. **Habitat:** Confined to a few places on Breckland in E. Anglia. **Notes:** Inflorescence glandular.

Wall Speedwell *V. arvensis* has erect habit, oval, coarsely toothed leaves and flowers in long, open inflorescence on short stalks. Very common on dry grassland, farmland and walls.

Common Cow-wheat
Scrophulariaceae *Melampyrum pratense*. **Habitat:** Locally abundant in woodland, on heaths and moors throughout British Isles. **Notes:** On acid soils. Flowers usually pale yellow, sometimes pink.
Small Cow-wheat *M. sylvaticum* is similar but found only in Scottish Highlands and Teesdale; flowers always deep yellow.

Eyebright Scrophulariaceae *Euphrasia nemorosa*. **Habitat:** Common on grassland, heaths and in open woodland in England and Wales; occasional in Scotland and Ireland. **Notes:** Variable.

Flowering Plants

Red Bartsia Scrophulariaceae *Odontites verna*. **Habitat:** Common on farmland, waste ground, roadsides and grassland throughout British Isles.

Lousewort Scrophulariaceae *Pedicularis sylvatica*. **Habitat:** Frequent on wet heaths and moors throughout British Isles. **Notes:** Not on calcareous or highly cultivated soils.

Yellowrattle (Hayrattle) Scrophulariaceae *Rhinanthus minor*. **Habitat:** Common in unimproved grassland throughout British Isles. **Notes:** Very variable species divided into four subspecies.

Water Mint Labiatae *Mentha aquatica*. **Habitat:** Marsh, wet woodland and by rivers and ponds throughout British Isles up to 500m, but less common in central and N. Scotland. **Notes:** Variable.

Red Dead-nettle Labiatae *Lamium purpureum*. **Habitat:** Abundant on farmland, waste ground, in hedgerows and gardens throughout British Isles.

Wild Thyme Labiatae *Thymus drucei*. **Habitat:** Common on dry chalk grassland, heaths, dunes and among rocks throughout much of British Isles up to 1200m; local in W. and central Ireland, central England and E. Anglia. **Notes:** Variable; aromatic; mat-forming.

Common Hemp-nettle Labiatae *Galeopsis tetrahit*. **Habitat:** Very common on farmland, in hedgerows, woodland and wetland throughout British Isles. **Notes:** Stem covered with sticky hairs; flowers pink or white.

White Dead-nettle *L. album* is taller with larger, deeply toothed, nettle-like leaves. It is very common in same habitats as *L. purpureum* in Britain; local in E. Ireland.

Yellow Archangel Labiatae *Galeobdolon luteum*. **Habitat:** Common in damp woodland in England and Wales; rare or absent in N. England, Scotland and Ireland. **Notes:** Usually on heavier soils. Sometimes locally dominant, especially after coppicing.

Marjoram Labiatae *Origanum vulgaris*. **Habitat:** Locally common in chalk grassland, scrub and hedgerows throughout British Isles, but rare in N. Scotland. **Notes:** In dry habitats. Aromatic.

Wild Basil Labiatae *Clinopodium vulgare*. **Habitat:** Locally common in chalk grassland, scrub, hedgerows and wood margins throughout British Isles, especially in S., up to 400m; becoming rare to absent in N. Scotland; scattered and rare in Ireland. **Notes:** In dry calcareous soils. Scented.

Flowering Plants

Common Skullcap Labiatae
Scutellaria galericulata.
Habitat: Common by streams
and ponds, damp meadows and
wet woodland in Britain; rare in
N.E. Scotland; occasional in
Ireland.

Ground Ivy Labiatae *Glechoma
hederacea.* **Habitat:** Very
common in woodland,
grassland, waste ground
throughout most of British Isles,
but rare in N.W. Scotland and W.
Ireland. **Notes:** Prefers damp,
heavy soils. Sometimes locally
dominant in oak woods
especially after coppicing.

Hedge Woundwort Labiatae
Stachys sylvatica. **Habitat:** Very
common in woodland,
hedgerows and shady waste
ground throughout British Isles
to 500m, but less common in N.
Notes: On rich soils.

Self-heal Labiatae *Prunella
vulgaris.* **Habitat:** Very common
in old grassland, woodland
rides, waste ground, gardens,
hedgerows throughout British
Isles up to 800m. **Notes:** Mainly
on basic and neutral soils.

Betony Labiatae *Betonica
officinalis.* **Habitat:** Common in
open woodland, heaths and
grassland in England and Wales,
but rare in E. Anglia; very rare in
Scotland and Ireland. **Notes:** On
calcareous and acid soils.

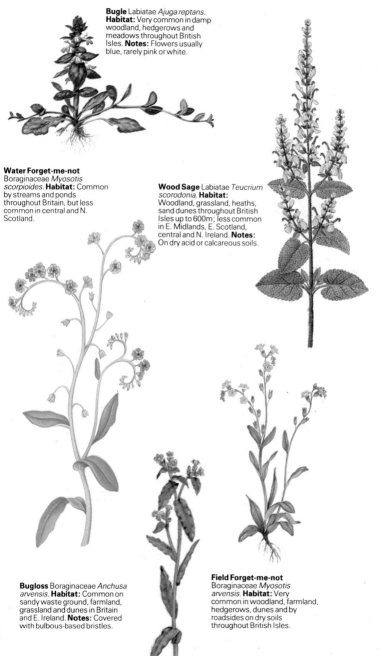

Bugle Labiatae *Ajuga reptans.*
Habitat: Very common in damp woodland, hedgerows and meadows throughout British Isles. **Notes:** Flowers usually blue, rarely pink or white.

Water Forget-me-not
Boraginaceae *Myosotis scorpioides.* **Habitat:** Common by streams and ponds throughout Britain, but less common in central and N. Scotland.

Wood Sage Labiatae *Teucrium scorodonia.* **Habitat:** Woodland, grassland, heaths, sand dunes throughout British Isles up to 600m; less common in E. Midlands, E. Scotland, central and N. Ireland. **Notes:** On dry acid or calcareous soils.

Bugloss Boraginaceae *Anchusa arvensis.* **Habitat:** Common on sandy waste ground, farmland, grassland and dunes in Britain and E. Ireland. **Notes:** Covered with bulbous-based bristles.

Field Forget-me-not
Boraginaceae *Myosotis arvensis.* **Habitat:** Very common in woodland, farmland, hedgerows, dunes and by roadsides on dry soils throughout British Isles.

107

Flowering Plants

Viper's Bugloss Boraginaceae *Echium vulgare*. **Habitat:** Common on rough, dry grassland and dunes in S. and E. Britain; rare in N. Scotland and E. Ireland. **Notes:** Covered with red-based bristles. Flower buds pink, opening bright blue.

Common Comfrey Boraginaceae *Symphytum officinale*. **Habitat:** Common by rivers and in marsh in Britain north to central Scotland; occasional in N. Scotland and Ireland. **Notes:** Flowers white or pink.

Lungwort Boraginaceae *Pulmonaria officinalis*. **Habitat:** Rare in woodland and hedgerows in Britain. **Notes:** On chalk or clay soils. White spots on leaves.

Common Butterwort Lentibulariaceae *Pinguicula vulgaris*. **Habitat:** Locally common in bogs, wet heaths and among wet rocks in N. and W. Britain up to 1000m; local elsewhere in British Isles. **Notes:** Leaves covered with sticky hairs for trapping and digesting insects.

Ribwort Plantain Plantaginaceae *Plantago lanceolata*. **Habitat:** Very common in grassland throughout British Isles. **Notes:** Can be hairy or hairless.

Greater Plantain
Plantaginaceae *Plantago major.*
Habitat: Abundant on farmland,
waste ground, and by roadsides
throughout British Isles. **Notes:**
Especially in well-trampled
places.

Buck's Horn Plantain
Plantaginaceae *Plantago
coronopus.* **Habitat:** Rocks, dry
sandy soils and waste ground
around British coasts and
scattered inland in England.

Nettle-leaved Bellflower
C. trachelium differs in having
shorter, sharply toothed leaves
and darker blue-purple flowers.
It is found in woodland margins
and hedgerows on calcareous
soils in Wales and central and S.
England, but is absent from the
S.W.

Harebell Campanulaceae
Campanula rotundifolia.
Habitat: Locally common in
grassland, fixed dunes, dry
places throughout much of
British Isles; scattered in S.W.
England, N.W. Scotland and
central and S. Ireland. **Notes:**
Often in poor, shallow, acid or
calcareous soils.

Giant Bellflower
Campanulaceae *Campanula
latifolia.* **Habitat:** Locally
common in woodland and
hedgerows in N. England, S.
Scotland and Wales. **Notes:**
Flowers blue-purple or white.

109

Flowering Plants

Twinflower Caprifoliaceae *Linnaea borealis.* **Habitat:** Rare in pinewoods in N.E. Scotland. **Notes:** Tiny, creeping plant; grows in mossy places.

Valerian Valerianaceae *Valeriana officinalis.* **Habitat:** Common in meadows, marsh and wetland, also on chalk grassland, throughout British Isles. **Notes:** Dry grassland form smaller.

Honeysuckle Caprifoliaceae *Lonicera periclymenum.* **Habitat:** Common in woodland, scrub and hedgerows throughout British Isles up to 650m. **Notes:** A twining shrub up to 6m; often trailing or scrambling.

Moschatel Adoxaceae *Adoxa moschatellina.* **Habitat:** Locally common in woodland, hedgerows and mountains up to 1200m in England, Wales, central and S. Scotland; only in Antrim in Ireland.

Hedge Bedstraw Rubiaceae *Galium mollugo*. **Habitat:** Chalk grassland, hedgerows, scrub and waste ground throughout British Isles to 400m, but only common in S., central and extreme N. England. **Notes:** Very variable.

Goosegrass, Cleavers Rubiaceae *Galium aparine*. **Habitat:** Very common in hedgerows, on farmland, waste ground, woodland and by the sea, throughout British Isles. **Notes:** On fertile soils. Fruits covered in hooked bristles that adhere tenaciously to passing animals or humans.

Lady's Bedstraw Rubiaceae *Galium verum*. **Habitat:** Common in dry, well-drained grassland, hedgerows and fixed dunes throughout most of British Isles, but less common in W., and in N. and S. Ireland. **Notes:** On weakly acid or calcareous soils. Smells of newly cut grass.

Squinancywort Rubiaceae *Asperula cynanchica*. **Habitat:** Locally common in chalk grassland and sand dunes in S. England and Wales, and W. Ireland up to 300m; rare in Midlands and N. England. **Notes:** Always on calcareous soils. Smells of vanilla.

Woodruff Rubiaceae *Galium odoratum*. **Habitat:** Common in woodland on calcareous soils in Britain, but occasional to rare in E. Anglia, N. Scotland and Ireland. **Notes:** Vanilla-scented when crushed.

Flowering Plants

Small Scabious Dipsacaceae *Scabiosa columbaria*. **Habitat:** Locally common in dry, calcareous grassland and hedgerows throughout England, N. and S. Wales. **Notes:** Colour varies from blue-lilac to pink or white.

Devil's Bit Scabious Dipsacaceae *Succisa pratensis*. **Habitat:** Common in wet meadows, damp woodland and marsh throughout British Isles. **Notes:** Flower colour varies from mauve to dark blue-purple. Attractive to butterflies.

Ragwort Compositae *Senecio jacobaea*. **Habitat:** Abundant in rough grassland, waste ground, dunes, roadsides throughout British Isles to 700m.

Groundsel Compositae *Senecio vulgaris*. **Habitat:** Abundant weed of waste ground, farmland and gardens throughout British Isles. **Notes:** Ray florets usually absent.

Golden Rod Compositae *Solidago virgaurea.* **Habitat:** Woodland, hedgerows, cliffs, rocky streamsides and dunes throughout the British Isles up to 1160m, but less common in E. and central England and central and E. Ireland. **Notes:** Usually on acid soils. Very variable. Visited by flies and bees.

Sea Aster Compositae *Aster tripolium.* **Habitat:** Common on coasts, salt marshes and cliffs throughout most of the British Isles, but confined to estuaries in N. England and Scotland.

Canadian Fleabane Compositae *Conyza canadensis.* **Habitat:** Locally common on waste ground, walls and dunes in S.E. and central S. England and E. Anglia; scattered in rest of England and Wales. **Notes:** Prefers light soils.

Ox-eye Daisy Compositae *Chrysanthemum leucanthemum.* **Habitat:** Common in rough grassland and on cliffs throughout British Isles, but less common in N.W. Scotland. **Notes:** Especially on better soils. Occasionally lacks white ray-florets.

Tansy Compositae *Chrysanthemum vulgare.* **Habitat:** Common in hedgerows, waste ground, and river banks throughout British Isles. **Notes:** Strong smelling. Flowers attract flies and beetles.

Flowering Plants

Daisy Compositae *Bellis perennis*. **Habitat:** Abundant in short grass throughout British Isles, up to 950m.

Coltsfoot Compositae *Tussilago farfara*. **Habitat:** Common on farmland, waste ground, woodland margins, by roadsides, dunes and streams throughout British Isles up to 1000m. **Notes:** Flowers close at night and appear before leaves in spring.

Yarrow, Milfoil Compositae *Achillea millefolium*. **Habitat:** Abundant in grassland, hedgerows and roadsides throughout British Isles. **Notes:** Strongly scented. Variable, especially with regard to hairiness and bract colour.

Hemp Agrimony Compositae *Eupatorium cannabinum*. **Habitat:** Common in marsh, wet woodland, on stream banks, throughout England and Wales; scattered in Ireland; rare in Scotland, absent from extreme N. **Notes:** Flowers white, pink or purplish.

Sneezewort Compositae *Achillea ptarmica*. **Habitat:** Locally common on heaths, scrub and in water meadows throughout British Isles. **Notes:** Prefers acid soils.

Scentless Mayweed Compositae *Tripleurospermum maritimum*. **Habitat:** On farmland, waste ground and by the sea throughout British Isles, but less common in N. Scotland and N. Ireland. **Notes:** On all soils. Very variable.

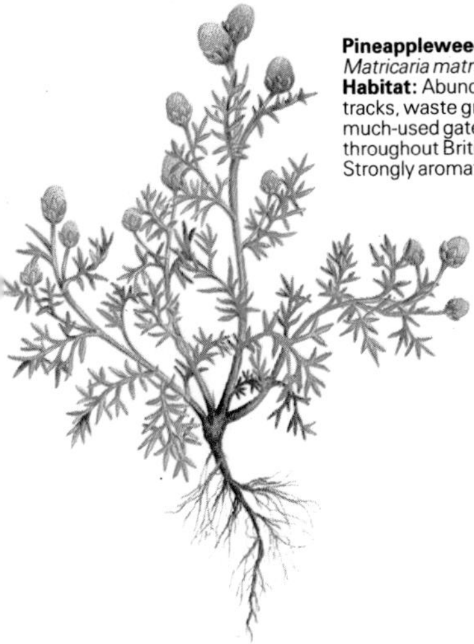

Pineappleweed Compositae
Matricaria matricarioides.
Habitat: Abundant on farmland,
tracks, waste ground and by
much-used gateways
throughout British Isles. **Notes:**
Strongly aromatic.

Mugwort Compositae
Artemisia vulgaris. **Habitat:**
Very common by roadsides, in
hedgerows and cultivated land
in most of British Isles; less
common in N. **Notes:** Leaf and
inflorescence variable in shape.

Marsh Thistle Compositae
Cirsium palustre. **Habitat:**
Meadows, marsh, wet
woodland and hedgerows
throughout British Isles up to
800m.

Creeping Thistle Compositae
Cirsium arvense. **Habitat:** Very
common on farmland, waste
ground and grassland
throughout British Isles up to
650m. **Notes:** Visited by
hoverflies and butterflies.

115

Flowering Plants

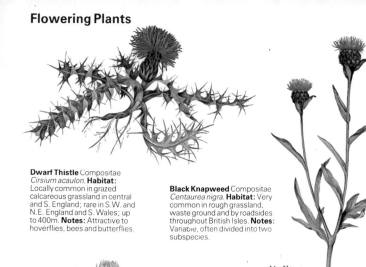

Dwarf Thistle Compositae
Cirsium acaulon. **Habitat:**
Locally common in grazed
calcareous grassland in central
and S. England; rare in S.W. and
N.E. England and S. Wales; up
to 400m. **Notes:** Attractive to
hoverflies, bees and butterflies.

Black Knapweed Compositae
Centaurea nigra. **Habitat:** Very
common in rough grassland,
waste ground and by roadsides
throughout British Isles. **Notes:**
Variable, often divided into two
subspecies.

Greater Knapweed *C. scabiosa*
is taller, with deeply lobed
leaves and long outer florets. It
is locally frequent to common
throughout British Isles on
calcareous soils.

Carline Thistle Compositae
Carlina vulgaris. **Habitat:**
Locally common on chalk
grassland throughout England
and Wales, central Ireland, and
on dunes on S., E. and W. coasts
of Scotland; up to 500m. **Notes:**
Biennial – first year's leaves die
before flowering.

Dandelion Compositae
Taraxacum officinale. **Habitat:**
Abundant on grassland, waste
ground etc., throughout British
Isles up to 1300m. **Notes:** Very
variable leaf shape and habit.

Chicory Compositae *Cichorium intybus*. **Habitat:** Frequent in rough grassland, waste ground and hedgerows in England; rare to local in rest of British Isles. **Notes:** On dry soils. Flowers very bright blue.

Rough Hawkbit Compositae *Leontodon hispidus*. **Habitat:** Common in grassland in England, Wales and S. Scotland up to 650m; scattered in central and S. Ireland. **Notes:** On base-rich or calcareous soils. Very variable, especially with regard to hairiness.

Nipplewort Compositae *Lapsana communis*. **Habitat:** Very common in hedgerows, woodland, waste ground and on walls throughout British Isles. **Notes:** Absent from mountains.

Beaked Hawksbeard Compositae *Crepis vesicaria*. **Habitat:** Common on chalk grassland, waste ground and by roadsides in S.E. England; locally common throughout England and Wales to 150m; scattered in S. Ireland. **Notes:** Very variable.

Mouse-ear Hawkweed Compositae *Pilosella officinarum*. **Habitat:** Very common on dry grassland, heaths, rocks and walls throughout British Isles. **Notes:** Undersurface of leaves covered with short, white hairs.

117

Flowering Plants

Perennial Sow Thistle
Compositae *Sonchus arvensis*.
Habitat: Very common on
farmland, waste ground,
hedgerows and in wetland
throughout British Isles. **Notes:**
Leaves edged with soft prickles.

Flowering Rush Butomaceae
Butomus umbellatus. **Habitat:**
Local in ponds, ditches and on
river margins in England, Wales,
central and S. Scotland and
Ireland.

Black Bryony Dioscoreaceae
Tamus communis. **Habitat:**
Common in woodland margins,
scrub and hedgerows in most of
England and Wales up to 250m;
known from one locality in
central Scotland and N.W.
Ireland. **Notes:** Prefers moist,
well-drained fertile soils.

Herb Paris Trilliaceae *Paris
quadrifolia*. **Habitat:** Locally
common in woodland in
England and E. Wales up to
400m; local in rest of Wales and
Scotland; absent from Ireland.
Notes: Prefers damp habitats
on calcareous soils.

Common Solomon's Seal
Liliaceae *Polygonatum multiflorum*. **Habitat:** Locally common in woodland in central and S. England and S. Wales; rare in rest of British Isles. **Notes:** Only on calcareous and sandy soils.

Butcher's Broom Liliaceae *Ruscus aculeatus*. **Habitat:** Locally common in dry woodland and among rocks in S. and E. England and S. Wales. **Notes:** Often cultivated.

Lily of the Valley Liliaceae *Convallaria majalis*. **Habitat:** Locally abundant in woodland in England; very rare in rest of British Isles. **Notes:** Only on calcareous and sandy soils. Fragrant.

Bluebell Liliaceae *Endymion non-scriptus*. **Habitat:** Locally common, often dominant, in woodland throughout most of British Isles up to 650m; less common in hedgerows and grassland, and in N.E. Scotland, S. and central Ireland. **Notes:** Prefers light, acid soils.

Flowering Plants

Bog Asphodel Liliaceae
Narthecium ossifragum.
Habitat: Common, often
abundant in bogs, on wet
heaths, moors and wet, acid
places on mountains up to
1000m in Scotland, Wales,
Ireland and N. England; very
local in rest of England. **Notes:**
Dominant on blanket bogs.

Star of Bethlehem Liliaceae
Ornithogalum umbellatum.
Habitat: Locally common in dry
grassland, hedgerows, and by
roadsides in Britain; absent
from N.W. Scotland. **Notes:**
Bulb surrounded by many
bulbils.

Ramsons, Wood Garlic
Liliaceae *Allium ursinum.*
Habitat: Common, sometimes
locally dominant, in damp
woodland throughout most of
British Isles up to 450m; only
local in N.E. Scotland and
Ireland. **Notes:** Strong smelling.

Snowdrop Amaryllidaceae
Galanthus nivalis. **Habitat:**
Scattered in damp woodland
and by streams throughout
Britain except N. Scotland;
probably extinct in Ireland.
Notes: Flowering begins in
January.

Wild Daffodil Amaryllidaceae
Narcissus pseudonarcissus.
Habitat: Locally common in
woodland and grassland
throughout England and Wales;
more common in W.; scattered
in Scotland and S. and E. Ireland.
Notes: Prefers damp habitats.

Yellow Flag Iridaceae *Iris
pseudacorus.* **Habitat:** Marsh,
wet woodland, shallow water
and wet river margins
throughout British Isles, but less
common in N. Scotland. **Notes:**
Outer flower segments variable.

**Cuckoo-pint, Lords and
Ladies** Araceae *Arum
maculatum.* **Habitat:**
Woodland, hedgerows, gardens
throughout England, Wales,
Ireland, S. and central to E.
Scotland. **Notes:** Can be a
persistent weed in gardens.
Prefers base-rich soils. Very
shade tolerant.

Flowering Plants

Marsh Helleborine
Orchidaceae *Epipactis palustris*.
Habitat: Local in calcareous grassland, marsh and dune slacks in England, S.E. Scotland, Wales except for centre, Ireland except for extreme S. and N.E.

Broad-leaved Helleborine
Orchidaceae *Epipactis helleborine*. **Habitat:** Locally common in woodland, scrub and on fixed dunes, throughout British Isles except N.E. Scotland. **Notes:** Usually on chalk or limestone with thin soil cover; very shade tolerant.

White Helleborine
Orchidaceae *Cephalanthera damasonium*. **Habitat:** Local in woodland on calcareous soils in S. and S.E. England and S. Midlands. **Notes:** Especially in beechwoods. Amount of flower opening depends on local weather conditions.

Bird's-nest Orchid
Orchidaceae *Neottia nidus-avis*.
Habitat: Local in woodland throughout British Isles except N. and E. Scotland and S. Ireland; most common in S. England. **Notes:** Usually in dark, bare-floored beechwoods, often on calcareous, humus-rich soils.

122

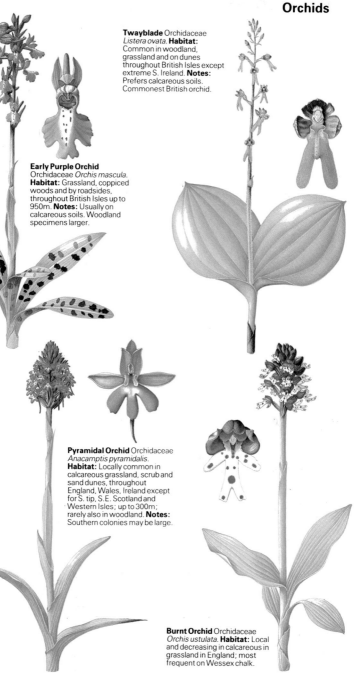

Twayblade Orchidaceae *Listera ovata*. **Habitat:** Common in woodland, grassland and on dunes throughout British Isles except extreme S. Ireland. **Notes:** Prefers calcareous soils. Commonest British orchid.

Early Purple Orchid Orchidaceae *Orchis mascula*. **Habitat:** Grassland, coppiced woods and by roadsides, throughout British Isles up to 950m. **Notes:** Usually on calcareous soils. Woodland specimens larger.

Pyramidal Orchid Orchidaceae *Anacamptis pyramidalis*. **Habitat:** Locally common in calcareous grassland, scrub and sand dunes, throughout England, Wales, Ireland except for S. tip, S.E. Scotland and Western Isles; up to 300m; rarely also in woodland. **Notes:** Southern colonies may be large.

Burnt Orchid Orchidaceae *Orchis ustulata*. **Habitat:** Local and decreasing in calcareous in grassland in England; most frequent on Wessex chalk.

Fragrant Orchid Orchidaceae
Gymnadenia conopsea.
Habitat: Locally common on
chalk grassland throughout
British Isles, up to 650m.
Notes: Colonies often large.

Musk Orchid Orchidaceae
Herminium monorchis.
Habitat: Rare in chalk grassland
in S. and S.E. England and S.
Wales. **Notes:** In short turf;
always in open.

Frog Orchid Orchidaceae
Coeloglossum viride. **Habitat:**
Locally common on chalk
grassland in S. England; rare in
neutral grassland, dunes, rocks
throughout rest of British Isles,
but more frequent in N.,
especially on N-facing slopes.

Bee Orchid Orchidaceae
Ophrys apifera. **Habitat:** Locally
common to rare in calcareous
grassland, dunes, quarries and
scrub in England, N. and S.
Wales, Ireland except for S.W.
Notes: Prefers open sites with
short grass and good drainage.

Common Spotted Orchid
Orchidaceae *Dactylorhiza
fuchsii*. **Habitat:** Meadows,
scrub, wetland, woodland and
roadsides throughout British
Isles. **Notes:** Most common on
calcareous soils.
Heath Spotted Orchid
D. maculata has flowers with
triangular lip. It replaces
D. fuchsii in acid wetland and
heaths.

Early Marsh Orchid
Orchidaceae *Dactylorhiza
incarnata*. **Habitat:** Local in
damp meadows and wetland
throughout British Isles. **Notes:**
Variable.

Flowering Plants

Woodland Meadow Grass Gramineae *Poa nemoralis*. **Habitat:** Woodland and hedgerows throughout Britain; in Ireland only common in E. **Notes:** Delicate grass of shady places. Often locally abundant.

Giant Fescue Gramineae *Festuca gigantea*. **Habitat:** Damp woodland, hedgerows and shady places throughout British Isles, but rare in N. Scotland.

Hairy Brome Gramineae *Zerna ramosa*. **Habitat:** Woodland, wood margins, hedgerows, and on roadsides that were originally woodland, throughout British Isles, except central and N. Scotland. **Notes:** In partial shade on moist soils.

Wood Sedge Cyperaceae *Carex sylvatica*. **Habitat:** Woodland, and scrub and grassland that were originally woodland; throughout British Isles, but rare in central and N. Scotland. **Notes:** On heavy, wet (and sometimes chalk with clay) soils.

Field Woodrush Juncaceae *Luzula campestris*. **Habitat:** Common in acid grassland throughout British Isles. **Notes:** Variable. In wet or dry situations.

Wood Melick Gramineae *Melica uniflora*. **Habitat:** Woodland and shady roadside banks throughout British Isles, except N. Scotland. **Notes:** Often very abundant, loosely carpeting beechwood floor. Albino form with white spikelets found in S. England and S. Wales.

Crested Hair-grass Gramineae *Koeleria cristata*. **Habitat:** Common on dry calcareous grassland and sandy places throughout British Isles, up to 650m

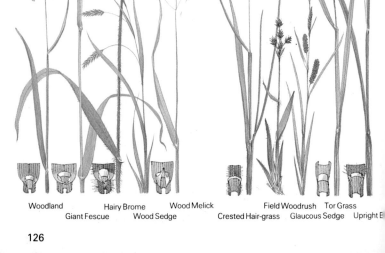

Woodland   Hairy Brome   Wood Melick   Field Woodrush   Tor Grass

Giant Fescue   Wood Sedge   Crested Hair-grass   Glaucous Sedge   Upright B

Grasses, Sedges and Rushes

Glaucous Sedge Cyperaceae *Carex flacca*. **Habitat:** Calcareous grassland, sand dunes and marsh throughout British Isles.

Tor Grass Gramineae (Poaceae) *Brachypodium pinnatum*. **Distribution:** Occurring in scattered localities in East Anglia, northern England, southern Scotland, Wales and Ireland.

Upright Brome Gramineae (Poaceae) *Zerna erecta*. **Distribution:** Central and southern England; rare in Wales and central Ireland. **Other habitats:** Roadside banks and verges; waste land.

Red Fescue, Creeping Fescue Gramineae *Festuca rubra*. **Habitat:** Very common on chalk grassland, coastal dunes, salt marsh, heaths, open woodland, road sides and waste ground, throughout British Isles.

Sheep's Fescue Gramineae *Festuca ovina*. **Habitat:** Grassland, heaths and moors throughout British Isles, up to 1300m.

Downy Oat Gramineae *Helictotrichon pubescens*. **Habitat:** Grasslands throughout British Isles.

Meadow Oat Grass Gramineae *Helictotrichon pratense*. **Habitat:** Dry calcareous grassland throughout British Isles, up to 1000m.

Yellow Oat Grass Gramineae *Trisetum flavescens*. **Habitat:** Rough grassland, roadside banks and verges throughout England and Ireland; less frequent in Wales; rare in Scotland.

Quaking Grass, Totter Grass Gramineae *Briza media*. **Habitat:** Calcareous or base-rich grassland throughout British Isles, up to 650m; more frequent in S.; rare in N. and N.W. Scotland.

Fine Bent Gramineae *Agrostis tenuis*. **Habitat:** Grassland, heaths, moors and waste ground throughout British Isles, up to 1300m.

Creeping Bent Gramineae *Agrostis stolonifera*. **Habitat:** Grassland, salt marsh, roadsides, inland and coastal sands, cliffs and open woodland, cultivated land throughout British Isles, up to 800m.

Fern Grass Gramineae (Poaceae) *Catapodium rigidum*. **Distribution:** Throughout England (especially the south); south Scotland; Wales; Ireland. **Other habitats:** Dry banks; walls; stony, rocky and sandy places.

Creeping Soft Grass Gramineae (Poaceae) *Holcus mollis*. **Distribution:** Throughout the British Isles.

Wood False-brome Grass Gramineae *Brachypodium sylvaticum*. **Habitat:** Woodland, hedgerows, shady places, and on grassland and roadsides that were originaly woodland

d Fescue   Downy Oat   Yellow Oat   Fine Bent   Fern Grass   Wood Melick
Sheep's Fescue   Meadow Oat   Quaking Grass   Creeping Bent   Creeping Soft Grass

Flowering Plants

Cocksfoot Gramineae *Dactylis glomerata*. **Habitat:** Grassland, roadsides and occasionally open woodland, throughout British Isles. **Notes:** Sometimes cultivated as a pasture grass.

Tufted Hair-grass Gramineae *Deschampsia caespitosa*. **Habitat:** Wet grassland, moors and wet woodland on poorly drained soils, throughout British Isles, up to 1300m. **Notes:** Coarse and variable.

Crested Dog's Tail Gramineae *Cynosurus cristatus*. **Habitat:** Common, often abundant, on grassland throughout British Isles, up to 650m. **Notes:** On wide range of soils.

Sweet Vernal Grass Gramineae *Anthoxanthum odoratum*. **Habitat:** Grassland, heaths, moors and open woodland throughout British Isles. **Notes:** Very variable. Flowers early; smells strongly of cut grass (coumarin).

Perennial Rye Grass Gramineae *Lolium perenne*. **Habitat:** Grassland, roadsides and waste ground throughout British Isles. **Notes:** Especially on rich, heavy soils. Variable in structure. The most important commercial pasture grass.

False Oat Grass Gramineae *Arrhenatherum elatius*. **Habitat:** Very common on rough grassland of hedgerows, roadsides, gravel and shingle banks and waste ground throughout British Isles.

Meadow Foxtail Gramineae *Alopecurus pratensis*. **Habitat:** Abundant in lowland grassland and water meadows throughout British Isles. **Notes:** On rich, moist soils.

Meadow Fescue Gramineae *Festuca pratensis*. **Habitat:** Lowland grassland, water meadows, and by roadsides throughout British Isles, but rare in N. Scotland. **Notes:** Most common on loam or heavy soils.

Smooth Meadow Grass Gramineae *Poa pratensis*. **Habitat:** Grassland, roadsides, cultivated land, waste ground, walls and shady places, throughout British Isles, up to 1300m. **Notes:** Mainly on well-drained sand, gravel or loam soils. Variable. An important hay and pasture grass.

Rough Meadow Grass Gramineae *Poa trivialis*. **Habitat:** Grassland, waste ground, cultivated land and by streams, throughout British Isles. **Notes:** Sometimes in partial shade; common on rich, moist soils.

Sea Couch Grass Gramineae *Agropyron junceiforme*. **Habitat:** Sandy coasts all round British Isles. **Notes:** Very salt tolerant, grows closer to sea than other grasses; forms small dunes at top of beach.

Cocksfoot   Crested Dog's Tail   Perennial   Meadow Foxtail   Smooth Meadow
Tufted Hair-grass   Sweet Vernal   False Oat Grass   Meadow Fescue   Rough Meadow Grass

Sea Manna Grass Gramineae *Puccinellia maritima*. **Habitat:** Coasts and inland salt marsh around all British Isles; most abundant in S. and E.

Salt Mud Rush Juncaceae *Juncus gerardii*. **Distribution:** All British Isles coasts. **Other habitats:** Inland salt marshes. **Notes:** Salt marshes from the highest point of the highest tide and above; often abundant and locally dominant.

Sand Sedge Cyperaceae *Carex arenaria*. **Habitat:** Sandy coasts around British Isles and a few areas inland. **Notes:** A common species of fixed dunes and areas of wind-blown, low lime content sand.

Rice-grass Gramineae *Spartina anglica*. **Habitat:** Common on tidal mudflats around coasts of N.W., central and S. England and Wales, with restricted distribution around rest of British Isles. **Notes:** Often planted to stabilise mud.

Marram Grass Gramineae *Ammophila arenaria*. **Habitat:** Sand dunes around all British Isles. **Notes:** Often abundant, usually dominant. Planted to bind and consolidate drifting sand.

Timothy Gramineae *Phleum pratense*. **Habitat:** Grassland, field margins, roadsides and waste ground throughout British Isles, but less common in N.W. Scotland.

Reed Canary Grass Gramineae *Phalaris arundinacea*. **Habitat:** Water meadows and wetland throughout British Isles, but less common in N.W. Scotland.

Wood Small-reed Gramineae (Poaceae) *Calamagrostis epigejos*. **Distribution:** Throughout England, sparse in Scotland and Wales, rare in north and west Ireland. **Other habitats:** Open places in damp woods; thickets; ditches; fens. **Notes:** Grows in heavy soils; occasionally very abundant.

Common Rush Juncaceae *Juncus conglomeratus*. **Habitat:** Water meadows, bogs and damp woodland throughout British Isles.

Couch Grass Salt Mud Rush Rice-grass
Sea Manna Grass Sand Sedge

Timothy Grass Wood Small-reed
Marram Grass Reed Canary Grass Common Rush

Flowering Plants

Saw Sedge Cyperaceae
Cladium mariscus.
Distribution: Scattered
throughout the British Isles, but
common only in Norfolk. **Notes:**
Forms dense, pure stands in
reed-swamp and fenland;
usually on neutral or basic soil.

Common Cotton Grass
Cyperaceae *Eriophorum
angustifolium.* **Habitat:**
Wetland and marsh throughout
British Isles, but less common in
the Midlands. **Notes:** Prefers
very wet, acid conditions;
grows best in water; does not
survive in drained areas.

Bulrush Cyperaceae *Scirpus
lacustris.* **Habitat:** Rivers, lakes
and ponds throughout British
Isles, but less common in
Wales. **Notes:** Grows in very
silty conditions.

Bulbous Rush Juncaceae
Juncus bulbosus. **Habitat:**
Wetland, wet woodland and bog
pools throughout British Isles.
Notes: Always on acid soils.
Variable. Grows in or out of
water.

Soft Rush Juncaceae *Juncus
effusus.* **Habitat:** Wet
grassland, bogs and wet
woodland throughout British
Isles. **Notes:** Often dominant,
especially on acid soils. Stems
smooth; spathe above
inflorescence long.

Three Leaved Rush Juncaceae
Juncus trifidus. **Distribution:**
West Scotland.

Mountain Sedge Cyperaceae
Carex bigelowii. **Distribution:**
West and central Scotland;
north England; north Wales;
scattered in Ireland.

Mat Grass Gramineae *Nardus
stricta.* **Habitat:** Poor acid
grassland throughout British
Isles, up to 950m, but more
common in N. and W. **Notes:**
Often abundant, dominating
large areas.

Hare's Tail, Cotton Grass
Cyperaceae *Eriophorum
vaginatum.* **Distribution:**
Scotland, Wales; north, north-
west, south-west and central
southern England; Ireland
except for the south-east.

Deer Grass Cyperaceae
Trichophorum cespitosum.
Habitat: Blanket bogs, heaths
and moors throughout British
Isles, except the Midlands.
Notes: Often locally dominant
in damp, acid, peaty places.
Absent from base-rich soils.

Blunt-flowered Rush
Juncaceae *Juncus
subnodulosus.* **Distribution:**
Throughout England, but only
common in the east; occasional
in Wales and southern Scotland;
frequent in west and central
Ireland. **Notes:** Fens, marshes
and dune-slacks with ground
water; usually on calcareous
peat.

Saw Sedge Bulrush Soft Rush Mountain Sedge Hare's Tail
Common Cotton Bulbous Rush Three Leaved Rush Mat Grass Deer Grass

Grasses, Sedges and Rushes

Black Bog Rush Cyperaceae *Schoenus nigricans*. **Distribution:** Throughout the British Isles, but widespread in west Scotland, west Ireland and East Anglia. **Other habitats:** Salt marsh. **Notes:** On damp and usually peaty base rich soils; especially common near the sea.

Lesser Pond Sedge Cyperaceae *Carex acutiformis*. **Habitat:** Locally abundant in wetland throughout England and central Ireland; less common in Wales, Scotland and S.W. England. **Notes:** On peat or clay, base-rich soils. Often forms dense stands. Grows beside rather than in water.

Carnation Sedge Cyperaceae *Carex panicea*. **Habitat:** Wetland, upland grassland, heaths and moors throughout British Isles. **Notes:** Usually on acid soils. Most common on areas receiving continuous irrigation.

Reedsweet Grass Gramineae *Glyceria maxima*. **Habitat:** In still shallow water and on banks by running water throughout British Isles, but rare in S.W. England, Wales and N. Scotland. **Notes:** Forms large, pure stands in suitable habitats. Useful fodder grass.

Greater Tussock Sedge Cyperaceae *Carex paniculata*. **Habitat:** In marsh, wet woodland and slow-flowing water throughout British Isles, but infrequent in Scotland. **Notes:** Prefers peaty soil where water level is seasonally high. Can withstand some shade. Forms very dense tussocks.

Common Reed Gramineae *Phragmites communis*. **Habitat:** Wetland throughout British Isles. **Notes:** Especially common in lowland areas. Usually grows in water and often covers large areas of marsh. The tallest British grass; often used for thatching.

White Beaked Sedge Cyperaceae *Rhynchospora alba*. **Distribution:** Scattered throughout the British Isles; mainly in western Scotland; west, central and northern Ireland. **Notes:** Wet and usually peaty, acid soils; locally common.

Blunt-flowered Rush   Lesser Pond Rush   Reedsweet Grass   Common Reed
Black Bog Rush   Carnation Sedge   Greater Tussock Sedge   White Beaked Sedge

131

Flowering Plants

Reedmace Typhaceae *Typha latifolia*. **Habitat:** Reed-beds, lakes, ponds and slow-flowing water throughout British Isles, but becoming rarer to N. and eventually absent in N.W. Scotland **Notes:** Often abundant and dominant at edge of reed-beds.

Branched Bur-reed Sparganiaceae *Sparganium erectum*. **Habitat:** common on mud, in shallow water in ponds, ditches, slow-flowing rivers and ungrazed marsh, throughout British Isles, but rare in N.W. Scotland. **Notes:** Variable.

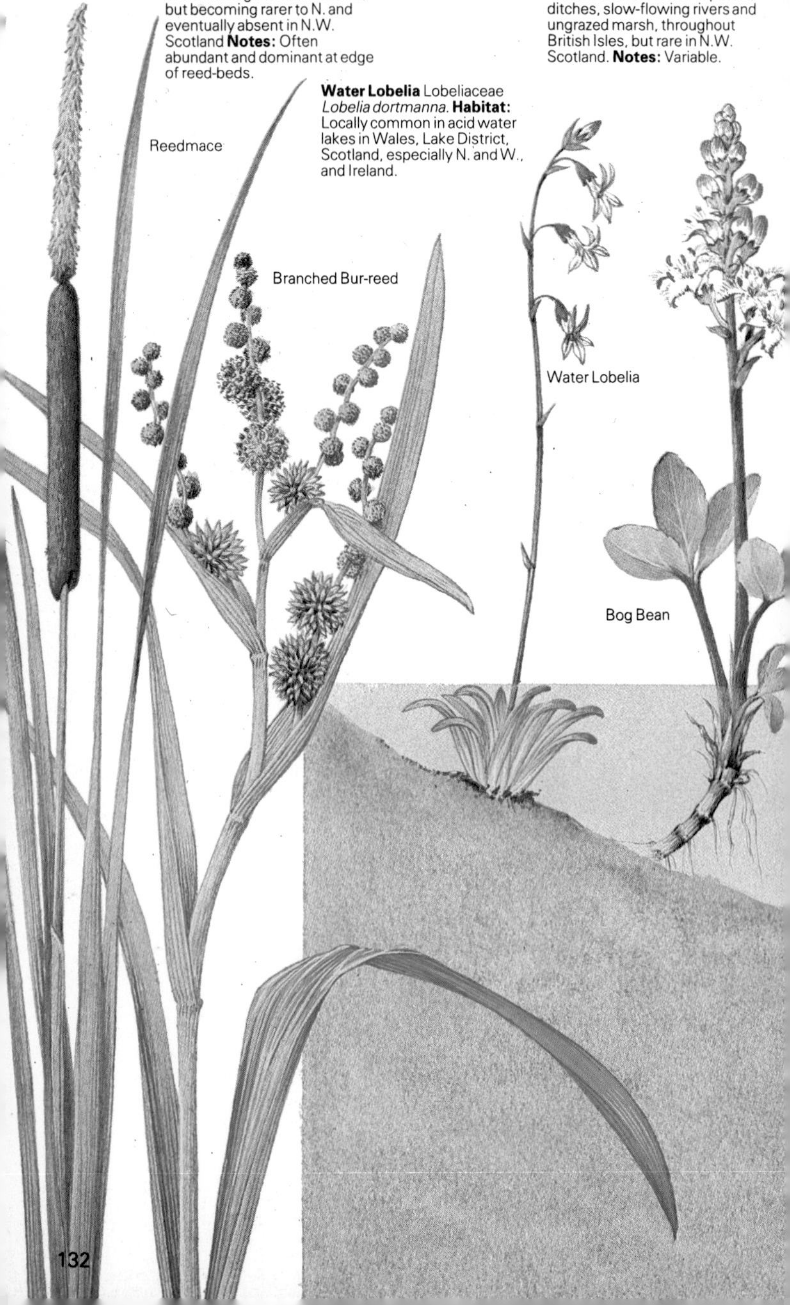

Water Lobelia Lobeliaceae *Lobelia dortmanna*. **Habitat:** Locally common in acid water lakes in Wales, Lake District, Scotland, especially N. and W., and Ireland.

Reedmace

Branched Bur-reed

Water Lobelia

Bog Bean

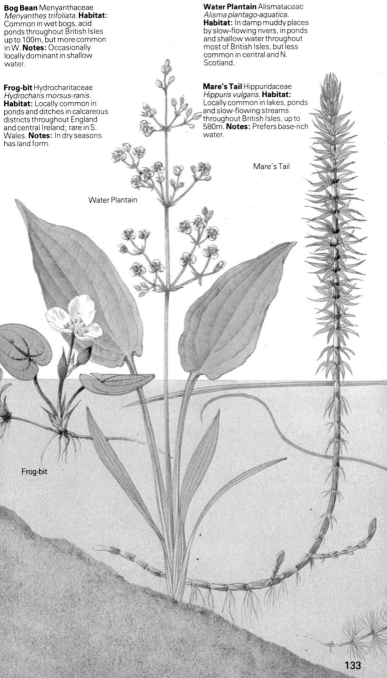

Bog Bean Menyanthaceae *Menyanthes trifoliata*. **Habitat:** Common in wet bogs, acid ponds throughout British Isles up to 100m, but more common in W. **Notes:** Occasionally locally dominant in shallow water.

Frog-bit Hydrocharitaceae *Hydrocharis morsus-ranis*. **Habitat:** Locally common in ponds and ditches in calcareous districts throughout England and central Ireland; rare in S. Wales. **Notes:** In dry seasons has land form.

Water Plantain Alismataceae *Alisma plantago-aquatica*. **Habitat:** In damp muddy places by slow-flowing rivers, in ponds and shallow water throughout most of British Isles, but less common in central and N. Scotland.

Mare's Tail Hippuridaceae *Hippuris vulgaris*. **Habitat:** Locally common in lakes, ponds and slow-flowing streams throughout British Isles, up to 580m. **Notes:** Prefers base-rich water.

Mare's Tail

Water Plantain

Frog-bit

133

Flowering Plants

Water Soldier
Hydrocharitaceae *Stratiotes aloides*. **Habitat:** Very local in ponds and ditches in calcareous districts in N. and central S. England, E. Anglia, S.W. Scotland and a few places in Ireland. **Notes:** Northern plants female, southern plants mostly male.

Floating Bur-reed
Sparganiaceae *Sparganium angustifolium.* **Habitat:** West of Britain and throughout Ireland. **Notes:** Peaty lake; mainly mountainous districts.

Hornwort Ceratophyllaceae
Ceratophyllum submersum. **Habitat:** Very local in ponds and ditches in central and S. England; very rare in N.

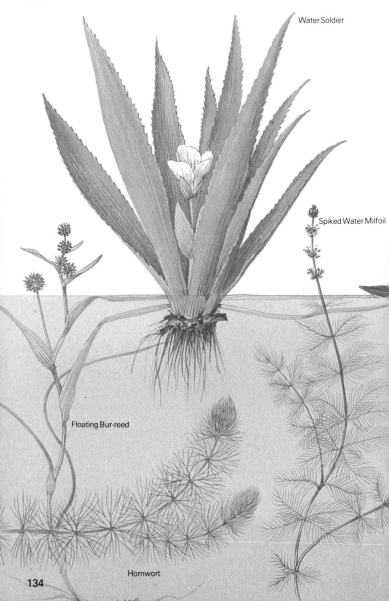

Water Soldier

Spiked Water Milfoil

Floating Bur-reed

Hornwort

Spiked Water Milfoil
Haloragaceae *Myriophyllum spicatum*. **Habitat:** Locally common in lakes, ponds and ditches throughout British Isles, up to 500m; more common in S. and E. **Notes:** Especially in calcareous waters.

White Water Lily
Nymphaeaceae *Nymphaea alba*. **Habitat:** Locally common on lakes and ponds throughout British Isles up to 350m, but rare in S.E. Ireland. **Notes:** Variable in size.

Arrow Head Alismataceae *Sagittaria sagittifolia*. **Habitat:** Locally common in shallow water in ponds and slow-flowing rivers, and on muddy soils in England except extreme N.; scattered in E. Ireland, Wales and S. Scotland.

Arrow Head

White Water Lily

135

Flowering Plants

Yellow Water Lily
Nymphaeaceae *Nuphar lutea*.
Habitat: Lakes, ponds and streams throughout British Isles up to 550m, but rare in N.W. Scotland. **Notes:** Smells of alcohol.

Western Bladderwort
Lentibulariaceae *Utricularia neglecta*. **Habitat:** Local in lakes, ponds and ditches throughout British Isles up to 650m, but rare in E. **Notes:** Usually in fairly deep water. Free-floating stems have small bladders that trap and digest aquatic organisms.

Floating Pondweed
Potamogetonaceae *Potamogeton natans*. **Habitat:** Lakes, ponds, rivers and ditches throughout British Isles. **Notes:** Especially on highly organic soils in water less than 1m deep.

Western Bladderwort

Floating Pondweed

Yellow Water Lily

Canadian Pondweed
Hydrocharitaceae *Elodea canadensis*. **Habitat:** Locally common in slow-flowing freshwater in England; rare in N., scattered in Ireland, Wales, S., central and E. Scotland.

Water Crowfoot
Ranunculaceae *Ranunculus fluitans*. **Habitat:** Very local in fast-flowing water in England and S. Scotland, and only Co. Antrim in Ireland. **Notes:** Variable.

Amphibious Bistort
Polygonaceae *Polygonum amphibium*. **Habitat:** Common in pools and slow-flowing water throughout the British Isles, but less common in N.W. Scotland. **Notes:** Also has terrestrial form on river banks. Flowers pink or red.

Shoreweed Plantaginaceae *Littorella uniflora*. **Habitat:** Locally common on lake shores and in shallow or deep water throughout British Isles, but more common in N. and W. **Notes:** Especially in calcareous districts. Often forms extensive turf in shallow water.

Lesser Duckweed Lemnaceae *Lemna minor*. **Habitat:** Floating in still, nutrient-rich water throughout British Isles, but rare in N. **Notes:** Often forms a green carpet. Only flowers in ditches exposed to sun.

Lesser Duckweed

Shoreweed

Amphibious Bistort

Water Crowfoot

Canadian Pondweed

Trees

Trees are usually the largest and most obvious living components of the countryside. They are basically of two kinds: the conifers and the broad-leaved species. Though collectively referred to as 'trees', these two groups are in fact very different.

Conifers

The conifers are gymnosperms (a word meaning 'naked seeds'), one of the oldest groups of plants which first evolved over 200 million years ago. Their seeds are borne on the surface of the woody scales which comprise the characteristic female cones. Their leaves consist of narrow, dark green 'needles' which are normally not shed over winter: hence the conifers are often referred to as 'evergreen' (though larches *do* lose their needles over winter). Their wood is comparatively soft, hence the general group name 'softwoods', and particularly useful for a wide range of products from furniture to paper.

Broad-leaved Trees

The broad-leaved trees are angiosperms, plants in which the seed develops hidden away inside an ovary. Often the seeds accumulate large stores of food material and are then popularly known as 'nuts'. Some seeds (e.g. those of the ash and sycamore) also develop blade-like extensions which serve as wings and allow the seeds to disperse on the wind. The leaves turn brown and are shed in the

Trees are the dominant component of the richest of our environments, the woodlands. Their shape and size creates a complete environment in which other plants and animals can prosper, and the products of their life cycle provides a steady stream of food for others to exploit.

autumn, so broad-leaved trees are often referred to as 'deciduous' (but note that some broadleaves, e.g. holly, retain leaves over winter). The leaves of these trees are usually soft, thin and with a broad distinctive shape characteristic of each species. Their wood is dense and very solid, hence the general name 'hardwoods' is often applied.

Range of Species

In Britain there are about 36 native tree species (including only one native conifer, the Scots Pine). But the scene is much complicated by introductions and extensive planting, especially of softwood species. Ornamental trees imported from all over the world mean that there are hundreds of species to be found here and in Europe, though only the commonest and most important types are described in this book. Their identification is based upon seed type, bark structure and leaf form.

Landscape

Conifers tend to grow more rapidly than broad-leaved trees and will thrive on poorer soils. Thus they are often chosen to be planted out in huge areas of the uplands (greatly altering landscape and ecology) and other places with little or no prospect of economic return from conventional farming. Conifers are also more able to resist cold and drought, so they tend to be found at high altitudes, higher latitudes and in drier places across Europe.

Trees are very important, because they are a major and distinctive part of the landscape. More than that, they are a three-dimensional home for hundreds of other species of animals and plants; they provide food for birds, mammals and insects; their decomposing remains are shelter for countless organisms and food for fungi; their roots bind the soil and the canopy breaks the wind and shields the ground. Trees are not just another group of plants, nor just an ecosystem component, but a whole habitat in their own right.

An acorn does its best to become an oak tree. The odds are not great; in one year an adult tree produces thousands of such seeds and will do so for 200-300 years. And yet in all that time only one progeny will reach full-grown status.

Trees

Juniper Cupressaceae *Juniperus communis*. **Habitat:** Usually in pine and birch woodland on chalk grassland, heaths and moors in S., S.E. and N. England, central and N. Scotland, W. Ireland; scattered in Wales, central and S.W. England; up to 1000m. **Notes:** Variable.

Yew Taxaceae *Taxus baccata*. **Habitat:** Pure stands in S.E. and N.W. England on calcareous or well-drained soils; with oak in deciduous woodland, parks, gardens, churchyards in S. and W. England, E. Wales, central Scotland; scattered in Ireland. **Notes:** Highly shade tolerant. Trunk often massive.

Western Red Cedar Cupressaceae *Thuja plicata*. **Habitat:** Throughout the British Isles. **Notes:** Grown for timber, for shelter in gardens and as a hedge; leaves are dark and glossy above and pale below.

Grand Fir Pinaceae *Abies grandis*. **Habitat:** Plantations and large country gardens throughout British Isles. **Notes:** Often planted as an ornamental.

Norway Spruce Pinaceae *Picea abies.* **Habitat:** Plantations, mixed woodland and gardens throughout British Isles. **Notes:** Timber crop (deal or whitewood); also for pulp, as source of turpentine, and for "Christmas trees". Foliage has hard, pointed needles and dark brown, round buds.

Cedar of Lebanon Pinaceae *Cedrus libani.* **Habitat:** Throughout the British Isles. **Other habitats:** Gardens and arboreta. **Notes:** Always planted; will tolerate poor and shallow soil; branches out-spreading and reach to ground level; rarely to 30 metres tall; cones open on tree.

Sitka Spruce Pinaceae *Picea sitchensis.* **Habitat:** Plantations and parks throughout British Isles, especially in N. and W. **Notes:** Tolerates poorest soils. An important forestry tree.

European Larch Pinaceae *Larix decidua.* **Habitat:** Coniferous woodland, gardens and country parks throughout British Isles. **Notes:** Often planted as an ornamental and for shelter. Foliage turns golden-yellow in November before falling. Twigs yellowish. Cone scales erect when ripe.

Trees

Scots Pine Pinaceae *Pinus sylvestris*. **Habitat:** Dominant tree in pine forests in Highlands of Scotland; elsewhere in coniferous woodland, plantations and parks throughout British Isles. **Notes:** Often forms woods on sandy soils. Variable.

Douglas Fir Pinaceae *Pseudotsuga menziesii*. **Habitat:** Plantations, parks and gardens throughout British Isles. **Notes:** Leaves dense, needle-like with blunt tips; have strong, fruity fragrance.

Corsican Pine Pinaceae *Pnus nigravar, maritima*. **Habitat:** Plantations, heaths and parks in S. England. **Notes:** Prefers sandy soils. An important forestry tree.

Lodgepole Pine Pinaceae *Pinus contorta*. **Habitat:** Throughout Britain especially the west. **Notes:** An important forestry tree; grows best in peaty soil; grows well on high ground.

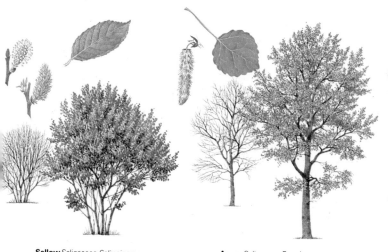

Crack Willow Salicaceae *Salix fragilis*. **Habitat:** River banks, water margins, wetland and damp woodland throughout British Isles; most common in England and E. Scotland. **Notes:** Tolerant of poor soils.

White Poplar *Populus alba*. Frequently planted in S. England. The undersides of the leaves are white.

Sallow Salicaceae *Salix cinerea*. **Habitat:** Damp woodland, water margins and hedgerows through British Isles, up to 650m. **Notes:** Variable, shrub or small tree.

Aspen Salicaceae *Populus tremula*. **Habitat:** Locally dominant in deciduous woodland on poorest soils, also in hedgerows throughout British Isles, but more common in N. and W., up to 530m.

143

Trees

Sweet Gale, Bog Myrtle
Myricaceae *Myrica gale*.
Habitat: Common in northern
Ireland, north-western England
and north-western Wales;
scattered in the rest of the
British Isles. **Notes:** Grows in
bogs, wet heaths and fens;
found up to 580 metres.

Black Poplar Salicaceae
Populus nigra var. *butulifolia*.
Habitat: Now rare in deciduous
woodland and by rivers,
occasionally in parks, gardens
and by roads throughout British
Isles. **Notes:** Bark nearly black.
Trunk and larger branches have
swollen bosses.

Walnut Juglandaceae *Juglans
regia*. **Habitat:** Usually in
plantations and gardens
throughout British Isles. **Notes:**
Cultivated for fruit and timber.
Number of pairs of leaflets per
leaf varies from 2 to 6.

Lombardy Poplar Salicaceae
Populus nigra var. *italica*.
Habitat: Woodland,
hedgerows, parks and gardens
throughout lowland British Isles.
Notes: Always planted, as it is a
male plant propagated by
cuttings. Prefers damp soils.
Bark grey. Characteristically tall
and thin.

Downy Birch Betulaceae *Butula pubescens*. **Habitat:** Wet heaths and damp places throughout British Isles, up to 800m. **Notes:** Tolerates wet, cold conditions. Forms pure stands in N. and W.

Silver Birch Betulaceae *Betula pendula*. **Habitat:** Woodland edges, heaths, scrub, moors and gardens; most common in S. England; rare in N. Scotland; scattered in Ireland. **Notes:** Prefers lighter soils; rare on chalk. Tolerates dry conditions.

Alder Betulaceae *Alnus glutinosa*. **Habitat:** Wetland, water margins and damp woodland throughout British Isles, up to 500m.

Hazel Betulaceae *Corylus avellana*. **Habitat:** Woodland, hedgerows, scrub and gardens throughout British Isles, but less common in E. Scotland.

Trees

Hornbeam Betulaceae *Carpinus betulus*. **Habitat:** Deciduous woodland, hedgerows, parks and gardens most common in S. England; rare in N. Scotland; scattered throughout Ireland.

Beech Fagaceae *Fagus sylvatica*. **Habitat:** Dominant in deciduous woodland, parks and gardens throughout British Isles, but less common in N.W. **Notes:** Often planted. Prefers well-drained calcareous loams and sandy soils.

Sweet Chestnut Fagaceae *Castanea sativa*. **Habitat:** Deciduous woodland and parks throughout British Isles; most common in S. and E.; rare to absent in N. and W. **Notes:** Often planted in pure stands, as a coppice crop.

Sessile Oak Fagaceae *Quercus petraea*. **Habitat:** Deciduous woodland, parks and gardens throughout British Isles up to 500m, but more common in W. **Notes:** Mainly on acid soils; rare on heavy clays; sometimes dominant or co-dominant with Pedunculate oak.

Sessile Oak

Pedunculate Oak

Pedunculate Oak Fagaceae *Quercus robur*. **Habitat:** Deciduous woodland, parks and gardens throughout British Isles but rare to absent in extreme N.W. Scotland; scattered in Ireland.

Evergreen Oak Fagaceae *Quercus ilex*. **Habitat:** Scattered throughout central and southern England, but more common in the south and east; rarely in Wales and Ireland. **Notes:** Evergreen; leaves variable in shape.

Turkey Oak *Q. cerris* has narrower crown and variable leaves. It is common in S.E. England; scattered in Wales, S. and W. Scotland and Ireland; prefers acid soils.

Trees

English Elm Ulmaceae *Ulmus procera*. **Habitat:** Woodland and hedgerows throughout British Isles, but rare to absent in central, N. and W. Scotland; most frequent in S. and E. England and Ireland. Now decimated by Dutch Elm disease.
Small-leaved Elm *Ulmus minor* is similar but has a narrower crown, greyer bark and smaller leaves.

Wych Elm Ulmaceae *Ulmus glabra*. **Habitat:** Deciduous woodland, hedgerows, parks, churchyards, especially near water, throughout British Isles, but more common in N. and W. **Notes:** Leaves rough on upper surface, hairy on lower; variable.

London Plane Platanaceae *Platanus x hispanica*. **Habitat:** City parks and roadsides throughout Britian. **Notes:** Grey-brown bark flakes to reveal characteristic cream patches on trunk. Usually planted.

Crab Apple Rosaceae *Malus sylvestris*. **Habitat:** Scattered in woodland throughout British Isles. **Notes:** Small, hard sour fruits are produced in autumn.

Mountain Ash, Rowan
Rosaceae *Sorbus aucuparia*.
Habitat: Deciduous woodland, mountains, parks, gardens and scrub throughout British Isles up to 1050m, but less common in Midlands and central and S. Ireland. **Notes:** Usually on light acid soils; rare or absent on clay.

Wild Service Tree Rosaceae *Sorbus torminalis*. **Habitat:** Local in old woodland and hedgerows in Britain. **Notes:** Bark grey, fissured. Produces small, brown berries in September.

Trees

Whitebeam Rosaceae *Sorbus aria.* **Habitat:** Scattered in deciduous woodland, scrub and gardens throughout British Isles; common only in S. **Notes:** Usually on chalk or limestone; also on sandstone hills.
Swedish Whitebeam *Sorbus intermedia* is a similar European species, occasionally planted in Britain.

Gean, Wild Cherry Rosaceae *Prunus avium.* **Habitat:** Deciduous woodland, parks, gardens and hedgerows throughout British Isles but rare in N. Scotland. **Notes:** Common on better soils. Suckers freely. Fruits bright or dark red, sweet or bitter.

Hawthorn Rosaceae *Crataegus monogyna.* **Habitat:** Woodland, hedgerows and scrub throughout British Isles up to 580m; rare in N. Scotland. **Notes:** Commonest shrub on all types of soil.

Sloe, Blackthorn Rosaceae *Prunus spinosa.* **Habitat:** Open woodland, hedgerows and scrub throughout British Isles, up to 435m; rare to absent in N. Scotland. **Notes:** On all soils except acid pear. Not shade tolerant.

Bird Cherry Rosaceae *Prunus padus*. **Habitat:** Woodland on calcareous soils in N. England and Scotland, Wales and E. Anglia. **Notes:** Bark smooth with a foetid odour. (17m)

Field Maple Aceraceae *Acer campestre*. **Habitat:** Hedgerows and deciduous woodland in England, except N. and S.W.; common in E. Wales, scattered in W.; scattered in S. and central Scotland and Ireland.

Sycamore Aceraceae *Acer pseudoplatanus*. **Habitat:** Woodland, parks, gardens in town and country, hedgerows and plantations throughout British Isles, but less common in N. Scotland. **Notes:** Prefers deep, moist, rich, well-drained soils, but grows on all but poorest types.
Norway Maple *Acer platanoides* is similar but has shiny, bright green leaves.

Trees

Horse Chestnut
Hippocastanaceae *Aesculus hippocastanum*. **Habitat:** Parks and gardens in town and country throughout British Isles, but less common in N. and W. and in Ireland. **Notes:** Planted as an ornamental.

Spindle(-tree) Celastraceae *Euonymus europaeus*. **Habitat:** Woodland, scrub, hedgerows and gardens in England, especially in S.; scattered throughout Wales, Ireland and S. Scotland; up to 340m. **Notes:** Usually on base-rich or calcareous soils.

Box Buxaceae *Buxus sempervirens*. **Habitat:** Locally abundant in woodland and scrub on calcareous soils in a few scattered localities in S. England; elsewhere in parks, gardens and scrub. **Notes:** Often planted. Evergreen.

Holly Aquifoliaceae *Ilex aquifolium*. **Habitat:** Beech and oak woodland, also scrub, hedgerows, among rocks; planted in gardens; throughout British Isles, but less common in N. and E. Scotland. **Notes:** Usually on well-drained soils.

Buckthorn Rhamnaceae
Rhamnus catharticus. **Habitat:**
Oak, ash and alder woodland,
scrub and hedgerows on damp,
peaty, calcareous soils
throughout England, especially
S. and E.; scattered in Ireland
and Wales. **Notes:** Thorny bush
or small tree.

Alder buckthorn Rhamnaceae
Frangula alnus. **Habitat:**
Wetland, wet heaths, damp
scrub and woodland throughout
Wales and England, especially in
S. **Notes:** Usually on acid or
peaty soils.

Small-leaved Lime Tiliaceae
Tilia cordata. **Habitat:**
Deciduous woodland,
particularly on limestone cliffs,
parks and gardens throughout
central and S. England and
Wales; scattered elsewhere.
Notes: Prefers limestone but
grows on other soils. Leaves
tough, blue-green beneath.
Large-leaved Lime *Tilia
platyphyllos* is very similar but
taller.

Trees

Ash Oleaceae *Fraxinus excelsior.* **Habitat:** Deciduous woodland, particularly with oak and beech, scrub, hedgerows, parks and gardens throughout British Isles, but less common in N. **Notes:** Common as woods on calcareous soils in wetter regions.

Wayfaring Tree Caprifoliaceae *Viburnum lantana.* **Habitat:** Woodland shrub layer, scrub, hedgerows, usually on dry calcareous soils in S. England; rarely scattered throughout rest of British Isles. **Notes:** Fruit red at first, turning black.

Elder Caprifoliaceae *Sambucus nigra.* **Habitat:** Woodland, hedgerows, waste ground, scrub and roadside verges throughout British Isles, up to 516m but rare in N. Scotland. **Notes:** Characteristic of base- and nitrogen-rich soils, especially in disturbed areas. Rarely a small tree.

Guelder Rose Caprifoliaceae *Viburnum opulus.* **HabitatL** Usually damp and alder woodland, scrub and hedgerows throughout British Isles, but less common in Ireland and scattered in Scotland. **Notes:** A sterile form is grown in gardens.

Marine Invertebrates

Thousands of species of marine invertebrates inhabitat the coasts of Britain and Europe, but the majority are not easy to find. Many live below the low water mark, while others – especially those of sandy and muddy shores – live hidden deep in burrows and will not be revealed without the energetic use of a spade. Even those that live in the open or are exposed at low tide are often hidden in crevices, under boulders or smothered by masses of seaweed.

However, many of these creatures (even those that normally live at sea) may be cast up on the shore after a storm. Similarly, their shells or other fragments are commonly washed up on the strandline, along with distinctive items such as whelk eggs (bunches of horny, hollow, yellow balls) and ''mermaid's purses'' (dark brown, horny rectangular packets with a prong at each corner) – the egg cases of skates and dogfish. As well as a rich collection of animals from around our shores the strandline may also contain animals and plants brought by tide and currents from far away. Coconut husks are occasionally swept to our shores by the Gulfstream all the way from the West Indies.

Of the living invertebrates found on British and European shores, the major groups are:

Gastropod molluscs typically have a coiled shell and live on rocks, piles and other fixed objects. They are especially abundant on rocky shores.

Bivalve molluscs have a hinged shell in two matched halves and normally burrow into sand or mud. They are very common on sandy shores. A few species (e.g. mussels) attach themselves to rocks and fixed objects.

Crustaceans. Crabs and shrimps are active animals that hide under rocks and in pools. Barnacles are sessile creatures that live permanently attached to rocks, etc. They form small pointed, open-topped cones. Sand-hoppers are among the small crustaceans found along the strandline and under stones.

The sea provides an environment every bit as complex and rich as we see on land. Here a hermit crab has taken over a whelk shell and sea anemones have joined in to exploit any food the crab may waste.

Jellyfish are ancient animals and are basically comparatively 'simple'. Even so, they can become very large and can propel themselves through water. They go through a number of stages, earlier stages being sedentary.

Marine Invertebrates

Worms mostly burrow in sand and mud. Occasionally, ragworms are found under stones. Several species live in straight tubes which they construct themselves and which can be found on the surface of sandy beaches. Other worms burrow into and eat sand, and squirt little coils of waste sand to the surface, just as earthworms produce "wormcasts" of soil. Other worms – especially the tube-makers – have a delicate fan of tentacles which filter minute particles of food from the surrounding water.

Echinoderms. These are the starfish, sea urchins and sea cucumbers. All three groups have distinctive "tube feet", delicate fleshy feelers each with a sucker-like tip. A starfish's tube feet project from the underside like a mass of legs, while a sea urchin's protrude through little holes in the shell among the spines. Sea cucumbers are unlikely to be found on the shore; they have tube feet round the mouth and along the sides of their sausage-like body. Echinoderms characteristically have a star-like, five pointed body symmetry not found in any other animals.

Soft-bodied invertebrates. Most of the animals mentioned have a shell or distinctive body shape, but many marine creatures are soft-bodied and slug-like. Although they belong to a variety of animal groups, they often look very similar and their differences are revealed only by a study of their internal anatomy. With practice they can be identified in the field, but it is often difficult.

Sea anemones are coloured columns of jelly which, when covered by water, have a mass of thick-tentacles around the mouth and a sticky base which attaches the animal to rocks and breakwaters.

Sea slugs crawl or swim slowly in shallow water and often have feathery tentacles or coloured projections on the back. They are shell-less gastropods. Sea squirts are yet another group, resembling sponges which often look more like plants than animals.

Many of the species of the intertidal zone are sensitive to the length of time that they are exposed to the air at low tide. Thus some occur only on the lower shore where they are uncovered for only a short time, while others live in the "splash-zone" on the upper part of the shore where they are rarely covered by water at all.

Many marine invertebrates, especially those that live in burrows or on rocks, have planktonic larvae which act almost like the seeds of plants and disperse the species around the coasts. Identification of these planktonic stages requires a microscope, but a hand lens will reveal clouds of little creatures buzzing about in a jar of sea water.

Starfish are a common animal found below the tide line of our shores. When washed up they may appear fairly inert, but on their undersides they have rows of tiny feet on which they clamber to find their prey, usually bivalve molluscs.

Marine Invertebrates

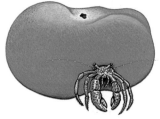

Sulphur Sponge, Sea-Orange
Suberites domuncula. **Habitat:**
From shallow water down to
200m; frequently associated
with hermit crabs; on most
British coasts. **Notes:** Sponge
encrusts hermit crab's whelk
shell, may gradually dissolve it
away to shelter crab directly.
(30cm diameter)

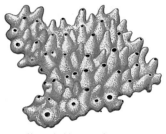

Hymeniacidon sanguinea.
Habitat: On rocks from middle
shore down to shallow water;
on all British coasts. **Notes:**
Variable in shape and colour
ranges from orange to scarlet;
surface furrowed or smooth.
(50cm)

Beadlet Anemone *Actinia
equina*. **Habitat:** Common on
rocks and in crevices from
middle shore down to 8m; on all
British coasts. **Notes:** About
200 densely packed retractile
tentacles; 24 blue spots on
outside or oral disc. Colour
variable, brown, red, orange or
green. (7cm high)

Breadcrumb Sponge
Halichondria panicea. **Habitat:**
On stones, seaweeds and shells
from middle shore down to
quite deep water; on all British
coasts. **Notes:** Colour varies
from grey to green or brown.
Often grows in large
encrustations. (20cm)

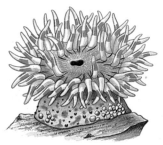

Dahlia Anemone *Tealia felina*.
Habitat: On hard substrates,
often in crevices; on all British
coasts. **Notes:** Prefers shade.
Coloration very variable, often
strikingly beautiful; tentacles
translucent, banded with
various colours. (15cm high)

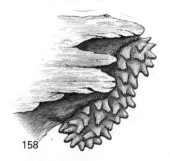

White Weed *Sertularia
cupressina*. **Habitat:** On
stones, shells and sometimes
on crabs in shallow and deeper
water; on all British coasts.
Notes: Large, branching
colonies; white or pink. (45cm
high)

Portuguese Man-o'-War
Physalia physalis. **Habitat:**
Pelagic on surface of Atlantic;
occasionally washed ashore.
Notes: Float conspicuous
above water surface; below are
long "tentacles" of polyps,
many armed with dangerous
stinging cells. (30cm wide)

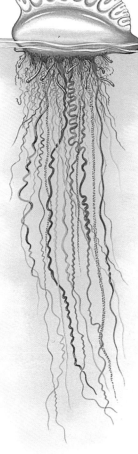

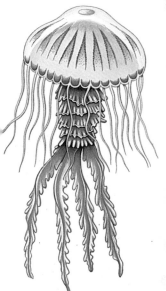

Compass Jellyfish *Chrysaora
hysoscella*. **Habitat:** Pelagic in
Atlantic, English Channel and
North Sea. **Notes:** Bell saucer-
shaped, bearing 24 tentacles; 4
mouth arms longer than
tentacles. (30cm)

Common Jellyfish *Aurelia
aurita*. **Habitat:** Pelagic in
Atlantic, English Channel and
North Sea. **Notes:** Frilly mouth
arms longer than the numerous
short tentacles. Four violet
horseshoe-shaped reproductive
organs clearly visible from
above. (25cm)

159

Marine Invertebrates

Snakelocks Anemone
Anemonia sulcata. **Habitat:** On
rocks and occasionally on
seaweeds from lower shore
down to 23m; Atlantic coast
north to W. Scotland; English
Channel east to Solent. **Notes:**
Prefers strong light. About 170
tentacles, often purple-tipped.
(10cm high)

Metridium senile. **Habitat:** On
rocks, wrecks and piers from 0.5
to 3m; on most British coasts.
Notes: Tentacles have
feather-duster appearance
because slender and very
crowded. Several colour
varieties. (8cm high)

Dead Man's Fingers *Alcyonium
digitatum.* **Habitat:** On rocks
and stones on lower shore
down to 100m; on most British
coasts. **Notes:** Polyps retract
when disturbed. Colour varies
from white to yellow, orange or
pink. (20cm high)

"Parasitic" Anemone *Calliactis
parasitica.* **Habitat:** On muddy
substrates from 3 to 100m;
Atlantic coasts north to W.
Ireland and Irish Sea; English
Channel coasts; frequently
found attached to shells
occupied by hermit crabs.
Notes: Not a true parasite,
anemone protects crab from
attack by predators and shares
food. (3cm)

Sea-mouse *Aphrodite aculeata.*
Habitat: Soft substrates in
shallow water; on all British
coasts. **Notes:** Bristles
brilliantly iridescent. (10-20cm)

Scale Worm *Harmothoë impar.*
Habitat: Under stones, rocks,
seaweeds on lower shore and in
shallow water; on all British
coasts. **Notes:** Scales
brown-green with yellow central
spot. (2.5cm)

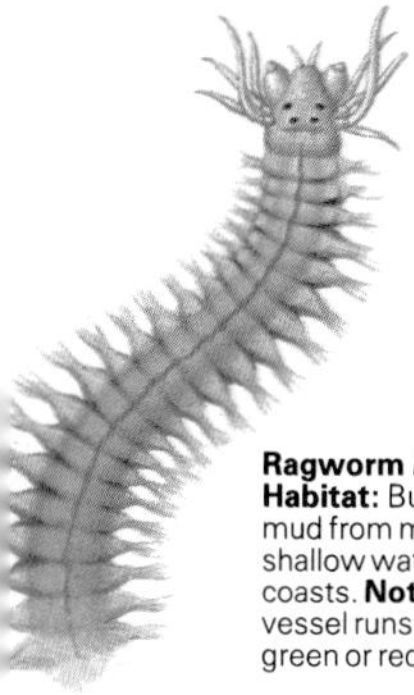

Ragworm *Nereis diversicolor*. **Habitat:** Burrows in sand or mud from middle shore to shallow water; on all British coasts. **Notes:** Distinct blood vessel runs down back. Colour green or red. (12cm)

Green Leaf Worm *Eulalia viridis*. **Habitat:** On lower shore and in shallow water in rock crevices; on all British coasts. **Notes:** Grass-green. (5-15cm)

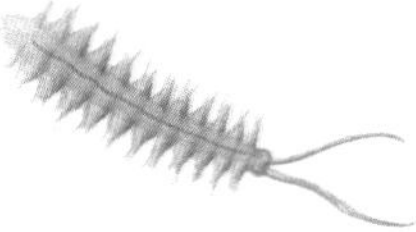

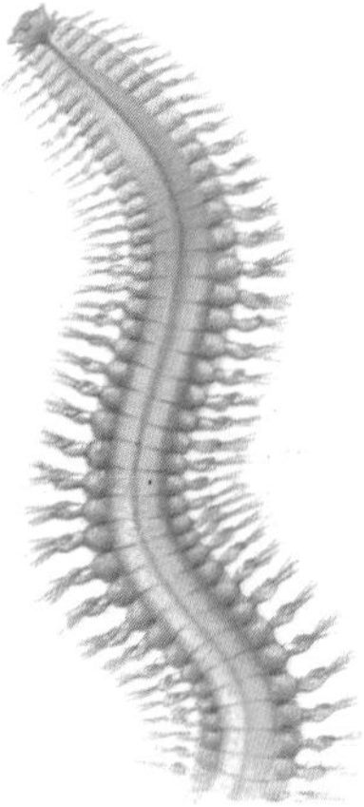

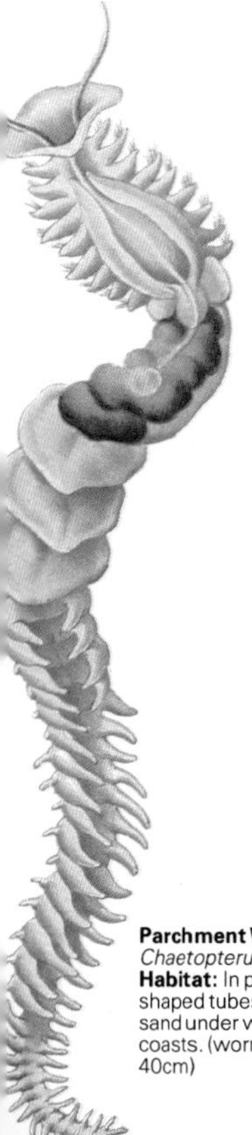

King Ragworm *Nereis virens*. **Habitat:** Lower shores and in shallow water; on all British coasts except S. **Notes:** Often burrows in sand. Pink underneath. (20-40cm)

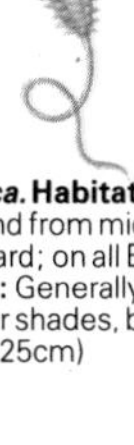

Parchment Worm *Chaetopterus variopedatus*. **Habitat:** In parchment-like U-shaped tubes buried in mud or sand under water; on all British coasts. (worm 25cm; tube 40cm)

***Nephtys caeca*. Habitat:** Burrows in sand from middle shore downward; on all British coasts. **Notes:** Generally pearly grey with other shades, but colour varies. (25cm)

161

Lugworm *Arenicola marina.*
Habitat: Burrows in sand from middle shore downward; on all British coasts. (20cm)

Sand Mason *Lanice conchilega.* **Habitat:** In tube of sand grains with frayed appearance at top, from middle shore downward; on all British coasts. (30cm)

Serpula vermicularis. **Habitat:** In free-standing tubes fixed to stones, rocks and shells on lower shore and in shallow water; on all British coasts. (7cm)

Pomatoceros triqueter. **Habitat:** In looped tube on stones and shells on lower shore and in shallow water; on all British coasts. (2.5cm)

Spirorbis borealis. **Habitat:** In coiled tube on seaweeds and rocks of middle and lower shore and in shallow water; on all British coasts. (35mm)

Coat of Mail Chiton *Lepidopleurus asellus.* **Habitat:** On shells and rocks from lower shore down to 150m; on all British coasts. (2cm)

Keyhole Limpet *Diodora apertura*. **Habitat:** On rocks from lower shore down to 20m; on all British coasts. (1.25cm)

Common Limpet *Patella vulgata*. **Habitat:** On rocks on middle and upper shore, often in exposed places; on all British coasts. **Notes:** Conical, rough, ribbed shell. Shell taller on more exposed coasts. (7cm)

Blue-rayed Limpet *Patina pellucida*. **Habitat:** Generally attached to fronds and holdfasts of *Laminaria* seaweed on lower shore and in shallow water; on all British coasts. (1.5cm)

Purple Topshell *Gibbula umbilicalis*. **Habitat:** On rocks on middle shore and upper lower shore; Atlantic and English Channel coasts only. (1.25cm high)

Grey Topshell *Gibbula cineraria*. **Habitat:** Under stones and on seaweeds on lower shore down to 20m; on all British coasts. (1.25cm high)

Toothed Topshell *Monodonta lineata*. **Habitat:** On rocks on middle shore; Atlantic coast, N. to Anglesey and W. English Channel. (2.5cm high)

Flat Periwinkle *Littorina littoralis*. **Habitat:** On seaweeds on lower middle and upper lower shores; on all British coasts. **Notes:** Colour varies from brown to orange or yellow. (1cm high)

Rough Periwinkle *Littorina saxatilis*. **Habitat:** In cracks, crevices, on stones on upper shore; on all British coasts. (0.8cm high)

Marine Invertebrates

Small Periwinkle *Littorina neritoides*. **Habitat:** Usually in crevices on extreme upper shore; on all British coasts. (0.5cm high)

Laver Spire Shell *Hydrobia ulvae*. **Habitat:** On mud in estuaries, on middle shore in brackish water; on all British coasts. (0.6cm high)

Edible Periwinkle *Littorina littorea*. **Habitat:** On rocks, stones and seaweeds on middle and lower shores; on all British coasts. (2.5cm high)

Pelican's Foot Shell *Aporrhais pespelecani*. **Habitat:** Burrows in mud, sand or gravel from lower shore down to 80m; on all British coasts. (3.5cm)

Tower Shell *Turritella communis*. **Habitat:** Partly buried in sand or mud on shore down to 80m; on all British coasts. (4.6cm high)

Violet Sea Snail *Ianthina exigua*. **Habitat:** Pelagic in Atlantic; occasionally washed up after westerly gales. (1.5cm high)

Slipper Limpet *Crepidula fornicata*. **Habitat:** Usually attached to others of same species and to bivalves in shallow water; on all British coasts. (2.5cm wide)

Cowrie *Trivia monacha*. **Habitat:** Among rocks on lower shore and in shallow water; on all British coasts. (1.2cm long)

Dogwhelk *Nucella lapillus.*
Habitat: In crevices and among barnacles on rocky shores in middle zone; on all British coasts. (3cm)

Sting Winkle, Oyster Drill
Ocenebra erinacea. **Habitat:** Muddy gravel, sand and rocks from lower shore down to 100m; on all British coasts. (6cm high)

Sea-hare *Aplysia punctata.*
Habitat: Among seaweeds in shallow water and occasionally swimming; on all British coasts.
Notes: Body almost encloses shell. Young reddish, older animals brown-green. May eject purple dye when disturbed. (14cm body)

Dendronotus frondosus.
Habitat: Among rocks and on sand in shallow water down to 100m; on all British coasts.
Notes: Many pairs of branched appendages along back. (5cm)

Elysia viridis. Habitat: On green seaweeds from middle shore downward; on all British coasts. **Notes:** Body flattened and soft. (3cm)

Common Whelk *Buccinum undatum.* **Habitat:** On sand, mud and in shallow water; on all British coasts. **Notes:** Empty shells often inhabited by hermit crabs. Spongy egg masses often washed up on shore. (8cm)

Marine Invertebrates

Common Grey Sea Slug
Aeolidia papillosa. **Habitat:** On
stony and rocky shores
between high and low water
marks; on all British coasts.
Notes: Many appendages on
back, "parted" in middle. (8cm)

Dog Cockle *Glycymeris
glycymeris*. **Habitat:** Burrows in
surface of mud, sand or gravel in
shallow water; mainly on S. and
W. coasts. (6.5cm long)

Common Mussel *Mytilus
edulis*. **Habitat:** Stones and
rocks in estuaries and in
extensive beds from middle
shore downward; on all British
coasts. **Notes:** Attached to
substrate by cluster of strong,
horny byssus threads. (1-10cm)

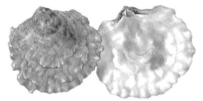

Common Oyster *Ostrea edulis*.
Habitat: Attached to rocks and
stones in shallow water down to
80m; on all British coasts.
(10cm)

Portuguese Oyster
Crassostrea angulata. **Habitat:**
On rocks and stones in shallow
water; on all British coasts.
(15cm wide)

Great Scallop *Pecten
maximus*. **Habitat:** On sand and
gravel, usually in deeper water;
on all British coasts. (15cm)

Spiny Cockle *Acanthocardia aculeata*. **Habitat:** In sand underwater from 10m downward; on all British coasts. (10cm)

Rayed Trough Shell *Mactra corallina*. **Habitat:** Burrows in sand and gravel from extreme lower shore down to 100m; on all British coasts. (5cm)

Common Cockle *Cerastoderma edule*. **Habitat:** Burrows in mud, sand or gravel in estuaries and from lower shore downward; on all British coasts. (5cm)

Thin Tellin *Tellina tenuis*. **Habitat:** Burrows in sand from middle shore to shallow water; on all British coasts. (2cm)

Banded Venus *Venus fasciata*. **Habitat:** Burrows in surface of sand or gravel underwater from 3 to 100m; on all British coasts. (2.5cm)

Baltic Tellin *Macoma balthica*. **Habitat:** Burrows in mud and sand in shallow brackish water; on all British coasts. (2.5cm)

Peppery Furrow Shell *Scrobicularia plana*. **Habitat:** Burrows in mud and sand between tidemarks; on all British coasts. (6cm)

Marine Invertebrates

Razor Shell *Ensis ensis.*
Habitat: Burrows in sand on extreme lower shore and in shallow water; on all British coasts. (12.5cm)

Grooved Razor Shell *Solen marginatus.* **Habitat:** Burrows in sand on lower shore and in shallow water; on all British coasts. (12.5cm)

Blunt Gaper *Mya truncata.*
Habitat: Burrows in mud and sand from middle shore down to 70m; on all British coasts. (7.5cm)

Common Piddock *Pholas dactylus.* **Habitat:** Bores into soft rock, wood, firm sand or peat on lower shore; on S. and S.W. coasts only. (15cm)

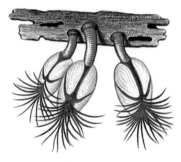

Goose Barnacle *Lepas anatifera.* **Habitat:** Attached to boats and driftwood in Atlantic, English Channel and North Sea. **Notes:** Long, retractable stalk, up to 20cm long.

Ship Worm *Teredo navalis.*
Habitat: Bores in submerged wooden structures; on all British coasts. **Notes:** Shell reduced; animal secretes chalky tube round body as it bores. (20cm tube)

Marine Invertebrates

Common Cuttlefish *Sepia officinalis.* **Habitat:** In shallow water over sand in bays and estuaries; on all British coasts. **Notes:** 10 tentacles round mouth; body broad, flattened. (30cm)

Common Squid *Loligo forbesi.* **Habitat:** Seldom found close to the shore around British Isles. **Notes:** Body torpedo-shaped with paired fins joining together at tip. Colour variable, predominantly pink, red and brown. (60cm)

Common Octopus *Octopus vulgaris.* **Habitat:** Among rocks and stones and often in constructed lair; offshore in Atlantic north to English Channel. **Notes:** Bag-like body with 8 tentacles, each with 2 rows of suckers. Colour variable. (Max. 1m)

Lesser Octopus *Eledone cirrhosa.* **Habitat:** Among rocks and stones offshore in Atlantic, English Channel and N. North Sea; occasionally on extreme lower shore. **Notes:** Body smooth or warty. One row of suckers on tentacles. Predominantly red-brown above, white below. (50cm)

Little Cuttlefish *Sepiola atlantica.* **Habitat:** Swims over and burrows into sand in shallow water; Atlantic and English Channel coasts only. **Notes:** Colour variable; body short and cup-shaped. (5cm)

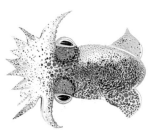

Marine Invertebrates

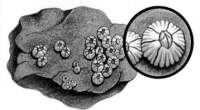

Acorn Barnacle *Semibalanus balanoides*. **Habitat:** Sessile on rocks on upper shore in N., middle shore in S.; on all British coasts. (1.5cm)

Parasitic Barnacle *Sacculina carcini*. **Habitat:** Parasitic on abdomen of Shore Crab on sandy and rocky shores; on all British coasts. **Notes:** Unlike other barnacles; a smooth conspicuous yellow-brown lump, which prevents crab from folding its abdomen closely under its body.

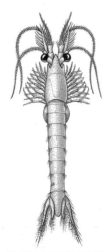

Leptomysis gracilis. Habitat: In pools on lower shore and in shallow water; on all British coasts. **Notes:** Transparent, colourless. (1.3cm)

Gammarus locusta. Habitat: Abundant under stones and seaweeds on middle and lower shores; on all British coasts. **Notes:** Body compressed laterally. (1.5-2cm)

Sand-hopper *Talitrus saltator*. **Habitat:** On rotting seaweeds on upper shore; on all British coasts. (1.6cm)

Sea-slater *Ligia oceanica*. **Habitat:** Among rocks, stones and seaweed debris above intertidal zone; on all British coasts. **Notes:** Very similar to woodlouse. (2.5cm)

Glass Prawn *Leander squilla.*
Habitat: In rock pools on lower shore, often among seaweeds, and in shallow water; on all British coasts. **Notes:** Main antennae 1½ times as long as body. Large pincers on 2nd pair walking legs. (5cm)

Common Shrimp *Crangon vulgaris.* **Habitat:** Lower shore and in shallow water and estuaries; on all British coasts. **Notes:** Main antennae almost as long as body. Largest pincers on 1st pair walking legs. (5cm)

Dublin Bay Prawn, Scampi, Norway Lobster *Nephrops norvegicus.* **Habitat:** In mud and sand offshore around Atlantic and North Sea coasts. **Notes:** Like a slender, pinkish lobster. Nippers have sharp spikes along ridges. (15cm)

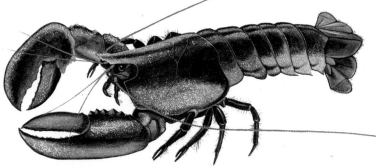

Lobster *Homarus gammarus.*
Habitat: Among rocks on lower shore and offshore; on all British coasts. **Notes:** Blue when alive. Massive pincers. (45cm)

Squat Lobster *Galathea squamifera.* **Habitat:** Under stones on lower shore down to 80m; on all British coasts. **Notes:** Abdomen folded under thorax, giving squat appearance. Very long pincer arms. (4.5cm)

Marine Invertebrates

Hermit Crab *Eupagurus bernhardus*. **Habitat:** In old mollusc shells, especially winkles and whelks, on lower shore; on most British coasts. **Notes:** Pincers unequal in size. Crabs move to larger shells as they grow. (10cm)

Common Shore Crab *Carcinus maenas*. **Habitat:** Common under stones, weeds and on mud; on all shores in British Isles. **Notes:** Angular carapace with sharp serrations along leading edge. (4cm)

Masked Crab *Corystes cassivelaunus*. **Habitat:** Usually buried in sand on lower shore; on most British coasts. **Notes:** Pincers longer than body (especially in male). Very long antennae are joined together. (4cm body)

Edible Crab *Cancer pagurus*. **Habitat:** Among rocks on lower shore; on most British coasts. **Notes:** Body 1½ times wider than long; crinkled carapace margin reminiscent of pie crust. Pincers heavy, black-tipped. (Max. 14cm)

Spider Crab *Macropodia tenuirostris*. **Habitat:** In shallow water among seaweeds; on most British coasts. **Notes:** Carapace often covered with weeds and encrusting organisms. Limbs very long, slightly hairy. (1.5cm body)

Chinese Mitten Crab *Eriocheir sinensis*. **Habitat:** In freshwater and estuaries; on most British coasts. **Notes:** Pincers covered with furry bristles giving appearance of mittens; other legs long and hairy. (7cm)

Marine Invertebrates

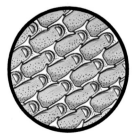

Sea-mat *Membranipora membranacea.* **Habitat:** On *Laminaria* and other seaweeds from middle shore down to shallow water; on most British coasts. **Notes:** Mat-like, encrusting colony of tiny animals, sometimes with "tower" growths.

Hornwrack *Flustra foliacea.* **Habitat:** On rocks and stones from shallow water down to 100m; on most British coasts. **Notes:** May form extensive communities. Leaf-like, branching colony of many tiny animals, often mistaken for seaweed. Often cast up on shore, where becomes white and brittle. (20cm high)

Astropecten irregularis. **Habitat:** Often burrows into sand from extreme lower shore downwards; on all British coasts. **Notes:** Body flattened with 5 arms, each edged with 2 layers of marginal plates bearing spines. Orange-brown above, white below. (12cm)

Scarlet Starfish *Henricia oculata.* **Habitat:** On soft substrates, among pebbles and small stones; on most British coasts. **Notes:** Arms nearly circular in cross-section and tapering. Blood-red to purple above, paler below. (10cm)

Sunstar *Crossaster papposus.* **Habitat:** On sand, stones, among mussel and oyster beds; on most British coasts. **Notes:** Between 8 and 13 short, blunt arms. Body surface covered with small spines. Colour variable. (25cm)

173

Marine Invertebrates

Ophiura texturata. Habitat:
Burrows in sand from lower
shore down to 200m; on all
British coasts. **Notes:** Two
conspicuous plates above origin
of each arm; arms up to 4 times
disc diameter, tapering, with
similarly tapering spines. (Disc
3cm)

Ophiocomina nigra. **Habitat:**
Among rocks, seaweeds and
sand from lower shore down to
400m; on all British coasts.
Notes: Arms not more than 5
times disc diameter and
tapering; arm spines fine,
glassy. Black, brown or orange-
yellow. (Disc 3cm)

Common Starfish *Asterias
rubens.* **Habitat:** On rocks and
stony ground, in mussel and
oyster beds from lower shore
down to 200m; on all British
coasts. **Notes:** Arms rounded,
tapering. Body covered with
irregularly arranged spines.
Brown-yellow above, paler
below. (Max. 50cm)

Common Brittle-star
Ophiothrix fragilis. **Habitat:**
Under stones, seaweeds and
shells from lower shore down to
350m; on all British coasts.
Notes: Disc often pentagonal.
Arms not more than 5 times disc
diameter, fragile, often broken;
arm spines conspicuous. Colour
variable. (Disc 2cm)

Paracentrotus lividus.
Habitat: On rocks and stones and among coralline seaweeds from lower middle shore, in rock pools, down to 30m; in Atlantic north to Channel Islands and W. coast of Ireland; rarely in W. English Channel. **Notes:** Spines up to 3cm. Colour variable. Frequently excavates hollows in rocks and sits there permanently. (6cm)

Purple Heart Urchin *Spatangus purpureus.* **Habitat:** In coarse sand and shell gravel underwater from 5 to 800m; on most British coasts. **Notes:** Five rows of tube feet; anterior row in shallow furrow leading to mouth. Spines mostly short; some paddle-shaped for burrowing in sand. (12cm)

Green Sea Urchin
Psammechinus miliaris.
Habitat: On rocks and under stones, often associated with coralline seaweeds, from lower middle shore down to 100m; on most British coasts. **Notes:** Spines up to 1.5cm with violet tips. Often covers itself with bits of shell and seaweed debris. (4cm)

Star Ascidian *Botryllus schlosseri.* **Habitat:** Encrusting stones, rocks and seaweeds on lower shore and in shallow water; on all British coasts. **Notes:** Individuals arranged in star-like groups of 3 to 12 in colonies of varying shapes and sizes; often flat, sometimes fleshy.

Ascidia mentula **Habitat:** Attached to rocks from lower shore down to 200m; on all British coasts. **Notes:** Sessile, solitary individuals encased in thick, cartilage-like tunic. (10cm)

Edible Sea Urchin *Echinus esculentus.* **Habitat:** On rocks and among seaweeds from extreme lower shore down to 50m; on most British coasts. **Notes:** Spines 1.5cm, short and solid, often with purple tips. Sex organs are edible. (10cm)

Sea-potato *Echinocardium cordatum.* **Habitat:** In sand from lower shore down to 200m; on most British coasts. **Notes:** 5 rows of tube feet; anterior row in deep furrow almost reaching the mouth. Spines mostly short, but some long, curved and backward pointing. (9cm)

175

Terrestrial and Freshwater Invertebrates

Although less obvious than the vertebrate fauna because of their generally small size, invertebrate animals are represented by many more species and individuals. Precise identification is often a job for the experienced specialist, using a microscope, but it is fairly easy in the field to identify the major group (or Family) to which a particular invertebrate belongs. Space does not permit illustrations of all the different invertebrate groups, but the most common and distinctive ones are featured. These are the cnidarians, flatworms, annelid worms, molluscs and arthropods. Most of the common invertebrates are arthropods and this group is represented largely by the insects, spiders and centipedes on land and by the crustaceans in water.

Cnidarians

These are soft-bodied, aquatic organisms with a hollow, sac-like body with a mouth at one end surrounded by a ring of tentacles used for trapping prey. Most cnidarians (e.g. jellyfish, corals and sea anemones) are marine, but a few, like the hydras, live in freshwater.

Hydra live under water attached to submerged stones and water weeds. Their tentacles are extended to catch small aquatic animals, but hydra shrink to a jelly-like mass if disturbed.

Right: Photography displays the agility of a lacewing's take-off. Flight is one of the great hallmarks of the insects: a group that successfully exploits virtually every niche of terrestrial habitat.

Flatworms

These are flat, somewhat worm-like, with no body segments, no legs and no shell. Some are parasitic in the bodies of animals, but many are aquatic. A few, like *Polycelis*, live in freshwater, typically near the bottom of ponds and streams, where they feed on other small invertebrates which they suck up through a tube (pharynx) on their under surface.

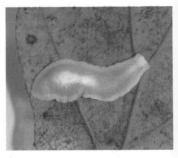

This aquatic flatworm browses over the detritus at the bottom of ponds but others feed on fish eggs and water snails, while yet others are parasitic within the body of larger animals.

Annelid worms

Annelids are typical worms with a segmented body, no legs and no shell. the common earthworm *Lumbricus* is a typical example of one group of annelids, the oligochaete worms. They vary in length from a few milimetres to several centimetres, have moist, slimy skins and are often red. They generally live in damp soil, leaf litter or under stones, or in shallow freshwater. Most feed on organic matter or micro-organisms.

Leeches are also annelids; they live in freshwater, are often slightly flattened and feed exclusively on the blood and body fluids of other animals.

Terrestrial and Freshwater Invertebrates

Molluscs

Molluscs are soft-bodied invertebrates, often without a recognisable head, with part of the body formed into a muscular foot, and usually with a shell. The distinctive shapes, colours and patterns of mollusc shells are often the only means of identifying them in the field.

Snails (gastropod molluscs) typically have a coiled shell from which only the head (which usually bears eyes on long stalks) and muscular foot protrudes. The closely related slugs are similar but do not have an external shell. Snails live on land and in freshwater; slugs are wholly terrestrial.

The freshwater mussels (bivalve molluscs) have two flattish shells joined at a hinge. They anchor themselves to the river bed and filter micro-organisms by pumping a current of water through their bodies through fringed tubes, or siphons, at one end of the shell.

These woodlice are crustaceans and are related to aquatic water fleas and crayfish. There are a number of aquatic woodlice-like creatures.

Crustaceans have a tough exoskeleton which is hard and chalky in larger species like crayfish and shrimps, but often thin and transparent in small species like water fleas and copepods, so that the internal organs are visible through it.

Most freshwater crustaceans are tiny, only a few millimetres long. They often occur in large numbers: a single pond can contain many millions of water fleas, for example. While water fleas swim through the water by beating their feathery antennae, tiny copepods like *Cyclops* and shrimps like *Gammarus* swim over the river bed with a crawling motion of their many legs.

The molluscs have exploited the plant life of ponds very successfully with about 70 species present in Britain. About half of these are gastropods, such as this great ram's-horn snail, whilst the remainder are bivalves.

Crustaceans

With the exception of the woodlice, which live on land, all British crustaceans are aquatic, living either in fresh or sea water. All crustaceans have a segmented body divided into head, thorax and abdomen. Many have a saddle-like covering, or carapace, extending from the head over the thorax. There are two pairs of antennae on the head and both thorax and abdomen bear several pairs of legs, some or all of which are used in locomotion.

The crayfish is a close relative of the marine lobster. It lives in clean rivers, especially in south-east England.

Insects

While crustaceans are the aquatic representatives of the Arthropoda, insects are, at least as adults, their terrestrial counterparts. An insect's body is divided into head, thorax and abdomen and covered with a tough, horny exoskeleton. The head bears one pair of antennae and the thorax three pairs of legs and often one or two pairs of wings.

Although few adult insects live in water, the larval stages of many develop there (e.g. dragonflies, mayflies, caddis flies, mosquitoes and many beetles). The diversity of species is fantastic and only the most common or distinctive insects found in the British Isles are illustrated here.

hunters; all ticks and many mites are parasitic on other animals. With a few exceptions arachnids are terrestrial, but one group, the water-mites, is common in freshwater. The adults feed on small crustaceans, while the larvae are parasitic on aquatic insects and molluscs.

A Cross Spider waits for its prey on its well-designed web. All spiders eat other animals, but some do not spin webs; they ambush their prey as they visit plants or flowers.

Myriapods

These are the centipedes and millipedes. Their bodies are typically long and thin, divided into many segments and bear numerous legs. Most live in damp habitats in soil, wood or under stones.

Moths and butterflies adopt a complex but effective life cycle to exploit their environment. The caterpillars form the "eating" component; whereas the later moth or butterfly provides the "reproductive" element. These are newly hatched Privet Hawk Moth larvae.

Arachnids

These are the spiders, scorpions, mites, ticks and harvestmen. They differ from insects in having the body divided into only two parts – a combined head and thorax and an abdomen – except in mites where head, thorax and abdomen are all combined. The combined head-thorax bears four pairs of legs but no wings.

Spiders normally spin webs or silken lines to ensnare prey, though some are

Millipedes are slow-moving grazers of decaying vegetation, whereas their relatives the centipedes are fast-moving carnivores that prey on mites and small insects.

Common Earthworm
Lumbricidae *Lumbricus terrestris*. **Habitat:** Most numerous in heavy soils under grassland and woodland; also common in gardens; throughout British Isles. **Notes:** Active all year, but burrows deeply in winter, as much as 2.5m below surface. Markedly flattened at hind end. (Up to 30cm; 110-160 segments.)

Common Garden Snail
Helicidae *Helix aspersa.* **Habitat:** Common on walls, in hedgerows, waste ground and gardens in S. Britain and Ireland; rare in N.; coastal only in Scotland. **Notes:** Hibernates in crevices and under stones. Garden pest. (35mm)

Roman Snail Helicidae *Helix pomatia.* **Habitat:** Calcareous rough grassland, woodland and hedgerows in parts of S.E. England. **Notes:** Active spring to autumn; hibernates in winter, and rests in sealed shell in very dry weather. Regarded as a delicacy in Europe.

Rounded Snail Endodontidae *Discus rotundatus.* **Habitat:** Common almost everywhere under ground litter in woodland, waste ground, hedgerows and among rocks, but not in Scottish Highlands. **Notes:** Easily recognised by regular brown stripes, and relatively large hollow on underside. (7mm)

Brown-lipped Snail Helicidae. *Cepaea nemoralis.* **Habitat:** Common in woodland, grassland and hedgerows throughout British Isles north to Great Glen. **Notes:** Very variable in colour and banding (often plain). Predated by thrushes. (22mm)
White-lipped Snail *Cepaea hortensis* is very similar but shell has white lip.

Heath Snail Helicidae *Helicella itala.* **Habitat:** Local (declining) on dry, calcareous and sandy grassland and hedgerows, often common on dunes, in S. and E. England and S. Ireland; elsewhere coastal. **Notes:** Fastens itself to plant stems in dry, sunny weather. (18mm)

Striped Snail Helicidae *Cernuella virgata.* **Habitat:** Dry, calcareous and sandy grassland, stubble, hedgerows, in S. and E. England and S. Ireland; coastal elsewhere. **Notes:** Fastens itself to plant stems in dry, sunny weather. (15mm)

Wrinkled Snail Helicidae *Candidula intersecta.* **Habitat:** Dry calcareous and sandy grassland, hedgerows and dunes in S. England and Ireland; elsewhere mainly coastal. **Notes:** Fastens itself to plant stems in dry, sunny weather.

Garden Slug Arionidae *Arion hortensis.* **Habitat:** Almost everywhere in woodland, grassland, and hedgerows, and especially common on cultivated land, less common in Scottish mountains. **Notes:** Recognised by orange sole. A serious crop and garden pest.

Black Slug Arionidae *Arion ater.* **Habitat:** Woodland, grassland, hedgerows and gardens throughout British Isles. **Notes:** Colour very variable; red or orange varieties very common in S.; black forms more typical of mountains and uncultivated places.

Swallowtail Papilionidae *Papilio machaon*. **Habitat:** Wetland in Norfolk Broads and Wicken Fen (recently re-introduced). **Flight time:** May, June; sometimes August, September; in two broods. **Larval foodplant:** Milk parsley.

Green-veined White Pieridae *Artogeia napi*. **Habitat:** Common almost everywhere throughout British Isles, except Shetland. **Flight time:** May, June; July to September; in two broods. Overwinters as pupa. **Larval foodplant:** Garlic mustard, lady's smock, charlock, etc. **Notes:** Male has only one black spot on forewing.

Small White Pieridae *Artogeia rapae*. **Habitat:** Common almost everywhere throughout British Isles; local in extreme N. **Flight time:** March to May; June to September; in two broods. Overwinters as pupa. **Larval foodplant:** Cabbage, nasturtium.

Wood White Pieridae *Leptidea sinapis*. **Habitat:** Woodland and cliffs in S. and S.W. England, Midlands, S.E. Wales. **Flight time:** May, June; July, August; usually in two broods. **Larval foodplant:** Tuberous pea and other vetches.

Orange Tip Pieridae *Anthocharis cardamines*. **Habitat:** Hedgerows, gardens and damp woodland rides throughout England and Wales, except Lancashire and N.E.; in Scotland only in Aberdeenshire and adjacent counties. **Flight time:** May, June. Overwinters as pupa. **Larval foodplant:** Lady's smock, hedge mustard, garlic mustard. **Notes:** Only male has orange tip to forewing.

Large White Pieridae *Pieris brassicae*. **Habitat:** Common almost everywhere in British Isles. Resident population sometimes reinforced by large-scale immigration. **Flight time:** April to June; July to September; in two broods. Overwinters as pupa. **Larval foodplant:** Cabbage, nasturtium.

Pale Clouded Yellow Pieridae *Colias hyale*. **Habitat:** Uncommon in lucerne and clover fields in S.E. England; immigrant. **Flight time:** May, June; August, September; in two broods. Does not overwinter in Britain. **Larval foodplant:** Clover, lucerne. **Notes:** Male pale yellow; female almost white.

Clouded Yellow Pieridae *Colias crocea*. **Habitat:** Chalk grassland, roadside verges and gardens, especially with clover, throughout British Isles, but especially in S. **Flight time:** August, September. Overwinters as larva. **Larval foodplant:** Clovers, melilot, lucerne.

Brimstone Pieridae *Gonepteryx rhamni*. **Habitat:** Woodland rides, hedgerows and gardens in England and Wales. **Flight time:** August to October and, after hibernation, March to June. Overwinters as imago. **Larval foodplant:** Buckthorn, alder buckthorn. **Notes:** Female pale green.

Berger's Clouded Yellow Pieridae *Colias australis*. **Habitat:** Chalk grassland and clover meadows in S. England; occasional visitor. **Flight time:** August, September. Overwinters as larva. **Larval foodplant:** Horseshoe vetch.

Terrestrial Invertebrates

Purple Emperor Nymphalidae *Apatura iris.* **Habitat:** Woodland rides in central S. England. **Flight time:** July, August. Overwinters as larva. **Larval foodplant:** Goat willow.

White Admiral Nymphalidae *Limenitis camilla.* **Habitat:** Woodland rides and coppice in England south of Severn-Humber line. **Flight time:** June to August. Overwinters as larva. **Larval foodplant:** Honeysuckle.
Poplar Admiral *Limenitis populi* is similar but larger with orange as well as white spots on wings. It is common in woodland in W. and central Europe and Scandinavia but absent from Britain.

Camberwell Beauty Nymphalidae *Nymphalis antiopa.* **Habitat:** Coastal and inland grassland of S.E. England; occasionally more widespread. A rare immigrant from Fennoscandia. **Flight time:** August onwards. Overwinters as imago but only rarely in Britain. **Larval foodplant:** Sallows, willow.

Comma Nymphalidae *Polygonia c-album.* **Habitat:** Hedgerows, woodland rides and gardens in England and Wales south of Mersey-Humber line. **Flight time:** March, April; June to August; in two broods. Overwinters as imago. **Larval foodplant:** Hop, nettle, currant.

Large Tortoiseshell
Nymphalidae *Nymphalis polychloros*. **Habitat:**
Woodland edges in S. Britain.
Flight time: July to October
and, after hibernation, March to
May. Overwinters as imago.
Larval foodplant: Elm, poplar,
aspen, willow.

Small Tortoiseshell
Nymphalidae *Aglais urticae*.
Habitat: Very common almost
everywhere in British Isles,
except Shetland. **Flight time:**
March to November; in two or
more broods. Overwinters as
imago. **Larval foodplant:**
Nettle.

Peacock Nymphalidae *Inachis
io*. **Habitat:** Common
throughout England and Wales,
except N.E.; local in Scotland
but spreading. **Flight time:**
March to November in two
broods. Overwinters as imago.
Larval foodplant: Nettle.

Red Admiral Nymphalidae
Vanessa atalanta. **Habitat:**
Grassland and gardens
throughout British Isles. A
common immigrant. **Flight
time:** March to November.
Rarely overwinters as imago in
Britain. **Larval foodplant:**
Nettle.

185

Terrestrial Invertebrates

Painted Lady Nymphalidae *Cynthia cardui*. **Habitat:** Coastal cliffs and grassland inland throughout Britain. Regular immigrant, numbers vary greatly. **Flight time:** May to October. Probably does not overwinter in Britain. **Larval foodplant:** Thistles.

Silver-washed Fritillary Nymphalidae *Argynnis paphia*. **Habitat:** Woodland rides and hedgerows in S. and W. England and Wales. **Flight time:** June to August. Overwinters as larva. **Larval foodplant:** Dog violet.

Dark Green Fritillary Nymphalidae *Mesoacidalia aglaja*. **Habitat:** Chalk grassland, moors and cliffs throughout British Isles, except Shetland. **Flight time:** July, August. Overwinters as larva. **Larval foodplant:** Violet.

High Brown Fritillary Nymphalidae *Fabriciana adippe*. **Habitat:** Woodland in S. England, Lake District, Wales. **Flight time:** June to August. Overwinters as egg. **Larval foodplant:** Dog violet.

Queen of Spain Fritillary
Nymphalidae *Issoria lathonia.*
Habitat: Coastal grasslands of
S. and S.E. England. Rare
immigrant. **Flight time:** May to
October. Does not overwinter in
Britain. **Larval foodplant:**
Violets.

Pearl-bordered Fritillary
Nymphalidae *Clossiana
euphrosyne.* **Habitat:**
Woodland rides and coppice in
S., W. and N.W. England; Wales
and central Scotland. **Flight
time:** May, June. Overwinters
as larva. **Larval foodplant:** Dog
violet.

Glanville Fritillary
Nymphalidae *Melitaea cinxia.*
Habitat: Coastal grassland and
landslips in S. Isle of Wight.
Flight time: May, June.
Overwinters as larva. **Larval
foodplant:** Sea plantain.

**Small Pearl-bordered
Fritillary** Nymphalidae
Clossiana selene. **Habitat:**
Woodland rides and coppice in
S., W. and N.W. England; Wales
and Scotland. **Flight time:**
June, July. Overwinters as larva.
Larval foodplant: Dog violet.

Marsh Fritillary Nymphalidae
Eurodryas aurinia. **Habitat:**
Local in water meadows and
damp grassland in S. and S.W.
England, W. Wales, Cumbria
and W. Scotland. **Flight time:**
May, June. Overwinters
gregariously as larva. **Larval
foodplant:** Devil's-bit scabious.

Heath Fritillary Nymphalidae
Mellicta athalia. **Habitat:** Very
local in woodland rides and
coppice in Kent, Devon and
Cornwall. **Flight time:** June,
July. Overwinters as larva.
Larval foodplant: Plantains,
cow-wheat.

Duke of Burgundy Fritillary
Riodinidae *Hamearis lucina.*
Habitat; Woodland, especially
on chalk, in England; very local
except in S. **Flight time:** May,
June. Overwinters as pupa.
Larval foodplant: Cowslip.

Terrestrial Invertebrates

Purple Hairstreak Lycaenidae *Quercusia quercus.* **Habitat:** Oak woodland in England, Wales, and W. Scotland south of Great Glen. **Flight time:** July, August. Overwinters as egg. **Larval foodplant:** Oak.

Brown Hairstreak Lycaenidae *Thecla betulae.* **Habitat:** Woodland rides and hedgerows in S. and midland England, W. Wales. **Flight time:** August to October. Overwinters as egg. **Larval foodplant:** Blackthorn.

White-letter Hairstreak Lycaenidae *Strymonidia w-album.* **Habitat:** Woodland rides and margins and wooded roadsides in England below Mersey-Humber line and in Wales. **Flight time:** July, August. Overwinters as egg. **Larval foodplant:** Wych elm, elm.

Green Hairstreak Lycaenidae *Callophrys rubi.* **Habitat:** Chalk grassland, moors, hedgerows and open woodland throughout much of British Isles. **Flight time:** April to July. Overwinters as pupa. **Larval foodplant:** Gorse, bird's-foot trefoil, rock-rose.

Small blue Lycaenidae *Cupido minimus.* **Habitat:** Chalk grassland and sand dunes in localised colonies in S. England; very local in S. Wales. **Flight time:** May, June. Overwinters as larva. **Larval foodplant:** Kidney vetch.

♂

♀

Holly Blue Lycaenidae *Celastrina argiolus.* **Habitat:** Gardens and open woodland in S. England and Wales; local in N. England. **Flight time:** April, May; July to September; in two broods. Overwinters as pupa. **Larval foodplant:** Flowers, buds and berries of holly, ivy, snowberry.

Small Copper Lycaenidae *Lycaena phlaeas.* **Habitat:** Grassland, hedgerows and gardens throughout British Isles. **Flight time:** April, May; July, August; sometimes September, October. Overwinters as larva. **Larval foodplant:** Dock, sorrel.

♂   ♀

Silver-studded Blue
Lycaenidae *Plebejus argus*.
Habitat: Heaths in S. and S.W.
England, Norfolk, Suffolk and N.
Wales. **Flight time:** June to
August. Overwinters as egg.
Larval foodplant: Bird's-foot
trefoil, gorse, ling (usually
feeding on flowers).

Brown Argus Lycaenidae *Aricia
agestis*. **Habitat:** Grassland,
especially on chalk, in S.
England and N. Wales. **Flight
time:** May, June; July to
September. Overwinters as
larva. **Larval foodplant:** Rock-
rose, common storksbill.

♂

♂

♀

♀

Chalkhill Blue Lycaenidae
Lysandra coridon. **Habitat:**
Chalk and limestone grassland
in England south of Severn-
Wash line, west to Somerset.
Flight time: July to September.
Overwinters as egg. **Larval
foodplant:** Horseshoe vetch
and other legumes.

Adonis Blue Lycaenidae
Lysandra bellargus. **Habitat:**
Chalk and limestone grassland
in S. England. **Flight time:** May,
June; August September; in
two broods. Overwinters as
larva. **Larval foodplant:**
Horseshoe vetch.

♂

♀

Mazarine Blue Lycaenidae
Cyaniris semiargus. **Habitat:**
Meadows and grassy hillsides in
W. Europe. Now extinct in
Britain. **Flight time:** June to
August. **Larval foodplant:**
Clover, vetches, thrift.

Common Blue Lycaenidae
Polyommatus icarus. **Habitat:**
Rough grassland, especially on
calcareous soils, throughout
British Isles. **Flight time:** May
to July; August, September.
Overwinters as larva. **Larval
foodplant:** Bird's-foot trefoil.

Marbled White Satyridae *Melanargia galathea*. **Habitat:** Rough grassland in England south of Severn-Wash line. **Flight time:** July, August. Overwinters as larva. **Larval foodplant:** Grasses, e.g. cocksfoot and timothy.

Grayling Satyridae *Hipparchia semele*. **Habitat:** Heaths and sand dunes in S. and W. England and Wales; coastal in N. England and Scotland. **Flight time:** July to September. Overwinters as larva. **Larval foodplant:** Grasses.

Mountain Ringlet Satyridae *Erebia epiphron*. **Habitat:** Grassy mountain tops in Lake District and Scotland. **Flight time:** Late June, July. Overwinters as larva. **Larval foodplant:** Mat grass.

Scotch Argus Satyridae *Erebia aethiops*. **Habitat:** Upland grassland and coniferous woodland in Cumbria, central and W. Scotland. **Flight time:** Late July, August. Overwinters as larva. **Larval foodplant:** Blue moor grass.

Meadow Brown Satyridae *Maniola jurtina*. **Habitat:** Grassland throughout British Isles, except at high altitudes. **Flight time:** June, July; August, September; in two broods. Overwinters as larva. **Larval foodplant:** Grasses.

Ringlet Satyridae *Aphantopus hyperantus*. **Habitat:** Hedgerows and woodland rides in S. and central England and Wales; local in N.W. England. **Flight time:** June to August. Overwinters as larva. **Larval foodplant:** Grasses.

Gatekeeper Satyridae *Pyronia tithonus.* **Habitat:** Hedgerows and woodland rides in England and Wales to Lake District, but not Pennines or N.E. **Flight time:** July to September. Overwinters as larva. **Larval foodplant:** Grasses.

Pearly Heath Satyridae *Coenonympha arcania.* **Habitat:** Open woodland and hedgerows in W. Europe and occasionally Britain. **Flight time:** June, July. **Larval foodplant:** Grasses, especially mellicks.

Small Heath Satyridae *Coenonympha pamphilus.* **Habitat:** Grassland throughout British Isles. **Flight time:** May to September, probably in two broods. Overwinters as larva. **Larval foodplant:** Grasses.

Speckled Wood Satyridae *Pararge aegeria.* **Habitat:** Woodland, hedgerows and gardens in England and Wales, mainly south of the Mersey, and S.W. Highlands of Scotland. **Flight time:** April, May; July-September; in two broods. Overwinters as pupa. **Larval foodplant:** Grasses, e.g. common couch grass and cocksfoot.

Large Wall Brown Satyridae *Lasiommata maera.* **Habitat:** Scrub and rocky places in W. Europe; absent from Britain. **Flight time:** June, July. **Larval foodplant:** Grasses.

Wall Satyridae *Lasiommata megera.* **Habitat:** Grassland and rough ground throughout England and Wales. **Flight time:** May, June; July, August; in two broods. Overwinters as larva. **Larval foodplant:** Annual meadow grass, cocksfoot and others.

Terrestrial Invertebrates

Grizzled Skipper Hesperiidae *Pyrgus malvae*. **Habitat:** Chalk grassland, waste ground, roadsides and grassy places in S. England and Wales. **Flight time:** Late April to June. Overwinters as pupa. **Larval foodplant:** Wild strawberry, bramble.

Dingy Skipper Hesperiidae *Erynnis tages*. **Habitat:** Grassland throughout much of England and Wales; very local in Scotland. **Flight time:** April to June. Overwinters as larva. **Larval foodplant:** Bird's-foot trefoil.

Essex Skipper *Hesperiidae Thymelicus lineola*. **Habitat:** Grassland in S.E. England. **Flight time:** July, August. Overwinters as egg. **Larval foodplant:** Grasses.

Large Skipper Hesperiidae *Ochlodes venatus*. **Habitat:** Grassland throughout England and Wales; local in N. **Flight time:** June to August. Overwinters as larva. **Larval foodplant:** Grasses.

Small Skipper Hesperiidae *Thymelicus flavus*. **Habitat:** Grassland in England and Wales north to Cheshire and Yorkshire. **Flight time:** June to August. Overwinters as larva. **Larval foodplant:** Grasses.

Silver-spotted Skipper Hesperidae *Hesperia comma*. **Habitat:** Chalk grassland in S. and S.E. England. Much less common than formerly. **Flight time:** July, August. Overwinters as egg. **Larval foodplant:** Sheep's fescue grass.

Moths

Ghost Moth Hepialidae *Hepialus humuli*. **HabitatL** Grassland throughout British Isles. **Flight time:** June, July. Overwinters as larva. **Larval foodplant:** Roots of grasses, burdock, dead-nettle, dock, dandelion, nettle. **Notes:** Male white; female yellow.

Leopard Moth Cossidae *Zeuzera pyrina*. **Habitat:** Woodland, gardens, hedgerows in S. and E. England and S. Wales; local north to Cheshire. **Flight time:** June, July. Overwinters as larva. **Larval foodplant:** Internally in stems of elm, apple, birch and other trees.

Green Longhorn *Incurvariidae Adela reaumurella*. **Habitat:** Deciduous woodland in England and Wales; local in E. central Scotland. **Flight time:** May, June. Overwinters as larva. **Larval foodplant:** Leaf litter. **Notes:** Male has very long antennae.

Six-spot Burnet Zygaenidae *Zygaena filipendulae*. **Habitat:** Grassland, particularly on chalk, throughout British Isles except Orkney and Shetland. **Flight time:** Mid-June to August. Overwinters as larva. **Larval foodplant:** Bird's-foot trefoil.

Brown China Mark Pyralidae *Nymphula nymphaeata*. **Habitat:** Adults in wetland; larvae in ponds; throughout much of British Isles. **Flight time:** June to August. Overwinters as larva. **Larval foodplant:** Pondweed, frog-bit, bur-reed.

Forester Zygaenidae *Adscita statices*. **Habitat:** Chalk grassland in Britain south of Argyll and Inverness-shire. **Flight time:** Late May to early July. Overwinters as larva. **Larval foodplant:** Common sorrel.

Green Oak Tortrix Moth Tortricidae *Tortrix viridana*. **Habitat:** Wherever oak trees grow throughout British Isles. **Flight time:** June to August. **Larval foodplant:** Oak. **Notes:** Larvae roll up oak leaves to form shelters. If disturbed, they drop down on silken life-lines. Often numerous.

Small Ermine Moth Yponomeutidae *Yponomeuta padella*. **Habitat:** Hedgerows, etc., throughout British Isles. **Flight time:** June to August. **Larval foodplant:** Hawthorn and blackthorn. **Notes:** Larvae (greenish-grey with black spots) feed in colonies, each colony covered with large silken web. Whole hedgerows may be covered.

Common Grass-veneer Pyralidae *Agriphila tristellus*. **Habitat:** Grassland throughout British Isles except Shetland. **Flight time:** July, August. Overwinters as larva. **Larval foodplant:** Grasses.

Currant Clearwing Sesiidae *Synanthedon salmachus*. **Habitat:** Gardens and orchards in British Isles north to Dumfries. **Flight time:** Late May to July. Overwinters as larva. **Larval foodplant:** Internally in stems of blackcurrant, possibly feeding for two years.

Pyrausta purpuralis Pyralidae **Habitat:** Scrub and rough grassland, especially on lime-rich soils, throughout British Isles. **Flight time:** May to August, in two broods. Flies by night and day. **Larval foodplant:** Mint, thyme, and other labiates.

Large White Plume Moth Pterophoridae *Pterophorus pentadactyla*. **Habitat:** Gardens and hedgerows throughout England and Wales. **Flight time:** June, July. Overwinters as larva. **Larval foodplant:** Bindweed.

Terrestrial Invertebrates

Lappet Lasiocampidae *Gastropacha quercifolia.* **Habitat:** Deciduous woodland and hedgerows on chalk and limestone, south of Severn-Wash line; very local elsewhere in Wales and Midlands. **Flight time:** June. Overwinters as larva. **Larval foodplant:** Hawthorn, blackthorn, sallow.

Fox Moth Lasiocampidae *Macrothylacia rubi.* **Habitat:** Heaths throughout mainland Britain; widespread but local. **Flight time:** May, June. Overwinters as larva. **Larval foodplant:** Heather, bramble, grasses. **Notes:** Male dark brown; female greyer.

Northern Eggar Lasiocampidae *Lasiocampa quercus callunae.* **Habitat:** Moors from S. Pennines to Orkney. **Flight time:** End May, June. Overwinters as larva in first winter, pupa in second winter (life cycle 2 years). **Larval foodplant:** Heather, bramble, other herbaceous plants.

Drinker Moth Lasiocampidae *Philudoria potatoria.* **Habitat:** Grassland, roadsides, especially where damp, in S. and midland England and Wales; local in N. England and W. Highlands of Scotland. **Flight time:** July, August. Overwinters as larva. **Larval foodplant:** Grasses.

December Moth Lasiocampidae *Poecilocampa populi.* **Habitat:** Deciduous woodland throughout British Isles, except Orkney and Shetland. **Flight timeL** November, December. Overwinters as egg. **Larval foodplant:** Oak, birch, poplar.

Emperor Moth Saturnidae *Saturnia pavonia.* **Habitat:** Heaths, moors, woodland edges throughout British Isles. **Flight time:** April, May. Overwinters as pupa. **Larval foodplant:** Heather, bramble, blackthorn, sallow.

Pebble Hook-tip Drepanidae *Drepana falcataria.* **Habitat:** Deciduous woodland in England and Wales; local in Scotland. **Flight time:** May, August; in two broods. Overwinters as pupa. **Larval foodplant:** Birch, oak, sallow.

Peach Blossom Thyatiridae *Thyatira batis.* **Habitat:** Gardens and hedgerows throughout British Isles except extreme N. Scotland. **Flight time:** June, July; sometimes August, September, as second brood. Overwinters as pupa. **Larval foodplant:** Bramble.

Magpie Moth Geometridae *Abraxas grossulariata.* **Habitat:** Gardens, hedgerows, etc., throughout British Isles. **Flight time:** July, August. Overwinters as larva. **Larval foodplant:** Blackthorn, hawthorn, heather, currants and gooseberries on which it is sometimes a serious pest.

Peppered Moth Geometridae *Biston betularia.* **Habitat:** Woodland, gardens and parks throughout British Isles to central Scotland. Black form (ab. *carbonaria*) occurs especially in industrial areas. **Flight time:** May to July. Overwinters as pupa. **Larval foodplant:** Oak, birch, elm, beech, sallow.

March Moth Geometridae *Alsophila aescularia.* **Habitat:** Gardens, hedgerows, open woodland throughout British Isles, north to Perthshire. **Flight time:** March to May. Overwinters as pupa. **Larval foodplant:** Many trees and shrubs, e.g. lilac, privet, rose, oak, hornbeam. **Notes:** Female wingless.

Terrestrial Invertebrates

Green Carpet Geometridae *Colostygia pectinaria*. **Habitat:** Grassland, hedgerows and scrub throughout British Isles except Shetland. **Flight time:** June, July. Overwinters as larva. **Larval foodplant:** Bedstraw.

Light Emerald Geometridae *Campaea margaritata*. **Habitat:** Deciduous woodland throughout British Isles except Orkney and Shetland. **Flight time:** June, July. Overwinters as larva. **Larval foodplant:** Oak, birch, beech, hazel.

Common Heath Geometridae *Ematurga atomaria*. **Habitat:** Heaths throughout British Isles except Shetland. **Flight time:** May, June; July, August; in two broods. Overwinters as pupa. **Larval foodplant:** Heather, clover, trefoils.

Canary-shouldered Thorn Geometridae *Ennomos alniaria*. **Habitat:** Deciduous woodland throughout much of Britain, north to Morayshire. **Flight time:** August to October. Overwinters as egg. **Larval foodplant:** Birch, alder.

Mottled Umber Geometridae *Erannis defoliaria*. **HabitatL** Deciduous woodland throughout British Isles to S. Scotland. **Flight time:** October to December. Overwinters in egg stage. **Larval foodplant:** Birch, oak, other trees; larvae feed in colonies and may defoliate trees.

Narrow-winged Pug Geometridae *Eupithecia nanata*. **Habitat:** Heaths throughout British Isles. **Flight time:** May, June; July, August; in two broods. **Larval foodplant:** Heather.

Winter Moth Geometridae *Operophtera brumata*. **Habitat:** Gardens, orchards, hedgerows throughout British Isles. **Flight time:** October to February. **Larval foodplant:** Many trees and shrubs. **Notes:** Important orchard pest. Female flightless.

Large Emerald Geometridae *Geometra papilionaria*. **Habitat:** Deciduous woodland throughout British Isles except N. Scotland. **Flight time:** June, July. Overwinters as larva. **Larval foodplant:** Birch, hazel, beech.

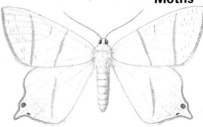

Brimstone Moth Geometridae *Opisthograptis luteolata.* **Habitat:** Deciduous woodland throughout British Isles. **Flight time:** April to August; October; in two broods. Overwinters as pupa (from 1st brood) and larva (from 2nd brood). **Larval foodplant:** Hawthorn.

Swallow-tailed Moth Geometridae *Ourapteryx sambucaria.* **Habitat:** Gardens, hedgerows and woodland throughout England, Wales and S. Scotland. **Flight time:** July, August. Overwinters as larva. **Larval foodplant:** Hawthorn, blackthorn, elder.

Grass Emerald Geometridae *Pseudoterpna pruinata.* **Habitat:** Heaths throughout much of England, Wales and S.W. Scotland. **Flight time:** June, July. Overwinters as larva. **Larval foodplant:** Petty whin, broom, gorse.

Twin-spot Carpet Geometridae *Perizoma didymata.* **Habitat:** Woodland and grassland in lowlands and mountains throughout British Isles. **Flight time:** July, August. Overwinters as larva. **Larval foodplant:** Primrose, red campion, bilberry.

Death's Head Hawk-moth Sphingidae *Acherontia atropos.* **Habitat:** Farmland and hedgerows throughout British Isles. Regular immigrant recorded in most years. **Flight time:** May to September. Probably does not overwinter in Britain. **Larval foodplant:** Potato, deadly and woody nightshade.

Latticed Heath Geometridae *Semiothisa clathrata.* **Habitat:** Grassland in S. and E. England; local elsewhere north to Clyde valley. **Flight time:** April, May; July, August; in two broods. Overwinters as pupa. **Larval foodplant:** Clovers, trefoils.

Terrestrial Invertebrates

Garden Carpet Geometridae *Xanthorhoe fluctuata*. **Habitat:** Gardens, orchards and hedgerows throughout British Isles. **Flight time:** May, June; August, September; in two broods. Overwinters as pupa. **Larval foodplant:** Many herbaceous plants, currant, gooseberry.

Elephant Hawk-moth Sphingidae *Deilephila elpenor*. **Habitat:** Throughout England and Wales, local in Scotland. **Flight time:** June; occasionally later as a second brood. Overwinters as pupa. **Larval foodplant:** Willowherb, bedstraw.

Humming-bird Hawk-moth Sphingidae *Macroglossum stellatarum*. **Habitat:** Grassland and gardens (especially by sea) in some years throughout Britain; most frequent in S. Immigrant; numbers vary greatly. **Flight time:** All year except winter. Occasionally overwinters as imago in extreme S.W. England. **Larval foodplant:** Bedstraw, wild madder.

Broad-bordered Bee Hawk-moth Sphingidae *Hemaris fuciformis*. **Habitat:** Local in deciduous woodland rides in England and Wales; apparently decreasing. **Flight time:** May, June. Overwinters as pupa. **Larval foodplant:** Honeysuckle, bedstraw, snowberry.

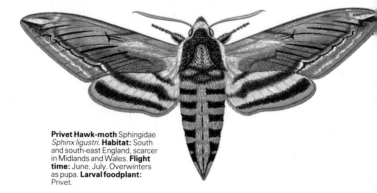

Privet Hawk-moth Sphingidae *Sphinx ligustri*. **Habitat:** South and south-east England, scarcer in Midlands and Wales. **Flight time:** June, July. Overwinters as pupa. **Larval foodplant:** Privet.

Convolvulus Hawk-moth
Sphingidae *Agrius convolvuli*.
Habitat: A regular immigrant of
coastal regions. **Flight time:**
July to November. **Larval
foodplant:** Field bindweed.

Poplar Hawk-moth Sphingidae
Laothoe populi. **Habitat:**
Throughout the British Isles.
Flight time: May, June;
occasionally later as a second
brood. Overwinters as pupa.
Larval foodpland: Poplar,
sallow.

Lime Hawk-moth Sphingidae
Mimas tiliae. **Habitat:** England
as far north as the Mersey-
Humber line; rare in Wales.
Flight time: May, June.
Overwinters as pupa. **Larval
foodplant:** Lime, elm, alder.

Pine Hawk-moth Sphingidae
Hyloicus pinastri. **HabitatL** Pine
forests in Dorset, Hampshire,
Surrey, Norfolk and Suffolk.
Flight time: End June to
August. Overwinters as pupa.
Larval foodplant: Scots pine,
Norway spruce.

199

Terrestrial Invertebrates

Eyed Hawk-moth Sphingidae *Smerinthus ocellata*. **Habitat:** Widespread, often in gardens, throughout England and Wales; local in N. **Flight time:** May to August. **Larval foodplant:** Willow, apple.

Puss Moth Notodontidae *Cerura vinula*. **Habitat:** Woodland, gardens and hedgerows throughout British Isles, except Shetland. **Flight time:** May to July. Overwinters as pupa. **Larval foodplant:** Sallow, poplar. **Notes:** Hindwing in male white; in female grey.

Poplar Kitten Notodontidae *Furcula bifida*. **Habitat:** Deciduous woodland in England south of Mersey-Humber line, and in Wales. **Flight time:** Late May to July. Overwinters as pupa. **Larval foodplant:** Poplar, aspen.

Buff Tip Notodontidae *Phalera bucephala*. **Habitat:** Woodland and gardens in England and Wales; local in Scotland. **Flight time:** Late May to July. Overwinters as pupa. **Larval foodplant:** Many deciduous trees.

Swallow Prominent Notodontidae *Pheosia tremula*. **Habitat:** Deciduous woodland throughout British Isles except Orkney and Shetland. **Flight time:** May, June; August in S. Britain. Overwinters as pupa. **Larval foodplant:** Poplar, aspen, willow.

Pale Prominent Notodontidae *Pterostoma palpina*. **Habitat:** Deciduous woodland in S. England; local in N. and Wales. **Flight time:** May; August in S. England. Overwinters as pupa. **Larval foodplant:** Poplar, aspen, willow.

Coxcomb Prominent
Notodontidae *Ptilodon
capucina*. **Habitat:** Deciduous
woodland throughout British
Isles except Orkney and
Shetland. **Flight time:** May,
June; August; in two broods.
Overwinters as pupa. **Larval
foodplant:** Birch, poplar, hazel,
willow.

Lobster Moth Notodontidae
Stauropus fagi. **Habitat:**
Woodland, especially beech, in
S. England and N.W. Wales.
Flight time: May to July.
Overwinters as pupa. **Larval
foodplant:** Beech, oak, birch,
hazel.

Pale Tussock Lymantriidae
Dasychira pudibunda. **Habitat:**
Woodland, gardens, orchards
and hedgerows throughout
England and Wales south of
Lake District. **Flight time:** May,
June. Overwinters as pupa.
Larval foodplant: Many
deciduous trees, hop.

Yellow-tail Lymantriidae
Euproctis similis. **Habitat:**
Gardens, woodland and
hedgerows throughout England
except extreme S.W. and N.E.;
Wales; very local in S. Scotland.
Flight time: July, August.
Overwinters as larva. **Larval
foodplant:** Hawthorn,
blackthorn, oak, birch, sallow.

Vapourer Lymantriidae *Orgyia
antiqua*. **Habitat:** Woodland,
parks, hedgerows and gardens
throughout British Isles. **Flight
time:** July, August; September,
October; in two broods; one in
N. Overwinters as egg. **Larval
foodplant:** Most deciduous
trees and shrubs.

Black Arches Lymantriidae
Lymantria monacha. **Habitat:**
Deciduous woodland in S.
England; very local in Wales.
Flight time: August.
Overwinters as egg. **Larval
foodplant:** Oak.

Garden Tiger Arctiidae *Arctia
caja*. **Habitat:** Gardens and
hedgerows throughout British
Isles except Shetland. **Flight
time:** July, August.
Overwinters as larva. **Larval
foodplant:** Herbaceous plants.

Terrestrial Invertebrates

Four-spotted Footman
Arctiidae *Lithosia quadra*.
Habitat: Deciduous woodland in S. England; elsewhere an immigrant as far north as Ross-shire. **Flight time:** August, September. Overwinters as larva. **Larval foodplant:** Lichens. **Notes:** Male grey; female white.

White Ermine Arctiidae
Spilosoma lubricipeda. **Habitat:** Gardens, hedgerows, waste ground, etc., throughout British Isles, except Shetland. **Flight time:** Late May to July. Overwinters as pupa. **Larval foodplant:** Herbaceous plants.

Cinnabar Moth Arctiidae *Tyria jacobaeae*. **Habitat:** Gardens, grassland, etc., on well-drained soils in S. and midland England and Wales; mainly coastal in N. England and Scotland. **Flight time:** Late May to July. Overwinters as pupa. **Larval foodplant:** Ragwort, groundsel.

Mullein Noctuidae *Cucullia verbasci*. **Habitat:** Grassland throughout England and Wales, north to S. Lake District and Yorkshire. **Flight time:** Late April, May. Overwinters as pupa. **Larval foodplant:** Mullein, figwort.

Ruby tiger Arctiidae
Phragmatobia fuliginosa.
Habitat: Rough grassland, including moors and heaths throughout British Isles, except Shetland. **Flight time:** May, June; occasionally September as second brood. **Larval foodplant:** Dock, dandelion, golden rod.

Buff Ermine Arctiidae
Spilosoma lutea. **Habitat:** Gardens, hedgerows, waste ground, etc., throughout Britain; local in Scotland. **Flight time:** Late May to July. Overwinters as pupa. **Larval foodplant:** Dock, dandelion, etc.

Silver Y Noctuidae *Autographa gamma*. **Habitat:** Grassland, woodland rides and gardens throughout British Isles. Regular, abundant immigrant. **Flight time:** Early spring to late autumn. Probably does not overwinter in Britain. **Larval foodplant:** Many herbaceous plants.

Turnip Moth Noctuidae *Agrotis segetum*. **Habitat:** Gardens and arable farmland throughout British Isles except Orkney and Shetland. **Flight time:** May, June; occasionally September, October, as second brood. Overwinters as larva. **Larval foodplant:** Roots of turnip, beet, swede, carrot.

Red Underwing Noctuidae *Catocala nupta.* **Habitat:** Damp woodland, wetland and hedgerows in England and Wales south of Mersey-Humber line; absent from S.W. **Flight time:** August, September. Overwinters as egg. **Larval foodplant:** Willow, poplar.

Burnished Brass Noctuidae *Diachrysia chrysitis.* **Habitat:** Gardens, hedgerows and waste ground throughout British Isles except Shetland. **Flight time:** June to September. Overwinters as larva. **Larval foodplant:** Nettle.

Merveille du Jour Noctuidae *Dichonia aprilina.* **Habitat:** Deciduous woodland throughout England and Wales; more local in Scotland and absent from extreme N. **Flight time:** September, October. Overwinters as egg. **Larval foodplant:** Oak.

Large Yellow Underwing Noctuidae *Noctua pronuba.* **Habitat:** Gardens, hedgerows, etc., throughout British Isles. **Flight time:** June to September. Overwinters as larva. **Larval foodplant:** Many herbaceous plants and grasses.

Green Silver Lines Noctuidae *Pseudoips fagana.* **Habitat:** Deciduous woodland in England and Wales; local in S. Scotland. **Flight time:** June, July. Overwinters as pupa. **Larval foodplant:** Oak, birch, beech, hazel.

Pine Beauty Noctuidae *Panolis flammea.* **Habitat:** Pine forests throughout British Isles. **Flight time:** March to May. Overwinters as pupa. **Larval foodplant:** Pine. **Notes:** Sometimes a serious forest pest.

Golden Plusia Noctuidae *Polychrisia moneta.* **Habitat:** Gardens throughout much of England and Wales; very local in S. Scotland. **Flight time:** June, July; sometimes August, September, as second brood. Overwinters as larva. **Larval foodplant:** Larkspur, monkshood.

Terrestrial Invertebrates

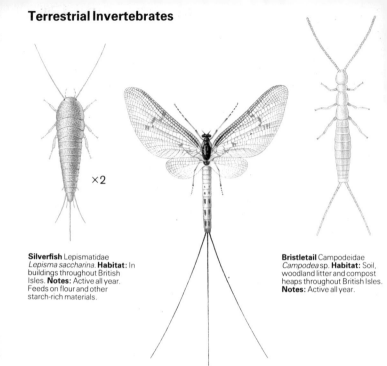

Silverfish Lepismatidae *Lepisma saccharina.* **Habitat:** In buildings throughout British Isles. **Notes:** Active all year. Feeds on flour and other starch-rich materials.

Bristletail Campodeidae *Campodea* sp. **Habitat:** Soil, woodland litter and compost heaps throughout British Isles. **Notes:** Active all year.

Greendrake Ephemeridae *Ephemera danica.* **Habitat:** Lakes and streams with sandy bottoms throughout British Isles. **Flight time:** May to September, but individuals live for only a few hours or days.

Springtail Poduridae *Podura aquatica.* **Habitat:** Surface of weed-covered ponds throughout British Isles. **Notes:** Has forked "spring" at hind end, which flicks out and sends insect through the air when disturbed.

Large Stonefly Perlodidae *Perlodes mortoni.* **Habitat:** Stony rivers throughout much of British Isles. **Flight time:** March to July.

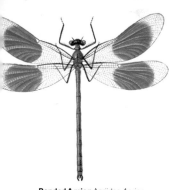

Banded Agrion Agriidae *Agrion splendens*. **Habitat:** Slow-flowing freshwater, clean lakes and ponds in British Isles, except Scotland. **Flight time:** Summer. **Notes:** Wings of female brown, body green.

Green Lestes Lestidae *Lestes sponsa*. **Habitat:** Weedy ponds and canals throughout British Isles. **Flight time:** Summer. **Notes:** Female lacks blue patches.

Common Coenagrion Coenagriidae *Coenagrion puella*. **Habitat:** Lakes, canals and slow-flowing streams in England and Wales. **Flight time:** Summer. **Notes:** Female has blacker body.

Large Red Damselfly Coenagriidae *Pyrrhosoma nymphula*. **Habitat:** Ponds, bogs, marshes, slow-flowing water throughout Britain; rare in Ireland. **Flight time:** Summer. **Notes:** Female has blacker body.

Common Sympetrum Libellulidae *Sympetrum striolatum*. **Habitat:** Anywhere near water in England and Wales; rare in Scotland and Ireland. **Flight time:** Summer. **Notes:** Darting flight. Female browner.

Gold-ringed Dragonfly
Cordulegasteridae
Cordulegaster boltonii. **Habitat:**
Fast-flowing shallow streams
and some lowland heaths in W.
Britain. **Flight time:** Summer.

Four-spotted Libellula
Libellulidae *Libellula
quadrimaculata.* **Habitat:**
Ponds, canals and wet heaths
throughout British Isles. **Flight
time:** Summer.

Emperor Dragonfly Aeshnidae
Anax imperator. **Habitat:**
Lakes, rivers, woodland and
hedgerows in S. England. **Flight
time:** Summer.

Common Field Grasshopper
Acrididae *Chorthippus
brunneus.* **Habitat:** Dry
grassland, dunes and rough
ground with some grass
throughout British Isles. **Notes:**
Active June to October.

Dragonflies, Grasshoppers and Crickets

Mole Cricket Gryllotalpidae *Gryllotalpa gryllotalpa*. **Habitat:** Very rare in damp meadows and cultivated land, usually near rivers; confined to a few places in S. Britain. **Notes:** Active April to August, mostly in underground burrow but may fly on warm evenings. Male makes churring call while sitting at mouth of burrow.

House Cricket Gryllidae *Acheta domesticus*. **Habitat:** Houses, bakeries, rubbish tips (especially in summer), throughout British Isles. **Notes:** Active all year in buildings; mainly nocturnal. Female has slender ovipositor. An introduced species.

Dark Bush Cricket Tettigoniidae *Pholidoptera griseoaptera*. **Habitat:** Hedgerows, gardens, woodland edges and clearings, scrub, in much of England and Wales. **Notes:** Flightless. Active July to November (or first frosts). Male has saddle-like wings perched on back.

Great Green Bush Cricket Tettigoniidae *Tettigonia viridissima*. **Habitat:** Hedgerows, gardens, coastal dunes, cliffs, woodland clearings and scrub in S. England and S. Wales. **Notes:** Active July to October.

Common Green Grasshopper Acrididae *Omocestus viridulus*. **Habitat:** Grassland, woodland rides, roadsides throughout British Isles. **Notes:** Active June to September.

Meadow Grasshopper Acrididae *Chorthippus parallelus*. **Habitat:** Grasslands and damp heaths throughout British Isles. **Notes:** Flightless. Active June to October. Male has longer wings.

Terrestrial Invertebrates

Common Cockroach Blattidae *Blatta orientalis*. **Habitat:** Houses, buildings, rubbish tips during summer, throughout British Isles. **Notes:** Flightless. Active all year in buildings. Female almost wingless.

German Cockroach Pseudomopidae *Blatella germanica*. **Habitat:** In buildings, and on rubbish tips in summer, throughout most of British Isles. **Notes:** Active all year in buildings.

Common Earwig Forficulidae *Forficula auricularia*. **Habitat:** Gardens, hedgerows, buildings, etc., throughout British Isles. **Notes:** Active spring to autumn. Hibernates underground. Female has straighter and more slender cerci.

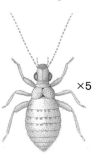

×5

×10

×10

Book Louse Trogiidae *Trogium pulsatorium*. **Habitat:** In food stores in buildings nearly everywhere. **Notes:** Active most of year. Feeds on microscopic fungi on various stored materials.

Biting Louse Philopteridae *Columbicola claviformis*. **Habitat:** Always in association with woodpigeons. **Notes:** Active all year. Feeds on skin and feathers.

Body Louse Pediculidae *Pediculus humanus*. **Habitat:** Always in association with man. **Notes:** Active all year. Sucks human blood from head or body.

Gorse Shield Bug Pentatomidae *Piezodorus lituratus*. **Habitat:** Heaths, woodland, sea-cliffs and waste ground in most of British Isles. **Notes:** Active all year but hides in leaf litter when very cold. Pink and green in autumn. On gorse, broom and other legumes.

Forest Bug Pentatomidae *Pentatoma rufipes*. **Habitat:** Woodland, hedgerows and gardens in most of British Isles. **Notes:** Active July to October

Birch Shield Bug Acanthosomidae *Elasmostethus interstinctus*. **Habitat:** Woodland (with Birch) throughout British Isles. **Notes:** Active spring to late autumn. Hibernates in leaf litter.

Cockroaches, Bugs and Aphids

Tree Damsel Bug Nabiidae *Himacerus apterus*. **Habitat:** Woodland and hedgerows in S. England and Wales. **Notes:** Active July to October. Individuals with long wings occur occasionally.

Heath Assassin Bug Reduviidae *Coranus subapterus*. **Habitat:** Heaths and sand dunes in most of Britain. **Notes:** Active July to October. Fully winged individuals occur occasionally.

Common Flower Bug Cimicidae *Anthocoris nemorum*. **Habitat:** Hedgerows, woodland, waste ground and gardens throughout British Isles. **Notes:** Active March to November. Hibernates in leaf litter.

Capsid Bug Miridae *Lygus pratensis*. **Habitat:** Hedgerows, woodland, heaths and gardens throughout British Isles. **Notes:** Active March to October.

Common Froghopper Cercopidae *Philaenus spumarius*. **Habitat:** Anywhere with varied plant cover throughout British Isles. **Notes:** Active June to October. Nymph on plant stems and leaves in "cuckoo spit".

Froghopper Cercopidae *Cercopis vulnerata*. **Habitat:** Hedgerows, woodland and gardens in England and Wales. **Notes:** Active April to July. Nymphs on plant roots in hardened froth, often living gregariously.

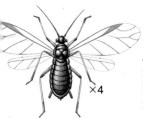

×4

Black Bean Aphid Aphididae *Aphis fabae*. **Habitat:** Grassland, cultivated land, hedgerows, etc., throughout British Isles. **Notes:** Active spring to autumn, but all year in sheltered places. Especially on beans, docks and spinach in summer; shrubs in winter. Summer insects all female, winged or wingless. Males occur only in autumn.

×17

Cabbage Whitefly Aleyrodidae *Aleyrodes proletella*. **Habitat:** On cabbages and related plants (usually on undersides of leaves) in much of British Isles. **Notes:** Active in summer. A serious crop pest.

Scale Insects Coccoidea. **Habitat:** Various herbaceous plants, trees and shrubs. **Notes:** Tiny bugs covered by horny or waxy scales or shields. Remain motionless on plants, and suck sap. Males very rare, very tiny and fragile with one pair of wings; females wingless, often legless.

Terrestrial Invertebrates

Common Alderfly Sialidae *Sialis lutaria.* **Habitat:** Vegetation, rocks and walls around ponds, canals and slow rivers throughout British Isles. **Notes:** Active May to July.

Snakefly Raphidiidae *Raphidia notata.* **Habitat:** Woodland, especially pine and oak, throughout British Isles. **Flight time:** May to August. **Notes:** Female has long, slender ovipositor.

Green Lacewing Chrysopidae *Chrysopa* sp. **Habitat:** Everywhere with good vegetation cover throughout British Isles. **Flight time:** Spring to autumn. **Notes:** Often hibernates in houses in winter.

Caddisfly Limnephilidae *Halesus radiatus.* **Habitat:** Flowing water throughout British Isles. **Flight time:** Autumn. **Notes:** Adult may fly to lights at night.

Crane-fly Tipulidae *Tipula maxima.* **Habitat:** Damp, shady places throughout much of British Isles. **Flight time:** Summer. **Notes:** Often comes into houses.

Common Scorpion Fly Panorpidae *Panorpa communis.* **Habitat:** Woodland, nettle-beds, hedgerows, gardens and areas of lush vegetation throughout British Isles. **Flight time:** May to August. **Notes:** Abdomen in female pointed, not turned up.

Mosquito Culicidae *Theobaldia annulata*. **Habitat:** Near freshwater throughout most of British Isles; females sometimes hibernate in houses. **Flight time:** Most of year unless very cold. **Notes:** The largest British mosquito. Female feeds on blood; male on nectar.

Chironomid Midge Chironomidae *Chironomus annularius*. **Habitat:** Common throughout British Isles. **Notes:** Active all year, but mainly in winter and spring; males in large swarms. Often confused with mosquitoes, but do not take blood. Larvae, known as bloodworms, bright red, in stagnant water.

Black-fly Simuliidae *Simulium* sp. **Habitat:** By running water nearly everywhere, often in huge numbers. **Notes:** Active spring to autumn, often forming large swarms around mammals and birds. Female sucks blood from many animals, including man. Larvae in running water.

×10

Moth-fly Psychodidae *Psychoda* sp. **Habitat:** Almost everywhere throughout British Isles. **Notes:** Active all year, but most common in spring and autumn. Often come to lighted windows at night, and run when disturbed with wings swept back like an arrowhead. Larvae in water and decaying matter, including compost heaps.

Winter Gnat Trichoceridae *Trichocera annulata*. **Habitat:** In houses, and most other habitats throughout British Isles. **Flight time:** All year, but especially in winter; swarm in afternoons.

211

Terrestrial Invertebrates

Thrips Thysanoptera. **Habitat:** On various plants including fungi, throughout British Isles. **Notes:** Very small, slender insects, usually with 4 feathery wings in female; males wingless. Adult females often hibernate in houses, getting under loose wallpaper and into picture frames. About 150 British species.

St Mark's Fly Bibionidae *Bibio marci*. **Habitat:** Hedgerows, grassland and gardens in most of British Isles. **Flight time:** Spring, often in large swarms.

Cleg-fly Tabanidae *Haematopota pluvialis*. **Habitat:** Woodland, meadows and marsh throughout British Isles, but more common in S. **Flight time:** May to September, especially in thundery weather. **Notes:** Feeds on mammalian blood. A silent flier.

Horse-fly Tabanidae *Tabanus bromius*. **Habitat:** Woodland, meadows and by rivers throughout England and Wales; most common in S. **Flight time:** May to September. **Notes:** Feeds on mammalian blood.

Bee-fly Bombyliidae *Bombylius major*. **Habitat:** Hedgerows, woodland clearings, waste ground and gardens in S. British Isles. **Flight time:** Early spring, visiting various flowers.

Long-legged fly Dolichopodidae *Poecilobothrus nobilitatus*. **Habitat:** Very common in damp places, garden ponds, etc., from Yorkshire southwards. **Flight time:** Spring to autumn. **Notes:** Female lacks the prominent genitalia and dark wing markings.

Robber-fly Asilidae *Asilus crabroniformis*. **Habitat:** Dry heaths, woodland clearings (especially pine), chalk grassland and dunes in S. British Isles. **Flight time:** Summer. **Notes:** Captures other flies in mid-air.

Soldier-fly Stratiomyidae *Chloromyia formosa*. **Habitat:** Wetland, damp woodland, hedgerows and gardens throughout much of British Isles. **Flight time:** May to July. **Notes:** Male has golden abdomen.

Dance fly Empididae *Empis tessellata*. **Habitat:** Hedgerows and woodland, especially with Hawthorn, in most of lowland British Isles. **Flight time:** Spring and early summer. **Notes:** Catches other small flies.

Flies

Hover-fly Syrphidae *Rhingia campestris*. **Habitat:** Woodlands, meadows, gardens, etc., throughout British Isles. **Flight time:** Summer. **Notes:** Larvae in dung.

Hover-fly Syrphidae *Volucella bombylans*. **Habitat:** Woodland and anywhere with flowers throughout British Isles. **Flight time:** Summer.

Hover-fly Syrphidae *Syrphus ribesii*. **Habitat:** Woodland, gardens and anywhere with flowers, especially umbellifers, throughout British Isles. **Flight time:** Summer. **Notes:** Larvae eat aphids.

Fly Sepsidae *Sepsis punctum*. **Habitat:** Hedgerows, woodland, farms, rubbish tips, in much of British Isles. **Flight time:** Spring to autumn. **Notes**. Closely related species often swarm on plants in vast numbers. Larvae in dung and carrion.

×5

Fruit-fly Drosophilidae *Drosophila* sp. **Habitat:** Houses, orchards and anywhere fruit is available, throughout British Isles. **Flight time:** All year in buildings. **Notes:** A tiny fly.

Drone-fly Syrphidae *Eristalis tenax*. **Habitat:** Woodland, gardens, hedgerows, etc., especially near freshwater, throughout British Isles. **Flight time:** All year unless very cold. **Notes:** Very common on spring flowers. Pale marks on abdomen very variable. Larvae in muddy water.

Greenbottle Calliphoridae *Lucilia caesar*. **Habitat:** In houses, farms, around sheep and other animals, throughout British Isles. **Flight time:** All year unless very cold.

Bluebottle Calliphoridae *Calliphora vomitoria*. **Habitat:** Wherever carrion can be found, in houses and other buildings, throughout British Isles. **Flight time:** All year unless very cold. **Notes:** One of several very similar species. A nuisance at slaughter houses.

Cluster-fly Calliphoridae *Pollenia rudis*. **Habitat:** Houses, caves, open country in summer, throughout British Isles. **Flight time:** Early spring to late autumn. **Notes:** Hibernates in houses and caves. Larvae parasitic in earthworms or predatory in soil.

Terrestrial Invertebrates

Gooseberry Sawfly
Tenthredinidae *Nematus ribesii*.
Habitat: Gardens, orchards and nearby woodlands and scrub throughout British Isles. **Flight time:** April to September.
Notes: Female broader with orange body. Larvae feed on gooseberry and currant leaves.

Flesh-fly Calliphoridae *Sarcophaga carnaria*. **Habitat:** Near houses and anywhere carrion can be found, throughout British Isles. **Flight time:** All year unless very cold.

House-fly Muscidae *Musca domestica*. **Habitat:** Houses, farms and rubbish tips throughout British Isles. **Flight time:** All year unless very cold

Chalcid wasp Torymidae *Torymus* sp. **Habitat:** Anywhere that oak galls occur, throughout British Isles. **Flight time:** Spring and early summer, or later, according to species.
Notes: Larvae parasitise gall wasp grubs in oak galls. Male lacks ovipositor.

Horntail Siricidae *Uroceras gigas*. **Habitat:** Pine woods throughout British Isles; also in timber yards. **Flight time:** Summer, or all year in buildings. **Notes:** Larvae in pine trunks. Male lacks ovipositor and black on abdomen.

Ruby-tailed wasp Chrysidida *Chrysis ignita*. **Habitat:** Anywhere, but usually near trees, throughout British Isles. **Flight time:** Spring and early summer. **Notes:** Larvae parasitise solitary bees.

Sawfly Tenthredinidae *Tenthredo atra*. **Habitat:** Hedgerows, woodland, gardens throughout British Isles. **Flight time:** May to August.

Yellow Dunfly Scathophagidae *Scathophaga stercoraria*.
Habitat: Grassland, hedgerows and farmland throughout British Isles. **Flight time:** Early spring to autumn. **Notes:** Carnivorous. Larvae in dung. Adult males swarm on dung.

Ichneumon wasp
Ichneumonidae *Rhyssa persuasoria*. **Habitat:** Pine woods throughout British Isles. **Flight time:** Summer. **Notes:** Larvae parasitise Horntail larvae. Female has long drill-like ovipositor and lays eggs on Horntail larvae, deep in pine trunks.

Galls. Growths that develop on various parts of plants in response to presence of insect grubs or other organisms, such as fungi or mites, in the tissues. The tissues swell up to form the galls around the invaders, providing them with nourishment. The plants do not seem to be harmed in any way.

Common Spangle Gall
Develops on the undersides of oak leaves, often in huge numbers, throughout British Isles. Caused by the larva of the gall wasp *Neuroterus quercusbaccarum*. Eggs are laid May-July and galls are well-formed by August. They fall with the leaves and then become detached. Adult females, like small winged ants, emerge from the galls February-March, lay eggs on oak buds and a new generation of galls develops on the young leaves and catkins April-June. These galls look like small currants – green at first and then red or purple. Male and female gall wasps emerge and, after mating, the female lays eggs which give rise to new spangle galls.

Oak Apple This gall matures on oak trees throughout British Isles, in midsummer. It has a spongy texture and contains numerous grubs of the gall wasp *Biorhiza pallida*. Winged adults emerge in July and females lay eggs in oak roots. Small rounded galls develop and grubs feed inside them. Wingless females emerge at end of second winter (18 months later) and climb up to lay eggs in the oak buds ready for another generation of oak apples.

Robin's Pincushion Gall Also known as the bedeguar gall, this growth develops on wild roses and is caused by grubs of the gall wasp *Diplolepis rosae*. Developing in early summer, the gall is bright red at first, later becoming brown and dry. Grubs remain inside through the winter. Adults emerge in spring and lay eggs in open leaf buds.

Rabbit Flea Pulicidae *Spilopsyllus cuniculi*. **Habitat:** Wherever rabbits are found throughout British Isles. **Notes:** Active all year. Feeds on rabbit blood. Transmits myxomatosis.

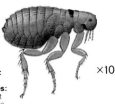

×10

Terrestrial Invertebrates

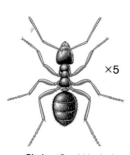

×5

×5

Black ant Formicidae *Lasius niger*. **Habitat:** Very common throughout British Isles, even in wet places. **Notes:** Active in all but the coldest months. Usually nests under stones, commonly under garden paths and pavements; often enters houses. Mating flight usually in August.

Meadow Ant Formicidae *Lasius flavus*. **Habitat:** Grassland, heaths and gardens throughout British Isles; most common in S. **Notes:** Active spring to autumn. Colonial. Construct large, conspicuous soil mounds.

Wood Ant Formicadae *Formic rufa*. **Habitat:** Usually in pine and oak woodland, building large mounds of twigs and leaf litter, in England and Wales, bu rare in N. and absent from Scotland. **Notes:** Active in all but coldest months. Mating flight usually in May or June.

Potter Wasp Eumenidae *Eumenes coarctata*. **Habitat:** Heaths in S. England. **Flight time:** Summer. **Notes:** Constructs small vase-shaped nest of mud.

Sand Wasp Sphecidae *Ammophila sabulosa*. **Habitat:** Sandy heaths, dunes and upper sea shores in most of British Isles. **Flight time:** Summer.

Digger Wasp Sphecidae *Ectemnius quadricinctus*. **Habitat:** Hedgerows, gardens, woodland and heaths throughout British Isles. **Flight time:** Summer. **Notes:** Nests in dead wood.

Common Wasp Vespidae *Paravespula vulgaris*. **Habitat:** Near buildings, in roots, hollow trees and anywhere it can nest underground without getting waterlogged; throughout British Isles, but less common in N. **Flight time:** Spring to late autumn. **Notes:** Colonial. Often build nests in attics or under floors. Only new queens survive winter.

Spider-hunting Wasp Pompilidae *Anoplius fuscus*. **Habitat:** Sandy heaths, waste ground, dunes and quarries in most of British Isles. **Flight time:** Summer.

Hornet Vespidae *Vespa crabro*.
Habitat: Hollow trees in
woodland and hedgerows, and
occasionally house roofs, in S.
England and Wales. **Flight
time:** Spring to autumn. **Notes:**
Colonial. Only young, mated
queens survive winter.

Buff-tailed Bumble Bee Apidae
Bombus terrestris. **Habitat:**
Almost anywhere in most of
Britih Isles, except N. Scotland.
Flight time: Early spring and
summer. **Notes:** Social; nests
underground.

Red-tailed Bumble Bee Apidae
Bombus lapidarius. **Habitat:**
Grassland, gardens and
hedgerows in England and
Wales; mainly coastal in
Scotland and absent from N.
Flight time: April to
September. **Notes:** Male found
only July-September, has
yellow collar.

Honey Bee Apidae *Apis
mellifera*. **Habitat:** Usually in
hives, but occasionally in hollow
trees in warmer parts; throughout British Isles. **Flight time:**
Early spring to autumn. **Notes:**
Social. Workers scour all
habitats for nectar and pollen.
Several races exist, with
different abdominal colours.

Cuckoo Bee Andrenidae
Nomada flava. **Habitat:** Sandy
places throughout British Isles.
Flight time: Summer. **Notes:**
Lays eggs in nests of other
solitary bees.

Mining Bee Andrenidae
Andrena armata. **Habitat:**
Woodland and gardens in most
of British Isles, but rare in N.
Flight time: Spring. **Notes:**
Solitary; nests underground in
light soils. Very fond of
gooseberry and currant flowers.
Male much less hairy, and
darker.

Terrestrial Invertebrates

Longhorn Beetle Cerambycidae *Rhagium bifasciatum*. **Habitat:** Woodland and hedgerows in most of British Isles. **Notes:** Active in summer.

Green Tiger Beetle Carabidae *Cicindela campestris*. **Habitat:** Sandy heaths and dunes in most of British Isles. **Notes:** Active in summer in sunshine.

Violet Ground Beetle Carabidae *Carabus violaceus*. **Habitat:** Woodland, grassland, gardens, hedgerows, throughout British Isles. **Notes:** Active all year, but hibernates when very cold. Nocturnal.

Devil's Coach Horse, Cocktail Staphylinidae *Ocypus olens*. **Habitat:** Woodland, grassland, hedgerows, gardens and in buildings throughout much of British Isles. **Notes:** Active most of year. Nocturnal. Feeds on other small invertebrates.

Stag Beetle Lucanidae *Lucanus cervus*. **Habitat:** Woodland, hedgerows and gardens in S. England and Wales. **Notes:** Active in early summer. Breeds in tree stumps and fence posts. Female lacks horns.

Click Beetle Elateridae *Agriotes obscurus*. **Habitat:** Hedgerows, grassland, farmland, and woodland throughout British Isles. **Notes:** Active May to July. Larvae (wireworms) are serious pests of root crops.

Dung Beetle Scarabaeidae *Aphodius rufipes*. **Habitat:** Grassland and woodland throughout British Isles. **Notes:** Active in summer. Often flies to light. Feeds on dung of hoofed mammals.

Carpet Beetle Dermestidae *Anthrenus verbasci*. **Habitat:** Houses and birds' nests, as larvae; flowery places as adults. **Notes:** Active spring and early summer. Not in large towns. Larvae (called woolly bears) eat wool, fur, etc.

Cockchafer Scarabaeidae *Melolontha melolontha*. **Habitat:** Hedgerows, woodland, parks, gardens, in most of British Isles, but not common in N. **Flight time:** May and June. **Notes:** Also called May-bug. Attracted to lights at night. Larvae damage crop roots; adults cause great damage to trees.

Rove Beetle Staphylinidae *Philonthus laminatus*. **Habitat:** Grassland and woodland throughout British Isles. **Notes:** Active in summer. Feeds on dung and associated insects.

218

Soldier Beetle Cantharidae *Cantharis rustica*. **Habitat:** Almost anywhere flowers occur in most of British Isles. **Flight time:** Summer. **Notes:** Often on flowers, but carnivorous.

22-spot Ladybird Coccinellidae *Thea 22-punctata*. **Habitat:** Almost anywhere, especially with nettles, in England, Wales and Ireland. **Notes:** Active spring to autumn. Feeds on aphids.

Seven-spot Ladybird Coccinellidae *Coccinella 7-punctata*. **Habitat:** Almost anywhere with vegetation throughout British Isles. **Notes:** Active spring to autumn. Feeds on aphids.

Burying Beetle Silphidae *Necrophorus vespillo*. **Habitat:** Grassland, hedgerows, woodland in most of British Isles. **Notes:** Active in summer. One of several similar species.

Elm Bark Beetle Scolytidae *Scolytus scolytus*. **Habitat:** Wherever elms are growing throughout British Isles. **Notes:** Active late spring to autumn. Larvae burrow in elm bark; adults carry fungi that cause Dutch elm disease.

Fur Beetle Dermestidae *Attagenus pellio*. **Habitat:** Houses and animal nests, as larvae; in flowery places as adults; throughout British Isles. **Notes:** Active in spring. Larvae feed on flour, fur, wool, etc.

Eyed Ladybird Coccinellidae *Anatis ocellata*. **Habitat:** Coniferous woodland in most of British Isles. **Notes:** Active in summer. Feeds on aphids.

Wasp Beetle Cerambycidae *Clytus arietus*. **Habitat:** Woodland, hedgerows and gardens throughout British Isles. **Notes:** Active in spring and summer.

Dor Beetle Geotrupidae *Geotrupes stercorarius*. **Habitat:** Grassland and woodland throughout British Isles. **Notes:** Active April to October. Feeds on dung.

Rove Beetle Staphylinidae *Emus hirtus*. **Habitat:** Grassland and farmland near cows in S. and E. England. **Notes:** Active in summer. Feeds on cow dung.

Colorado Beetle Chrysomelidae *Leptinotarsa decemlineata*. **Habitat:** A serious pest of potato crops in Europe; not established in Britain. **Notes:** Active spring to autumn in two generations; adult hibernates. Native of N. America. Larva bright pink; feeds (like adult) on potatoes and nightshades.

Terrestrial Invertebrates

Glow-worm Lampyridae *Lampyris noctiluca*. **Habitat:** Very local on grassland, in hedgerows and open woodland on calcareous soils in S. England and Wales. **Notes:** Active July and August. Female wingless, slug-like; produces green light at tip of abdomen to attract male.

Cardinal Beetle Pyrochroidae *Pyrochroa serraticornis*. **Habitat:** Local in woodland, hedgerows and anywhere with tree stumps in England, Wales and Ireland. **Notes:** Active in summer; adults often on flowers; larvae under bark.

Woodworm, Furniture Beetle Anobiidae *Anobium punctatum*. **Habitat:** Houses, hedgerows, woodlands and anywhere with dead wood, throughout British Isles. **Notes:** Active mainly in early summer. Larvae tunnel in dead wood.

Weevil Apionidae *Apion miniatum*. **Habitat:** Local in hedgerows, waste ground, damp places and on coasts in much of British Isles. **Notes:** Active in summer. Feeds on dock leaves.

Weevil Curculionidae *Otiorhynchus clavipes*. **Habitat:** Hedgerows and woodland in much of British Isles. **Notes:** Active in summer.

Green Tortoise Beetle Chrysomelidae *Cassida viridis*. **Habitat:** Hedgerows, marsh, damp woodland in much of British Isles. **Notes:** Active July and August. Especially on mint.

Leaf Beetle Chrysomelidae *Chrysolina polita*. **Habitat:** Hedgerows and damp places in most of British Isles. **Notes:** Active in summer. Feeds on mint.

Woodlouse Porcellionidae *Porcellio scaber*. **Habitat:** Under decaying vegetation in woodland, heaths, grassland, gardens and sand dunes throughout British Isles. **Notes:** Active all year except when very cold. Often climbs on walls and tree trunks on damp nights to browse on algae.

False scorpion Neobisiidae *Neobisium muscorum*. **Habitat:** In moss and decaying vegetation in woodland, hedgerows, river banks and gardens throughout British Isles.

Garden Spider Argiopidae *Araneus diadematus*. **Habitat:** On vegetation and fences, wherever there is space to build an orb web, throughout British Isles. **Notes:** Active late summer and autumn.

House Spider Agelenidae *Tegenaria saeva*. **Habitat:** In buildings, on rocks and walls in most of England and Wales; rare in Scotland. **Notes:** Active all year in buildings. Traps prey on sheet web.

Meta segmentata Argiopidae. **Habitat:** Low-growing plants in woodland, gardens and hedgerows in Britain; less common in Ireland. **Notes:** Active late summer and autumn, sometimes in spring. Traps prey on orb web.

Enoplognatha ovata
Theridiidae. **Habitat:** Low-growing plants throughout British Isles; one of the commonest spiders. **Notes:** Active in June and July. Abdomen may or may not be marked with carmine. Traps prey on web.

Linyphia triangularis
Linyphiidae. **Habitat:** Low-growing plants and bushes throughout British Isles. **Notes:** Active late summer and autumn. Traps prey on domed sheet or hammock-shaped web.

Amaurobius fenestralis
Amaurobiidae. **Habitat:** Walls, buildings, tree trunks, under stones throughout British Isles. **Notes:** Active all year. Traps prey on web.

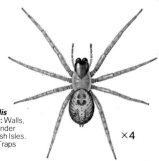

×4

Trochosa ruricola Lycosidae. **Habitat:** Under stones and logs almost everywhere in British Isles. **Notes:** Active all year. Hunts prey by night.

Crab spider Thomisidae *Misumena vatia*. **Habitat:** On flowers throughout S. England and Wales and S. Ireland. **Notes:** Active May to July or August. Changes colour between white and yellow to match different flowers. Male much smaller than female. Ambushes prey.

Wolf Spider Pisauridae *Pisaura mirabilis*. **Habitat:** On plants in woodland, grassland, heaths and roadsides throughout British Isles. **Notes:** Active May to July. Hunts prey.

Daddy-long-legs Pholcidae *Pholcus phalangioides*. **Habitat:** In buildings in S. England, Wales and S. Ireland. **Notes:** Active all year but may be dormant in winter. Traps prey on web.

Zebra Spider Salticidae *Salticus scenicus*. **Habitat:** Walls, rocks and exposed tree trunks throughout British Isles, except N. Scotland. **Notes:** Active May to September. Hunts prey by jumping on to it.

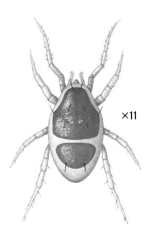

×11

Harvestman Phalangiidae *Phalangium opilio*. **Habitat:** Shrubby vegetation throughout British Isles. **Notes:** Active June to November.

Mite Parasitidae *Parasitus coleoptratorum*. **Habitat:** On dung and dung beetles throughout British Isles. **Notes:** Active most of year.

×2

Sheep Tick Ixodidae *Ixodes ricinus*. **Habitat:** On mammals, in woodland edges and rides, on rough grassland, throughout most of British Isles; most common on upland moors of N. and W. **Notes:** Active spring and summer. Feeds on mammalian blood.

Centipede Geophiliidae *Geophilus* sp. **Habitat:** In soil and leaf litter in woodland, grassland and gardens throughout British Isles. **Notes:** Active all year except when very cold.

Millipede Iulidae *Cylindroiulus* sp. **Habitat:** In decaying plant matter throughout British Isles. **Notes:** Active all year except when very cold.

Freshwater Invertebrates

Flatworm Planariidae *Polycelis nigra.* **Habitat:** Still and slow-flowing water throughout British Isles. **Notes:** Active all year. Glides over stones and leaves, even upside-down on underside of water surface. Colour varies from cream to dark brown or black. Usually 3 small rounded lobes at front, with numerous eyes around edges. (Up to 1cm)

Hydra Hydridae *Hydra* sp. **Habitat:** Still and slow-flowing water in most of British Isles Attaches itself to water plants, including undersides of water lily leaves. **Notes:** Active spring to autumn; passes water in egg stage in mud. Catches water fleas in tentacles armed with stinging cells.

Sludge Worm Tubificidae *Tubifex tubifex.* **Habitat:** In mud at bottom of ponds, streams, and ditches, even where polluted, in most of British Isles. **Notes:** Builds little mud tubes and lives head down in them, with tail waving in water. Active all year.

Medicinal Leech Gnathobdellidae *Hirudo medicinalis.* **Habitat:** Ponds and sluggish streams in England, but now rare. **Notes:** Active all year. Feeds on blood of mammals, including man – once used for blood-letting. Young stages feed on fishes, newts, and other small animals. (15cm when expanded; 3-4cm when contracted.)

Great Ramshorn Snail Planorbidae *Planorbis corneus.* **Habitat:** Locally common in well-lit weedy ponds, canals and slow-flowing rivers in most of British Isles; in quite stagnant waters. **Notes:** Active all year. Rarely needs to come up for air. Browses on algae.

Great Pond Snail Limnaeidae *Limnaea stagnalis.* **Habitat:** Common in ponds and other still and slow-flowing waters; often in stagnant swamps and ditches; throughout S. Britain; rare in N. **Notes:** Active all year. One of the largest water snails.

Freshwater Invertebrates

Painter's Mussel Unionidae *Unio pictorum*. **Habitat:** In mud in still and slow-flowing water in England and Wales. **Notes:** So-named because painters once used the shells as containers for paint.

Water Measurer Hydrometridae *Hydrometra stagnorum*. **Habitat:** Surface of ponds and edges of weedy streams throughout British Isles. **Notes:** Active most of year except when very cold.

Toothed Pondskater Gerridae *Gerris odontogaster*. **Habitat:** Surface of weedy ponds and canals throughout British Isles. **Notes:** Active spring to autumn.

Water Scorpion Nepidae *Nepa cinerea*. **Habitat:** Muddy ponds and lakes throughout British Isles, except N. Scotland. **Notes:** Active all year, but hides in mud when very cold. Will eat small fish.

Saucer Bug Naucoridae *Ilyocoris cimicoides*. **Habitat:** Weedy and muddy ponds and canals in S. England and Wales. **Notes:** Active all year unless very cold. May venture onto land at night.

Common Water Boatman Corixidae *Corixa punctata*. **Habitat:** Weedy ponds and slow-flowing rivers throughout British Isles. **Notes:** Active July to March; can fly.

Common Backswimmer Notonectidae *Notonecta glauca*. **Habitat:** Ponds and canals throughout British Isles. **Notes:** Active all year unless very cold. Swims on its back, belly uppermost. Can fly from pond to pond.

225

Freshwater Invertebrates

Whirligig Beetle Gyrinidae *Gyrinus marinus.* **Habitat:** Lakes, ponds, canals and (sometimes) rivers throughout British Isles. **Notes:** Active spring to autumn. Skates on water surface, often whizzing round and round in circles.

Great Diving Beetle Dytiscidae *Dytiscus marginalis.* **Habitat:** Ponds and canals throughout British Isles. **Notes:** Active all year, but hides in mud when very cold. Female has more striated elytra and lacks swellings on front legs.

Screech Beetle Hygrobiidae *Hygrobia hermanni.* **Habitat:** Local in muddy ponds as far north as Yorkshire. **Notes:** Active spring to autumn.

Silver Water Beetle Hydrophilidae *Hydrophilus piceus.* **Habitat:** Local in weedy ponds as far north as Yorkshire. **Notes:** Active all year, but hides in mud when very cold. Female lacks triangular lobes on front legs.

Water Mite Hygrobatidae *Arrhenurus buccinator.* **Habitat:** Ponds and slow-flowing water throughout British Isles. **Notes:** One of a large group of mites, mostly green or brown, in which males and females are markedly different. Female is plumply rounded; male is oval or pear-shaped with a distinct "tail". Swims actively thoughout the year.

Water Spider Agelenidae *Argyroneta aquatica.* **Habitat:** In still water throughout British Isles except far N. **Notes:** Active all year. Feeds on aquatic insects. Makes an air-filled balloon with web but leaves web to hunt. Only truly aquatic spider.

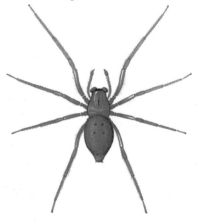

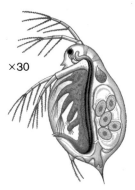

×30

×4

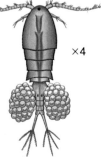

×4

Water Flea Daphnidae *Daphnia pulex*. **Habitat:** Ponds and lakes in most of British Isles; often in such immense numbers in summer that water becomes brown. **Notes:** Swims jerkily in upright position by beating branched antennae. Mainly females in summer; males appear in autumn. Active all year, but numbers fall drastically in autumn when mated females lay overwintering eggs.

Water Louse Asellidae *Asellus aquaticus*. **Habitat:** Weedy ponds and streams, even where polluted, in most of British Isles. **Notes:** Aquatic relative of woodlice. Crawls over mud and vegetation. Active all year. (Male 12mm; female 8mm.)

Cyclops strennus Cyclopidae. **Habitat:** Weedy ponds and other still water throughout British Isles. **Notes:** Swims jerkily. Females most easily recognised by paired egg sacs, males smaller. Active all year, but most numerous in summer.

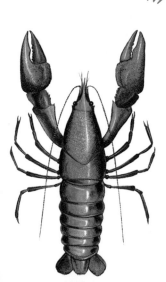

×5

Freshwater Shrimp Gammaridae *Gammarus pulex*. **Habitat:** Shallow, well-aerated streams and lakes in most of British Isles. **Notes:** Mostly under stones and debris, but swims strongly when disturbed. Active all year. One of several similar species.

Crayfish Potamobiidae *Potamobius pallipes*. **Habitat:** Mainly in lowland areas in shallow, well-aerated streams and rivers with firm beds and not too much vegetation; mostly in limestone regions of British Isles, but now rare in many places. **Notes:** Burrows in stream bed or bank and hides there by day. Hunts small animals, including fish, by night. Active spring to autumn; quiescent in winter.

227

Fishes

More than 150 species of fish are found in the freshwaters of Europe, of which about one third occur in Britain. An even greater number frequent the oceans and coasts. Only those most likely to be encountered by the amateur naturalist have been included here. Many of the freshwater species are found in only a very limited area and a lot of the marine forms will only be caught well out at sea or using special equipment. However, these more unusual types do turn up occasionally. Taking measurements and, where possible, counting the number of scales along the fish's lateral line and the number from belly to dorsal fin will help in identification.

The following notes are intended to amplify the remarks given in the notes beneath each illustration, but beware – many species are very difficult to distinguish (especially the Salmonids).

Appearance

Dead fish quickly lose their colours and look grey or white; only fresh specimens are as colourful as the illustrations. In certain species (e.g. stickleback and minnow) the males become very bright coloured in the breeding season, but fade to duller shades soon after. For most species, definitive identification may require counts of bones (rays) in the fins or the number of scales along or across the body. An *adipose* fin is one which contains no bones. The lateral line is often distinctive and consists of a line of special scales associated with sense organs.

Habitat

Most fish live either in freshwater (rivers, ponds, lakes) or in the sea. However, some (e.g. salmon, eel) migrate between the two (and may change appearance when they do) and a few (e.g. flounder, 15-spined stickleback) live in estuaries and may extend into both salt or freshwater. The marine species illustrated are those found near the coast in rockpools, or washed up, or easily caught from the shore.

Freshwater species in the fast-flowing headwaters of rivers experience quite different physical conditions to those fish that live in the muddy, slow-flowing lower reaches. Often the physical characteristics of a river or lake are determined by geological factors; deep lakes and fast-flowing streams are a feature of the hard rocks and high mountains of north and west Britain. The clays and sands of lowland Britain (especially in the south-east) are normally associated with static or slow-flowing, relatively shallow water. Such features are important to fish because flow rate, muddiness and temperature all greatly affect the oxygen content of the water, which in turn is a major determinant of which species are present or absent.

Pollution is a serious threat to fish and has severely restricted their diversity in many rivers. Generally it is the species that need cool, well-oxygenated water that are displaced. Some species are tolerant of low oxygen levels (e.g. tench, carp) and may be found in polluted water and in muddy or stagnant ponds.

Three-spined sticklebacks displaying their courting colours in the spring. The male builds a nest of fibrous materials and introduces one or more females to lay their eggs in it.

Useful aids to identification

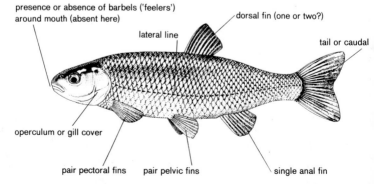

presence or absence of barbels ('feelers') around mouth (absent here)

lateral line

dorsal fin (one or two?)

tail or caudal

operculum or gill cover

pair pectoral fins

pair pelvic fins

single anal fin

sometimes useful to note the number of rays (bones) in the major fins

Fish

Basking Shark Cetorhinidae *Cetorhinus maximus*. **Habitat:** Open sea; summer visitor to N. and W. Britain. **Notes:** Cartilaginous. Solitary or in small shoals. Enormous; large, gaping mouth and enlarged gill slits (almost meet on top of neck) for filter feeding on plankton. Small eyes. No teeth. (Max. 11m.)

Blue Shark Carcharhinidae *Prionace glauca*. **Habitat:** Open sea; regular but uncommon visitor to N and W. British coastal waters. **Notes:** Cartilaginous. Small transverse constriction at base of tail. Pointed snout, prominent teeth; each with a single point and serrated edges. (Max. 4m.)

Spotted Dogfish Scyliorhinidae *Scyliorhinus canicula*. **Habitat:** Coastal and inshore waters, over weedy sand banks from 18-25m; all around British Isles. **Notes:** Cartilaginous. Back, sides and fins dark-spotted. Snout bluntly pointed. Teeth very small. (Max 1m.)

Thornback Ray Rajidae *Raja clavata*. **Habitat:** Coastal and inshore waters, on sea bed in muddy substrates from 20-100m; all around British Isles. **Notes:** Cartilaginous. Commonest British ray. Back has numerous smooth-based thorns. (Max. 120cm.)

Skate Rajidae *Raja batis*. **Habitat:** Coastal waters on sea bed in most substrates; all around British Isles. **Notes:** Cartilaginous. Long snout. Small thorns around eyes and rows along tail. (Max. 2.5m)

Sting Ray Dasyatidae *Dasyatis pastinaca*. **Habitat:** Shallow inshore water on sea bed, often buried in sand; off S. Britain; late summer visitor. **Notes:** Cartilaginous. Long, whip-like tail without fins or thorns but with poison spine. (Max. 2.5m)

Marine Fish

Sprat Clupeidae *Sprattus sprattus*. **Habitat:** Shallow coastal waters around British Isles, and in open water. **Notes:** Forms shoals. Slender with no visible lateral line. Base of pelvic fins in front of or below dorsal fin. Scales between pelvics and anal fin have sharp, pointed keels. (15-20cm)

Herring Clupeidae *Clupea harengus*. **Habitat:** Open sea in mid-water around British Isles as adults; young inshore. **Notes:** Slender; lateral line not visible. Base of pelvic fins behind front of short dorsal fin. Lower jaw projects; snout pointed. (Max. 40cm)

Garfish Belonidae *Belone belone*. **Habitat:** Open sea near surface and coastal waters around British Isles. **Notes:** Forms large shoals. Very long, pointed, toothed snout. Dorsal and anal fins set well back, no small finlets between these and tail. (Max. 90cm)

Pollack Gadidae *Pollachius pollachius*. **Habitat:** Open sea, near sea bed to 200m and inshore waters to 15cm; all around British Isles. **Notes:** Protruding lower jaw without barbel. Lateral line curves strongly above pectoral fins. Anus below middle of 1st dorsal fin. (Max. 1m)

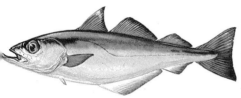

Cod Gadidae *Gadus morrhua*. **Habitat:** Open sea and coastal waters near sea bed to 600m, inshore to 18cm; all around British Isles. **Notes:** Protruding upper jaw, chin barbel, pale lateral line. Colour variable. (Max. 120cm)

Whiting Clupeidae *Merlangius merlangus*. **Habitat:** Open sea and coastal waters from eel-grass zone to 200m; all around British Isles. **Habitat:** Protruding upper jaw; no barbel on lower jaw. Black spot at base of pectoral fin. (20-40cm)

231

Fish

Seahorses Syngnathidae *Hippocampus* sp. **Habitat:** Shallow inshore waters in seaweed zone, around British Isles. **Notes:** Bony external skeleton; rigid box-like body. No tail fin. Abdomen coiled to grasp seaweed. Head 90° to body. Tubular snout. Fan-like dorsal fin. (Approx. 16cm)

Great Pipefish Syngnathidae *Syngnathus acus.* **Habitat:** Shallow inshore waters, seaweed zone, all around British Isles, commonest W. Scotland. **Notes:** Also called Mediterranean Pipefish. Extremely elongate with long snout, bony outer skeleton and 18-19 bony rings between head and dorsal fin. (Max. 45cm)

Grey Mullet Mugilidae *Crenimugil labrosus.* **Habitat:** Open sea, shallow coastal waters, over soft sea bed, estuaries; around most of Britain except Scotland and N. Ireland. **Notes:** Also called Thick-lipped Mullet. 1st dorsal fin four spiny rays; 2nd also short. Thick upper lip. Lateral line not visible. (Max. 60cm)

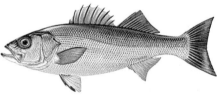

Bass Serranidae *Dicentrarchus labrax.* **Habitat:** Open sea, rocky inshore waters, estuaries; all around British Isles, commonest in S. and W. **Notes:** Two dorsal fins of same length, 1st very spiny. Large mouth. Prominent black marking on top of gill covers. (Max. 80cm)

Mackerel Scombridae *Scomber scombrus.* **Habitat:** Open sea and coastal waters near surface, all around British Isles. **Notes:** Form large shoals. Two dorsal fins widely separated; four to six finlets between 2nd and tail. No dots below lateral line; zebra-like stripes on flanks. (Max. 50cm)

Red Mullet Mullidae *Mullus surmuletus.* **Habitat:** Near sea bed in open and inshore waters over rocky and sandy substrates; around most of Britain in low numbers, except Scotland and N. Ireland. **Notes:** Bright, changeable colour. Two long barbels on lower jaw. 1st dorsal fin spiny. (Max. 40cm)

Dragonet Callionymidae *Callionymus lyra*. **Habitat:** Open sea and coastal waters, on sea bed in sandy substrates to 400m; all around British Isles. **Notes:** Brightly coloured. Broad head; eyes dorsal, directed upwards; small mouth; small gill opening. (Max. 30cm)

Ballan Wrasse Labridae *Labrus bergylta*. **Habitat:** Shallow, inshore waters, rocky coasts, seaweed zone, around British Isles, commonest in W. **Notes:** Large dorsal, spiny and jointed ray portions continuous. 40-50 large scales along lateral line. (Max. 60cm)

Corkwing Labridae *Crenilabrus melops*. **Habitat:** Shallow inshore waters, rocky coasts, seaweed zone; all around British Isles, commonest in S. and W. **Notes:** Large dorsal, spiny and jointed ray portions continuous. Dark spot behind eye and base of tail. Male base colour green, female brown. (15-20cm)

Sand Eel Ammodytidae *Ammodytes tobianus*. **Habitat:** Inshore waters from 0-30m, buried in sand by day, forming shoals in open water at night; all round British Isles. **Notes:** Elongate. Hind tips of pectorals reach behind front of dorsal fin. Protrusible mouth. (Max. 20cm)

Butterfish Pholidae *Pholis gunnellus*. **Habitat:** Very common in shallow inshore waters, rocky shores and seaweed zone from 0-30m; all around British Isles. **Notes:** Also called Gunnel. Very elongate and laterally flattened, with 9-13 dark spots along base of dorsal fin. (15-25cm)

Eelpout Zoarcidae *Zoarces viviparus*. **Habitat:** Shallow inshore waters, rocky shores, seaweed zone to 40m; mainly around E. coast, occasionally Scottish W. coast (northern species at southern limit). **Notes:** Also called Viviparous Blenny. Elongate. (Max. 50cm)

Shanny Blenniidae *Blennius pholis*. **Habitat:** Shallow inshore waters, rocky shores, rock pools, among seaweeds; all around British Isles. **Notes:** Spiny dorsal fin with dip in middle. No tentacles on head. (Max. 16cm)

Fish

Gurnards Triglidae *Trigla* sp.
Habitat: Near sea bed over soft
substrates in open sea, coastal
and inshore waters to 10-15m;
all around British Isles. **Notes:**
Strong bony head. Three
anterior pectoral fin-rays
separated into finger-like
processes, on which fish walks
over sea bed.

Rock Goby Gobiidae *Gobius
paganellus.* **Habitat:** Shallow
inshore waters and seaweed
zone of rocky shores, S.W.
England to W. Scotland. **Notes:**
Pelvics fused forming suckers.
Stocky, with short tail base.
Large head, eyes dorsal. Dorsal
fins distinctly edged with white.
(Max. 12cm)

Pogge Agonidae *Agonus
cataphractus.* **Habitat:** Open
sea and coastal waters on sea
bed in soft substrates to 300m;
all around British Isles. **Notes:**
Head and body covered in
keeled, bony plates. Short
bristles on underside of head.
Somewhat tadpole-shaped.
(Max. 20cm)

Lumpsucker Cyclopteridae
Cyclopterus lumpus. **Habitat:**
Shallow, inshore waters,
intertidal zone, near or on sea
bed; large specimens to 200m;
all around British Isles. **Notes:**
Ventral fins modified into
suction disc. Scaleless skin.
Dorsal fin near tail behind high
ridge. Flanks with row of thorns.
(Max. 60cm)

Montagu's Sea Snail Liparidae
Liparis montagui. **Habitat:**
Shallow inshore waters, and
seaweed zone on rocky shores;
all around Britain except S.W.
Notes: Small, tadpole-shaped.
Scaleless, soft and slimy.
Rounded pectorals extend
under neck. Ventral sucker for
adherence. (Max. 6cm)

Angler Fish Lophiidae *Lophius
piscatorius.* **Habitat:** Open sea
and coastal waters on the sea
bed in soft substrates from
5-1000m; all around British
Isles. **Notes:** Very broad
flattened head with wide mouth
and prominent teeth. 1st dorsal
fin-ray flexible and feathery
tipped. Small feathery
projections on soft, scaleless
skin. (Max. 1.75m)

Marine Fish

Plaice Pleuronectidae *Pleuronectes platessa*. **Habitat:** Coastal and shallow inshore waters on sea bed in mixed and sandy substrates from 10-120m; all around British Isles. **Notes:** Eyes only on right side. Ridge of 4 to 7 bony knobs between eyes. Spotted orange. Smooth, small scales. May hybridize with Flounder. (30-50cm)

Dab Pleuronectidae *Limanda limanda*. **Habitat:** Coastal and inshore waters on the sea bed in sandy substrates to 140m; all around British Isles. **Notes:** Eyes on right side. Scales rough on right side, lateral line arches above pectoral fin. (20-30cm)

Flounder Pleuronectidae *Platichthys flesus*. **Habitat:** Coastal and inshore waters on sea bed in mixed substrates from 5-25m; all around British Isles. **Notes:** Eyes usually only on right side. Rough, bony nodules along lateral line, dorsal and anal fin bases. Often enters rivers. (30-40cm) (Plaice/Flounder hybrids smoother skinned, orange-spotted.)

Halibut Pleuronectidae *Hippoglossus hippoglossus*. **Habitat:** Open sea on sea bed in mixed substrates from 50-200m; North Sea, N. and W. British Isles. **Notes:** Eyes only on right side. Large mouth, prominent teeth. Lateral line curved over pectoral fin. (Max. 3m)

Sole Soleidae *Solea solea*. **Habitat:** Coastal waters on sea bed in sandy and muddy substrates from 10-60m; all around British Isles, commonest in S. **Notes:** Eyes only on right side. Lateral line almost straight. Both pectoral fins well developed. (Max. 50cm)

235

Marine Fish

Turbot Scophthalmidae
Scophthalmus maximus.
Habitat: Coastal and inshore waters on sea bed in mixed substrates from 20-70m; all around British Isles. **Notes:** Eyes only on left side, which is scaleless but adorned with bony nodules. Body almost circular. (Max. 80cm)

Brill Scophthalmidae
Scophthalmus rhombus.
Habitat: Coastal and shallow inshore waters on sea bed in sandy and mixed substrates from 5-50m; all around British Isles. **Notes:** Eyes only on left side, which has small, smooth scales and no nodules. (Max. 65cm)

Topknot Scophthalmidae
Zeugopterus punctatus.
Habitat: Coastal and shallow inshore waters on sea bed in stony and rocky substrates within seaweed zone; all around British Isles. **Notes:** Eyes only on left side. Scales have five spiny outgrowths resembling coarse fur. (Max. 25cm)

Norwegian Topknot Bothidae
Phymorhombus norvegicus.
Habitat: In shallow inshore and coastal waters on sea bed in stony substrates within seaweed zone; all around British Isles. **Notes:** Eyes only on left side. Scales on right side rough. Dorsal fin begins above right eye. Often has irregular transverse bands. (Max. 12cm)

Fish

River Lamprey
Petromyzonidae *Lampetra fluviatilis*. **Habitat:** Open sea, estuaries, lakes and rivers throughout British Isles except W. Ireland. **Notes:** Oral sucker, no jaws. 7 paired gill openings. No paired fins. Very slimy. Single nostril on top of head. Marine, breeds in freshwater in spring. Larvae remain 3-5 years, metamorphose and return to sea. (Adult 50cm.)
Brook Lamprey *L. planeri* is similar, but found in streams, does not go to sea and is smaller. (15cm.)

Twaite Shad Clupeidae *Alosa fallax*. **Habitat:** Slow-flowing clean rivers (lower reaches) and estuaries; localised around British coast. **Notes:** Marine, breeds in freshwater in May. Young may remain for 1 year. upper jaw notched. Less than 70 lateral scales (Allis Shad similar but over 70 lateral scales). (Max. 60cm.)

Salmon Salmonidae *Salmo salar*. **Habitat:** Open sea; fast-flowing rivers and streams over gravel throughout British Isles. **Notes:** Migratory. Four distinct phases in development: in freshwater, young fish (fry) become parrs at 18 months when flanks develop blue-grey bands ("parr marks"). After 3-4 years parr marks disappear and silvery smolt migrates to sea. After 1-3 years becomes sexually mature adult and returns to breed in same rivers where spawned, making vigorous journey upstream. (Max. 1.5m.)

Rainbow Trout Salmonidae *Salmo gairdneri*. **Habitat:** Fast-flowing clean rivers, streams, and lakes throughout British Isles. **Notes:** Wild populations rarely breed in Britain. Dark spots on dorsal and caudal fins. Characteristic iridescent purple flank stripe. Adipose fin (fleshy posterior dorsal) not red. (Max. 120cm.)

Brown Trout Salmonidae *Salmo trutta fario*. **Habitat:** Most types of clean freshwater, especially fast-flowing rivers and streams; common throughout British Isles. **Notes:** Non-migratory sub-species, entirely freshwater. Adipose fin often red. White haloes around body pigment spots in adults and parr. 14-19 scales in forward oblique row from adipose fin to lateral line. (Max. 120cm.)

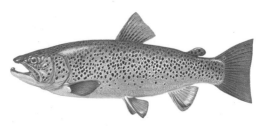

237

Fish

Sea Trout Salmonidae *Salmo trutta trutta*. **Habitat:** Coastal waters, lochs, stony rivers, clean estuaries throughout coastal British Isles. **Notes:** Silver smolt migrates to sea; many spots on operculum. Breeding adults return to freshwater in autumn. Female steel grey; male brownish. Parr and scale counts as *S. trutta fario*. (Max. 140cm.)

Char(r) Salmonidae *Salvelinus alpinus*. **Habitat:** Isolated deep lakes in upland Wales, Cumbria and Scotland. **Notes:** White leading edge to ventral fins; light coloured spots. Breeding males have crimson bellies in October. (Different races have evolved.) (Max 95cm.)

Cisco, Vendace Coregonidae *Coregonus albula*. **Habitat:** Some deep cold lakes in Scotland and Ireland. **Notes:** A shoaling, surface dweller with projecting lower jaw. (Max. 25cm)

Common Whitefish, Powan Coregonidae *Coregonus lavaretus*. **Habitat:** Large lakes in N. Wales, Cumbria and Scotland. **Notes:** Small mouth with no teeth. Migrates into rivers to spawn. (15-40cm.)

Grayling Thymallidae *Thymallus thymallus*. **Habitat:** Cool, clean, fast-flowing rivers and streams in Britain except N. Scotland. **Notes:** Very tall dorsal fin with 17-24 rays, and small adipose fin as in Salmonidae. (45cm.)

Pike Esocidae *Esox lucius*. **Habitat:** Medium- and slow-flowing rivers, canals, lakes and ponds throughout British Isles. **Notes:** Large pointed snout, flattened on top; prominent grooves forward from eyes; backward pointing teeth. Dorsal fin well back near tail above anal fin. (1.5m.)

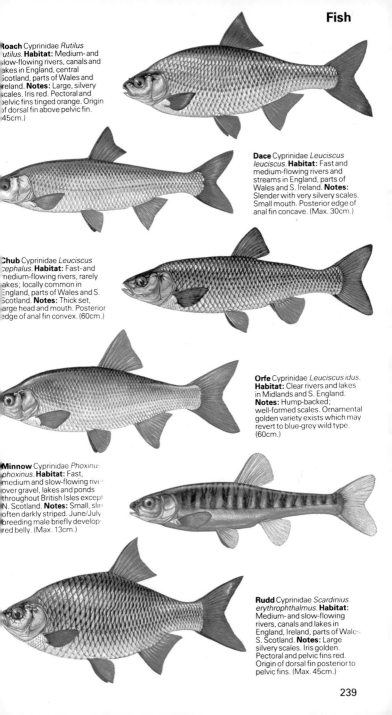

Roach Cyprinidae *Rutilus rutilus*. **Habitat:** Medium- and slow-flowing rivers, canals and lakes in England, central Scotland, parts of Wales and Ireland. **Notes:** Large, silvery scales. Iris red. Pectoral and pelvic fins tinged orange. Origin of dorsal fin above pelvic fin. (45cm.)

Dace Cyprinidae *Leuciscus leuciscus*. **Habitat:** Fast and medium-flowing rivers and streams in England, parts of Wales and S. Ireland. **Notes:** Slender with very silvery scales. Small mouth. Posterior edge of anal fin concave. (Max. 30cm.)

Chub Cyprinidae *Leuciscus cephalus*. **Habitat:** Fast- and medium-flowing rivers, rarely lakes; locally common in England, parts of Wales and S. Scotland. **Notes:** Thick set, large head and mouth. Posterior edge of anal fin convex. (60cm.)

Orfe Cyprinidae *Leuciscus idus*. **Habitat:** Clear rivers and lakes in Midlands and S. England. **Notes:** Hump-backed; well-formed scales. Ornamental golden variety exists which may revert to blue-grey wild type. (60cm.)

Minnow Cyprinidae *Phoxinus phoxinus*. **Habitat:** Fast, medium and slow-flowing rivers over gravel, lakes and ponds throughout British Isles except N. Scotland. **Notes:** Small, slim, often darkly striped. June/July breeding male briefly develops red belly. (Max. 13cm.)

Rudd Cyprinidae *Scardinius erythrophthalmus*. **Habitat:** Medium- and slow-flowing rivers, canals and lakes in England, Ireland, parts of Wales, S. Scotland. **Notes:** Large silvery scales. Iris golden. Pectoral and pelvic fins red. Origin of dorsal fin posterior to pelvic fins. (Max. 45cm.)

Fish

Tench Cyprinidae *Tinca tinca*. **Habitat:** Slow-flowing, weedy lakes, canals and ponds. Common in England, Ireland, parts of Wales, central and S. Scotland. **Notes:** Rounded tail; thick-set and slimy. One pair of barbels. Ornamental golden variety exists. (Max. 64cm.)

Gudgeon Cyprinidae *Gobio gobio*. **Habitat:** Fast- and medium-flowing rivers in England, Ireland, parts of Wales, S. Scotland. **Notes:** Elongate; wedge-shaped head; mouth below snout with 2 barbels. 38-44 scales along lateral line. (Max. 20cm.)

Barbel Cyprinidae *Barbus barbus*. **Habitat:** Fast and medium-flowing weedy rivers over gravel; locally common in England. **Notes:** Strong, elongate; mouth below snout with 4 barbels. 55-65 scales along lateral line. (Max. 90cm.)

Bleak Cyprinidae *Alburnus alburnus*. **Habitat:** Medium- and slow-flowing rivers, clean lakes in England and parts of Wales. **Notes:** Small, delicate; large silvery scales; upturned mouth. Long, concave anal fin with 16-20 branched rays. (Max. 20cm.)

White Bream Cyprinidae *Blicca bjoerkna*. **Habitat:** Medium- and slow-flowing rivers, weedy lakes in parts of England. **Notes:** Also called Silver Bream. 44-48 scales along lateral line. Long anal fin with 21-23 branched rays. (Max. 30cm.)

Common Bream Cyprinidae *Abramis brama*. **Habitat:** Medium- and slow-flowing rivers, canals and lakes in England, Ireland, parts of Scotland and Wales. **Notes:** Slimy, silver, deep-bodied, with dark fins. 51-60 scales along lateral line. Long anal fin with 24-30 branched rays. (Max. 60cm.)

Freshwater Fish

Bitterling Cyprinidae *Rhodeus amarus*. **Habitat:** Slow-flowing rivers, sandy lakes and ponds; spreading from Lancashire and Cheshire. **Notes:** Lateral line appears incomplete. Blue stripe on flank. April/May breeding female develops ovipositor; male becomes purple with red belly and fins. (Max. 9cm.)

Crucian Carp Cyprinidae *Carassius carassius*. **Habitat:** Slow-flowing rivers, weedy lakes and ponds in S. and E. England; localised elsewhere. **Notes:** No barbels. Convex anal fin. 15-19 branched dorsal fin-rays. 28-33 scales along lateral line. (Max. 50cm.)

Goldfish Cyprinidae *Carassius auratus*. **Habitat:** Slow-flowing rivers and ponds in parts of England. **Notes:** Usually brassy but golden varieties exist. First dorsal fin-ray strongly serrated, fin long and concave. Anal fin concave. No barbels. (Max. 30cm.)

Carp Cyprinidae *Cyprinus carpio*. **Habitat:** Ponds, lakes, slow-flowing rivers, canals in England, parts of Wales, Ireland and S. Scotland. **Notes:** 4 barbels. 17-22 branched dorsal fin-rays. 35-40 scales along lateral line. Partially scaled ("mirror carp") and elongate varieties exist. (Max. 1m.)

Stone Loach Cobitidae *Noemacheilus barbatulus*. **Habitat:** Medium-flow rivers and streams over stones in most of Britain except N. Scotland. **Notes:** Small, elongate, ventrally flattened. Six sizeable barbels. Dark brown-buff with irregular brown patches. (Max. 12cm.)

Spined Loach Cobitidae *Cobitis taenia*. **Habitat:** Rare and localised in weedy, stagnant, slow-flowing rivers in parts of N. and central England. **Notes:** Small, elongate, laterally flattened. Six small barbels. Retractable spine in groove below eye. Yellowish with dark spots along flank. (Max. 11cm.)

Fish

Wels Siluridae *Silurus glanis*.
Habitat: Weedy lakes in the Midlands; very localised.
Notes: Flat head, 2 long barbels on upper jaw, 4 shorter on lower jaw. Tiny dorsal fin; long anal fin. (Max. 3m)

Eel Anguillidae *Anguilla anguilla*.
Habitat: In all non-polluted freshwater throughout British Isles. **Notes:** Elongate, cylindrical, without pelvic fins. In spring elvers invade freshwater from sea; are yellow until sexual maturity (up to 20 years). In autumn migrate back to sea, eyes enlarged, flanks silvery. (Max 1.5m.)

Burbot Gadidae *Lota lota*.
Habitat: Rare in slow-flowing rivers (lower reaches) and estuaries from Yorkshire to E. Anglia. **Notes:** Elongate, flat head, single chin barbel, 2 shorter nostril barbels. Very long anal and posterior dorsal fins. (Max. 1m.)

3-Spined Stickleback
Gasterosteidae *Gasterosteus aculeatus*. **Habitat:** Most freshwater bodies, some brackish estuaries, throughout most of British Isles. **Notes:** Three dorsal spines anterior to fin. Long caudal peduncle. Breeding male in May/June develops red throat and belly, and prominent pale blue eyes. (6cm.)

Freshwater Fish

10-Spined Stickleback
Gasterosteidae *Pungitius
pungitius*. **Habitat:** Most
freshwater bodies and brackish
estuaries; sporadically common
in England, Ireland, N. Wales,
central Scotland. **Notes:**
Usually 9 (7-12) dorsal spines
anterior to fin. (Max. 6cm.)

Perch Percidae *Perca fluviatilis*.
Habitat: Medium- and
slow-flowing rivers, canals,
lakes, throughout British Isles.
Notes: Anterior dorsal fin spiny,
separate from posterior fin. Very
hump-backed. Often
prominently striped. Ventral fins
red. (Max. 50cm.)

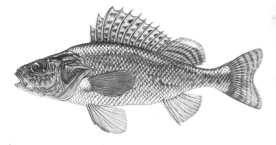

Pikeperch Percidae
Stizostedion lucioperca.
Habitat: Weedy lakes,
slow-flowing rivers; locally
common, spreading from
Midland lakes and E. Anglian
rivers and dykes. **Notes:** Also
called Zander. First dorsal fin
spiny, separate from second.
Prominent, sharp teeth.
(Max. 1m.)

Ruffe Percidae *Gymnocephalus
cernua*. **Habitat:** Medium- and
slow-flowing rivers, canals,
some lakes in England, except in
W. **Notes:** Also called Pope.
Small, anterior dorsal fin spiny
and continuous with posterior
fin. (Max. 25cm.)

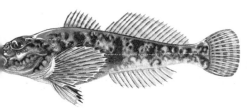

Bullhead Cottidae *Cottus
gobio*. **Habitat:** Stony rivers and
streams, some lakes in Britain
south of the Clyde. **Notes:** Also
called Miller's Thumb. Small
with broad head. Two dorsal
fins. (Max. 10cm.)

Amphibians and Reptiles

These are "cold-blooded" (poikilothermic) animals, whose activity is governed by environmental temperature. Thus in winter they are torpid and rarely seen. Their growth and breeding success also depend on temperature and consequently amphibians and reptiles are both more abundant and more diverse in the warmer regions of Europe. The species illustrated here occur in the cooler, more northerly parts of Europe; many more species are found in the Mediterranean area.

Amphibians

Amphibians have a soft, moist skin which offers only limited protection from water loss and which therefore restricts their habitat to damp places. Moreover, they normally need to lay their eggs in water, so are rarely found far from rivers and ponds. An amphibian's skin contains poison-secreting cells which help provide some protection against predators, but the poison is not normally harmful to humans.

Adult frogs, toads, salamanders and newts are not difficult to distinguish, but their aquatic larvae (tadpoles) are often very similar. Except in the breeding season, when male newts take on bright, distinctive colours, males and females of Britain's three species of newts are difficult to tell apart. Amphibians are normally silent but breeding male marsh and edible frogs make a very loud noise indeed.

Reptiles have a scaly skin which is quite dry to the touch. This offers full protection against water loss, so snakes and lizards are able to live in very dry regions. In fact, they thrive in hot, dry habitats and frequently bask in the sun.

Reptiles

Most reptiles lay eggs on land but at least two European species are viviparous, giving birth to living young. this adaptation has enabled these species to live in cooler areas at higher altitudes and further north than most. Most species are absent from Ireland and many Scottish islands.

Reptiles, like adult amphibians, are carnivorous and swallow their prey whole. Only one species (the adder) is poisonous, but its bite is rarely fatal to humans.

The different species are not difficult to identify provided they stay still long enough for their colours and form to be noted; usually they disappear from sight remarkably quickly. The slow-worm may be mistaken for a snake at a distance. It is, in fact, a legless lizard, quite harmless and gentle, and shares with other lizards the habit of shedding its tail if it is held roughly (which it then regrows). Unlike snakes, the slow-worm also has eyelids.

Right: A grass snake guards her brood of eggs. Though it has a preference for eating frogs and frequents wet places, it finds a warm dry spot in which to rear its young.

A female great crested newt deposits her eggs on a water plant. They will hatch into "newtpoles" and appear to be very similar to the tadpoles of frogs and toads.

Amphibians and Reptiles

Common (Smooth) Newt
Salamandridae *Triturus vulgaris*.
Habitat: Lowland wetlands,
especially weed-filled ponds, in
England, Wales and W.
Scotland; local in Ireland and E.
Scotland. **Notes:** Hibernates
October to March. (Max. 11cm)
Males of all 3 newts shown have
very distinctive breeding
colours; but rest of year male
looks more like female.

Crested Newt Salamandridae
Triturus cristatus. **Habitat:** Rare
and local, in ponds and slow-
moving streams in England and
Wales. **Notes:** Warty skin. Has
long, ragged dorsal crest in
breeding season. Largest British
newt. Hibernates September to
March. (15cm)

Palmate Newt Salamandridae
Triturus helveticus. **Habitat:**
Wetlands, ponds and slow-
moving rivers from sea level to
upland lakes throughout Britain,
except Lincolnshire and the
Midlands. **Notes:** No spots on
throat. Has webbed feet during
breeding season. (Max. 9cm)

Common Salamander
Salamandridae *Salamandra
salamandra*. **Habitat:** Damp
woodland, near water,
sometimes in grassland, in
central and S. Europe; absent
from Britain. **Notes:** Also called
Fire Salamander. Slow-moving
with soft, moist scaleless skin.
Usually black with golden
blotches but may be yellow with
black spots. Nocturnal. (20-
28cm)

Common Toad Bufonidae *Bufo
bufo*. **Habitat:** Pools and slow-
moving streams in lowland
areas, gardens and parks,
throughout Britain; the only
amphibian on Orkney. **Notes:**
Dry, warty skin. Bulbous glands
behind eyes. Hibernates mid-
October to mid-March. (Max.
15cm)

Natterjack Toad Bufonidae *Bufo calamita*. **Habitat:** Very rare in pools on sandy heaths and damp sand dunes in N.W. Norfolk and parts of S. England. **Notes:** Yellow stripe along back. Warty skin; short legs. Hibernates October to February. (Max. 10cm)

Green Toad Bufonidae *Bufo viridis*. **Habitat:** Dry grassland, gardens and farmland in lowland E. and S.E. Europe; absent from Britain. **Notes:** Similar to Natterjack Toad, but usually lacks dorsal stripe. Pinkish with large irregular green blotches. (10cm; males smaller)

Spadefoot Toad Pelobatidae *Pelobates fuscus*. **Habitat:** Sandy lowland, especially farmland and gardens, in central and E. Europe; absent from Britain. **Notes:** Colour very variable. Rotund body with smooth skin. Pupil vertical. Small "spade" or scraper on hind foot. (Up to 8cm)

Yellow-bellied Toad Discoglossidae *Bombina variegata*. **Habitat:** Usually in water at edge of ponds, streams and puddles in central and S. Europe; a few, short-lived colonies have been artificially established in England in the past. **Notes:** Flattened, very warty, with bright orange belly, fingertips and thighs. Pupil heart-shaped. Nocturnal. (Up to 5cm)

Marsh Frog Ranidae *Rana ridibunda*. **Habitat:** Common only in Romney Marsh, where replaces Common Frog; absent elsewhere in British Isles. **Notes:** No black patch behind eye. Very loud call in breeding season. Hibernates mid-October to early April. (Max. 15cm)

Amphibians and Reptiles

Common Frog Ranidae *Rana temporaria*. **Habitat:** Common in wetland, bogs, ponds, parks, gardens, ditches and drains from sea level to 1000m throughout Britain, and especially in Ireland. Skin smooth. Long hind legs. Black patch behind eye. Hibernates mid-October to late February. (Max. 10cm)

Moor Frog *Rana arvalis* is similar but shorter-legged with more pointed snout. It is found in wetland, wet grassland and bogs in lowland N.E. Europe, but is absent from Britain.

Green Tree Frog Hylidae *Hyla arborea*. **Habitat:** Scrub and damp woodland near water, reed-beds, in most of Europe including small artificially established colonies in England. **Notes:** Bright, pale green often with dark stripe down flanks. Suckers on fingertips. Regularly climbs high in trees. Males call loudly in breeding season. Nocturnal. (Up to 5cm)

Common (Viviparous) Lizard Lacertidae *Lacerta vivipara*. **Habitat:** Common on heaths, grassland, woodland rides, gardens and hedgerows in England and Wales, most of Scotland and parts of Ireland. **Notes:** Slender. Belly orange in male, yellow in female. Hibernates mid-October to late February. (Max. 6.5cm)

Sand Lizard Lacertidae *Lacerta agilis*. **Habitat:** Rare on dry, sandy heaths in S. and W. England and sand dunes in N.W. **Notes:** Large heavy head. Males very green. Hibernates early October to late March. (Max. 9cm)

Slow Worm Anguidae *Anguis fragilis*. **Habitat:** Grassland, scrub, dry heaths, hedgerows and gardens throughout Britain; commoner in S. **Notes:** Not a snake because has eyelids and can shed tail. Shiny, metallic brown. Hibernates mid-October to late February. (Max. 50cm)

Grass Snake Colubridae *Natrix natrix*. **Habitat:** Widely distributed in grassland, deciduous woodland, hedgerows and wetland in England and Wales. **Notes:** Has distinctive yellow collar. Hibernates October to March. (120-200cm)

Smooth Snake Colubridae *Coronella austriaca*. **Habitat:** Very rare on dry sandy heaths; local in S. and W. England. **Notes:** Hibernates early October to late March. (60-80cm)

Adder Viperidae *Vipera berus*. **Habitat:** Dry heaths, deciduous woodland and moors in England and Wales; sparse in Scotland. **Notes:** Has characteristic zig-zag markings. Colour variable, coppery red to black. Hibernates early October to late February. (65-90cm)

Birds

About 450 species of birds are seen regularly in north west Europe, of which 180 or so normally breed in the British Isles. These include several dozen species which come to Britain in the summer and leave again after breeding. During the winter the resident population may be swelled by migrants arriving from Europe and the Arctic to avoid harsh conditions. These immigrants include about 30 species that are winter visitors only and do not nest here. Unusual weather conditions, especially prolonged easterly winds, may cause several normally non-British birds also to visit Britain in winter.

With practice, the identification of birds is not difficult. It is best not to rely on a single distinctive feature but to take note of as many features as possible about a bird's appearance, behaviour, song and habitat.

Description

The colour illustration of each species in the following pages indicates its general appearance and the notes beneath draw attention to distinctive features recognisable in the field, e.g. white wing patches. In many birds the female has a duller version of the male's plumage, but in some (e.g. ducks) the two sexes appear quite different. As an added complication

A tawny owl is superbly adapted to its nocturnal, predatory way of life. Excellent vision complements good hearing while its soft plumage lessens the sound of its approach to the unwary prey.

some male ducks change plumage in summer and resemble females. Adult gulls, terns, gannets and swans have white or very pale plumage, whereas the juveniles are browner and often look quite different. A few species also look different according to season.

Habitat

Some birds are characteristically associated with particular habitats but birds, perhaps more than any other group of animals, are very mobile and can, and do, range widely. Some species change their habitat with the seasons; waders, for example, nest on moorland in summer but spend the winter in the lowlands and on the coast. Similarly, tits, finches and ducks, which live in pairs in summer, gather in large flocks in winter.

Some habitats, particularly woodland, are three dimensional with different species characteristically associated with different "levels" (e.g. pigeons in the canopy, woodpeckers on trunks and branches, pheasants on the floor). Similarly, some

Useful aids to identification

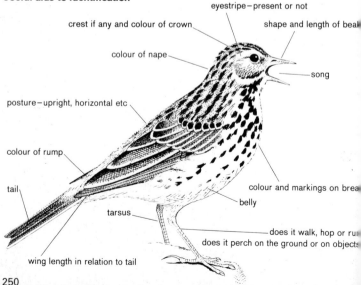

crest if any and colour of crown

colour of nape

posture—upright, horizontal etc

colour of rump

tail

tarsus

wing length in relation to tail

eyestripe—present or not

shape and length of beak

song

colour and markings on breast

belly

does it walk, hop or run

does it perch on the ground or on objects

Birds

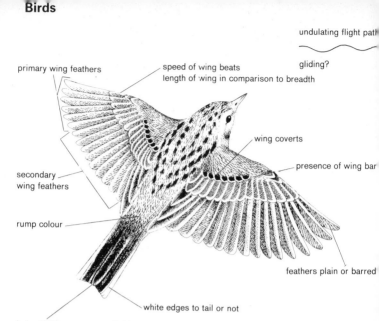

undulating flight path

gliding?

primary wing feathers

speed of wing beats
length of wing in comparison to breadth

wing coverts

presence of wing bar

secondary wing feathers

rump colour

feathers plain or barred

white edges to tail or not

forked tail? or square ended or rounded?

The great crested grebe is one of the British birds that have increased their numbers in recent years. Once exploited for their plumage, they now enjoy an increasing number of habitats of man-made reservoirs and flooded gravel pits.

ducks (e.g. pochard and tufted) prefer open water in the middle of ponds and lakes, while others (teal and mandarin) skulk in vegetation at the margins.

Status

Sometimes birds are described as "common" or "rare" as a guide to the likelihood of their being seen. "Common" and "abundant" birds are those which are likely to be seen without any special search. "Scarce" birds need searching for and will not be seen often. "Rare" species are normally only seen by accident or after a careful and deliberate search. Bear in mind that a species may be common in its normal habitat, but very rare elsewhere (e.g. coots are common on ponds and lakes, but not at sea).

Distribution

The notes suggest where a species is most likely to be found (e.g. golden plover in the north and west). But they *can* occur elsewhere, especially at different seasons. Obviously a migrant species like the osprey might be seen en route to its normal home in Scotland. Such species are referred to as "passage migrants".

Size

Size is often difficult to assess, especially at a distance or through binoculars. It is often useful to compare a bird to something whose approximate size is known (e.g. a bramble leaf, gate post, cockle shell). Sizes given in the notes are approximate lengths from tip of beak to tip of tail. "Small" or "tiny" means sparrow-sized or smaller. "Very big" means that sheer size rather than colour or behaviour is the most immediately striking feature.

Sounds

Songs and alarm calls are very difficult to describe, yet they are often the most distinctive and easiest recognition feature to use. Recognising a bird by its song only comes with practice; the notes draw attention to some of the most characteristic sounds of certain species.

Behaviour

Often posture, gait and flight patterns and other behavioural details are more easily recognised and more distinctive than colours, and will help to distinguish between birds whose outline and colours are very similar.

Many of Britain's birds are only here temporarily, migrating in and out according to season. The Bewick's swans fly in each winter from their breeding grounds in Siberia, to exploit our unfrozen water sites. Other migrants fly in for a summer's profitable feeding and breeding.

Black-throated Diver
winter

Black-throated Diver Gaviidae *Gavia arctica*. **Habitat:** Breed on large lakes in N.W. Scotland winters on coasts in S.E. England; rare. **Notes:** Bill mo slender than Great Northern Diver's. (56-58cm.)

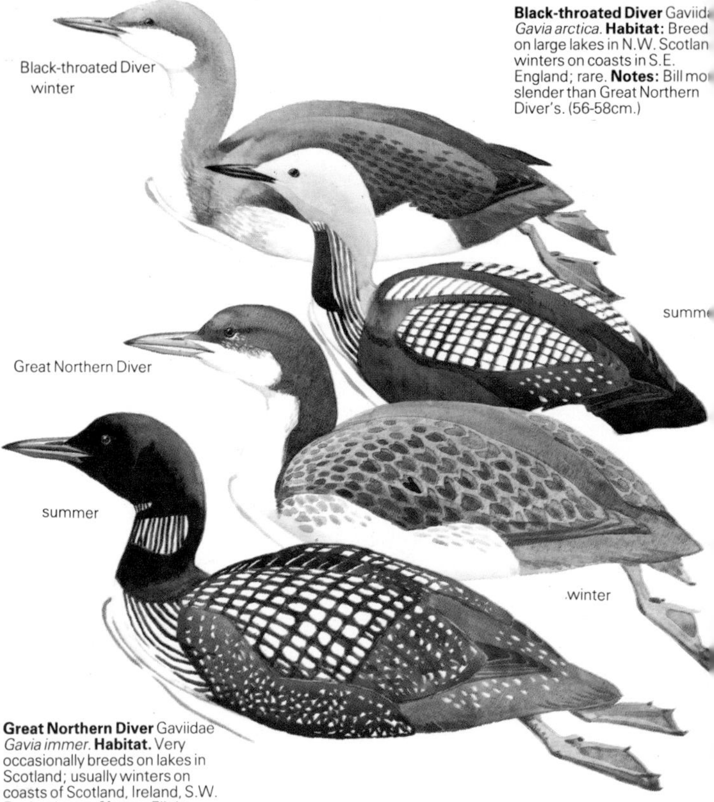

summe

Great Northern Diver

summer

winter

Great Northern Diver Gaviidae *Gavia immer*. **Habitat.** Very occasionally breeds on lakes in Scotland; usually winters on coasts of Scotland, Ireland, S.W. England; rare. **Notes:** Flight strong, but take-off difficult. (68-81cm.)

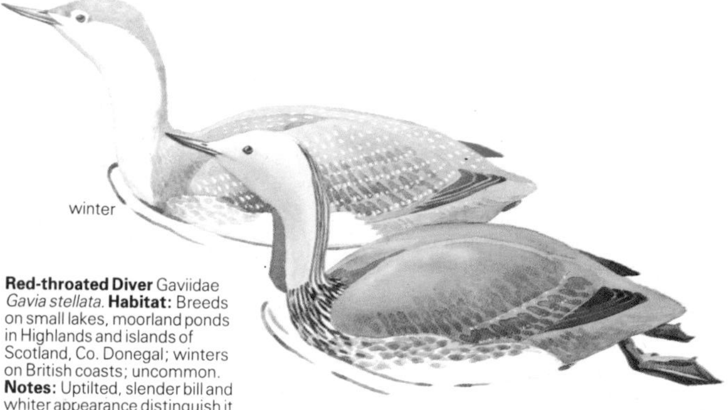

winter

Red-throated Diver Gaviidae *Gavia stellata*. **Habitat:** Breeds on small lakes, moorland ponds in Highlands and islands of Scotland, Co. Donegal; winters on British coasts; uncommon. **Notes:** Uptilted, slender bill and whiter appearance distinguish it from other divers in summer. (53-58cm.)

summer

Great Crested Grebe winter

Great Crested Grebe
Podicipedidae *Podiceps cristatus*. **Habitat:** Lakes, reservoirs, sheltered coasts, estuaries and lagoons in winter, in British Isles south of central Scotland. **Notes:** White wing-patches conspicuous in flight. Loses distinctive hood in winter. (48cm.)

Great Crested Grebe
summer

Red-necked Grebe
Podicipedidae *Podiceps grisegena*. **Habitat:** Chiefly sheltered coasts, sometimes lakes and reservoirs in E. Britain; rare winter visitor. **Notes:** Distinguished in winter from Great Crested Grebe by darker neck and black-tipped, yellow bill. Flight similar. (43cm.)

Red-necked Grebe
summer

Black-necked Grebe
winter

winter

summer

Slavonian Grebe
winter

Slavonian Grebe
Podicipedidae *Podiceps auritus*. **Habitat:** Rarely breeds on lakes and ponds in N.E. Scotland; winters on shallow lakes, coasts and estuaries around Britain. **Notes:** In winter distinguished from Black-necked Grebe by white cheeks and straight bill. (33cm.)

winter

Black-necked Grebe
Podicipedidae *Podiceps nigricollis*. **Habitat:** Breeds on lakes and ponds with thick vegetation in central Scotland; winters on shallow lakes and coasts in E. and S. Britain; uncommon. **Notes:** White wing-patch longer than Slavonian Grebe's in flight; dark wing-tips. Slightly uptilted bill. Winter plumage similar to other grebes. (30cm.)

summer

summer

Little Grebe Podicipedidae *Tachybaptus ruficollis*. **Habitat:** Breeds on lakes, ponds, reservoirs, slow-flowing rivers throughout British Isles; more coastal in winter. **Notes:** Stocky. No wing-patch visible in flight. In winter, resembles other grebes. (27cm.)

Birds

Manx Shearwater
Procellariidae *Puffinus puffinus*.
Habitat: Coastal waters and
remote islands and cliffs around
W. Britain and Ireland;
uncommon summer visitor.
Notes: Nocturnal at colonies,
spends day in nesting burrows
or fishing at sea. Long-winged,
slender-bodied. (35cm.)

juvenile

Gannet

adult

Cormorant Phalacrocoracidae
Phalacrocorax carbo. **Habitat:**
Common on coastal waters,
estuaries, inland lakes and
wetlands, all round British Isles.
Notes: White patch
on thighs in breeding
season; white throat.
Flight swift
and heavy;
rapid wing-beats.
(90cm.)

Gannet Sulidae *Sula bassana*.
Habitat: Breeds on islands,
occasionally mainland cliffs in
Scotland; migrant in rest of
Britain and Ireland. **Notes:** Long
wings with black tips. Feeds by
diving from a height. Immature
bird dark grey with white
speckles. (90cm.)

Shag Phalacrocoracidae
Phalacrocorax aristotelis.
Habitat: Coastal waters off
rocky coasts and islands in
Britain and Ireland, but rare
between Cleveland and Solent.
Notes: Crest on head in

breeding season. Faster wing-
beats and slimmer head and
neck than Cormorant.
Distinctive bottle-green gloss in
sunlight; no white throat patch.
(76cm.)

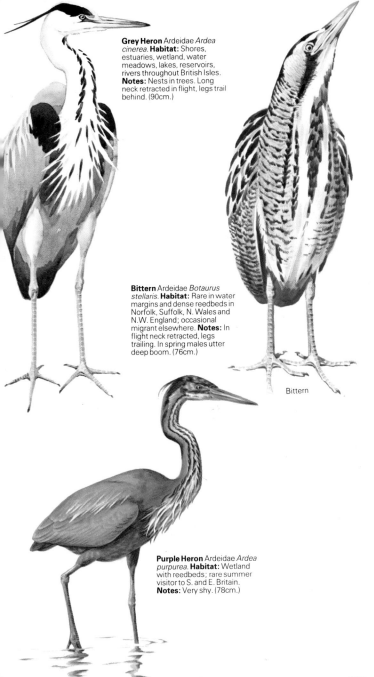

Grey Heron Ardeidae *Ardea cinerea*. **Habitat:** Shores, estuaries, wetland, water meadows, lakes, reservoirs, rivers throughout British Isles. **Notes:** Nests in trees. Long neck retracted in flight, legs trail behind. (90cm.)

Bittern Ardeidae *Botaurus stellaris*. **Habitat:** Rare in water margins and dense reedbeds in Norfolk, Suffolk, N. Wales and N.W. England; occasional migrant elsewhere. **Notes:** In flight neck retracted, legs trailing. In spring males utter deep boom. (76cm.)

Bittern

Purple Heron Ardeidae *Ardea purpurea*. **Habitat:** Wetland with reedbeds; rare summer visitor to S. and E. Britain. **Notes:** Very shy. (78cm.)

Birds

White-fronted Goose Anatidae *Anser albifrons.* **Habitat:** Grassland, wetland, water meadows and salt marshes in Ireland, W. Scotland, S.W. England and Wales; winter visitor. **Notes:** Juveniles lack bars on belly and white bill base. (66-76cm.)

Greylag Goose Anatidae *Anser anser.* **Habitat:** Breeds on moors in N.W. Scotland and in a few feral colonies in England; winter visitor to farmland, grassland, wetland and estuaries in N. and E. Britain and Ireland. **Notes:** Resembles other grey geese, but has orange beak and legs. (76-89cm.)

Spoonbill Threskiornithidae *Platalea leucorodia.* **Habitat:** Rare in wetland and reedbeds, coastal lagoons, estuaries in E. Anglia; passage migrant only. **Notes:** White colour and distinctive bill are diagnostic. Juveniles have black wing-tips. (86cm.)

White Stork Ciconiidae *Ciconia ciconia.* **Habitat:** Wetland, grassland; rare summer visitor to S. Britain. **Notes:** All white except black flight feathers and eye patch. Nests on roof-tops in Europe. (1m.)

Barnacle Goose Anatidae *Branta leucopsis*. **Habitat:** Coastal farmland and meadows in W. Scotland and Ireland; winter visitor. **Notes:** Easily recognised by contrasting plumage. (58-69cm.)

Brent Goose Anatidae *Branta bernicla*. **Habitat:** Mudflats and saltings on British E. and S. coasts; winter visitor. **Notes:** Neck and head black apart from whitish neck patch. (56-61cm.)

Canada Goose Anatidae *Branta canadensis*. **Habitat:** Lakes (natural and manmade), wetland and grassland near water in England and Wales; breeds in S. Britain; rare in Scotland and Ireland. **Notes:** Browner than other "black" geese. Sociable. (92-102cm.)

Bewick's Swan Anatidae *Cygnus columbianus*. **Habitat:** Lakes, rivers, flooded grassland and sheltered coasts mainly in England; rare winter visitor. **Notes:** Smaller yellow area on bill than Whooper Swan. Loud, honking call in flight. (122cm.)

Whooper Swan Anatidae *Cygnus cygnus*. **Habitat:** Breeds occasionally on moorland lakes and wetland in N. Scotland; mainly a scarce winter visitor to sheltered coasts and estuaries in N. Britain and Ireland. **Notes:** Large yellow area on bill. Neck held erect. A trumpeting "whoop-whoop" call; very vocal. (152cm.)

Mute Swan Anatidae *Cygnus olor*. **Habitat:** Common on well-vegetated lakes and rivers, sheltered coasts and estuaries throughout British Isles. **Notes:** Orange bill. Audible "sighing" sound in flight. (152cm.)

Birds

Bean Goose Anatidae *Anser fabalis.* **Habitat:** Wetland and water meadows in S.W. Scotland, Northumberland and E. Anglia; scarce winter visitor. **Notes:** Browner than other grey geese; orange legs. (71-89cm.)

Pink-footed Goose Anatidae *Anser brachyrhynchus.* **Habitat:** Farmland and wetland in central Scotland, Lincolnshire and E. Anglia; winter visitor. **Notes:** Distinguished from Bean Goose by pale, blue-grey upper parts; legs pink; head noticeably darker than body. (61-76cm.)

Mallard Anatidae *Anas platyrhynchos.* **Habitat:** Common on lakes, ponds, rivers, wetland throughout British Isles. **Notes:** White-bordered blue speculum visible in flight. Drake resembles duck in summer eclipse. Feeds at surface and by upending. (58cm.)

♂
Mallard

♀ Gadwall

Gadwall Anatidae *Anas strepera.* **Habitat:** Lakes, ponds, rivers and wetlands; breeds in England; winters throughout British Isles, except Scotland; uncommon. **Notes:** Dull plumage with black under tail. Black and white speculum. Surface feeder. (51cm.)

♂

♀

♂
Pintail

Pintail Anatidae *Anas acuta.* **Habitat:** Breeds on shallow lakes in Scotland and E. England; winters on coasts and estuaries throughout British Isles; uncommon. **Notes:** Male has green and white speculum; female has brown speculum. Long tail and long, thin neck distinctive in flight. (26cm.)

Eider Anatidae *Somateria mollissima.* **Habitat:** Common on coastal waters and offshore islands in N. Britain and Ireland; a few summer and winter in S. **Notes:** Diving duck. (58cm.)

♀

♂

Red-breasted Merganser Anatidae *Mergus serrator.* **Habitat:** Breeds on lakes and rivers in N.W. Scotland, Lake District and Ireland; widespread along sheltered coasts in winter. **Notes:** Large white wing-patches in flight. (58cm.)

♀

Red-breasted Merganser

♂

♀

Goosander ♂

Goosander Anatidae *Mergus merganser.* **Habitat:** Breeds and winters on lakes, reservoirs and large rivers, occasionally on estuaries in N. Britain and Wales; in S. in winter; uncommon. **Notes:** Appears very white in flight and when swimming. Feeds by diving. (66cm.)

♀

♂

Smew Anatidae *Mergus albellus.* **Habitat:** Large lakes, reservoirs and rivers in S. England; uncommon winter visitor. **Notes:** Female distinguished from grebes by white throat and cheeks. Diving duck. (41cm.)

Shelduck Anatidae *Tadorna tadorna.* **Habitat:** Coastal; sandy and muddy shores, estuaries, sand-dunes, around British Isles. **Notes:** Late summer moult in Germany, but a few go to Bridgewater Bay. Sexes similar all year. (61cm.)

Shelduck

Birds

Teal Anatidae *Anas crecca*.
Habitat: Breeds on small ponds
and streams on heaths and
moors; winters on lakes,
reservoirs and wetland
(generally skulks round margins)
throughout British Isles;
common. **Notes:** Yellow thigh
patch in male very distinctive. In
autumn male resembles
female. Both sexes have green
speculum. Feeds at surface.
(35cm.)

Teal

♀

♀

♂

♂

Garganey Anatidae *Anas
querquedula*. **Habitat:** Shallow
lakes and wetland in England
and Wales; uncommon
summer visitor. **Notes:** Both
sexes have blue-grey forewing
and green speculum in flight.
Feeds at surface. (38cm.)

Wigeon

♀

Wigeon Anatidae *Anas
penelope*. **Habitat:** Breeds on
lakes in N. Scotland; winters on
coastal lagoons and estuaries
throughout British Isles. **Notes:**
Conspicuous white patch and
green speculum on wings in
flight. Surface feeder, and often
comes ashore to graze grass.
(46cm.)

♂

♀

♂

Scaup Anatidae *Aythya marila*.
Habitat: Occasionally nests on
lochs in Scotland; winters on
coasts and estuaries around
British Isles; uncommon.
Notes: Diving duck. (48cm.)

♀

♂

Tufted Duck Anatidae *Aythya
fuligula*. **Habitat:** Breeds on
lakes, ponds, slow-flowing
rivers in E. Britain; winters in
larger lakes throughout British
Isles; common. **Notes:** Male
distinguished from Scaup by
black back; female by smaller
white facial mark; found inland
more than Scaup. Diving duck.
(43cm.)

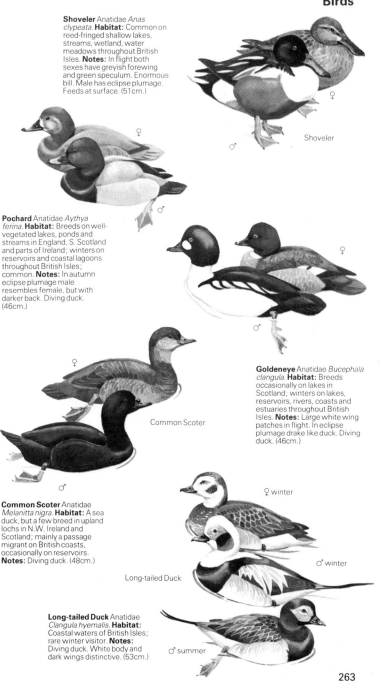

Shoveler Anatidae *Anas clypeata*. **Habitat:** Common on reed-fringed shallow lakes, streams, wetland, water meadows throughout British Isles. **Notes:** In flight both sexes have greyish forewing and green speculum. Enormous bill. Male has eclipse plumage. Feeds at surface. (51cm.)

♀

♂

Shoveler

Pochard Anatidae *Aythya ferina*. **Habitat:** Breeds on well-vegetated lakes, ponds and streams in England, S. Scotland and parts of Ireland; winters on reservoirs and coastal lagoons throughout British Isles; common. **Notes:** In autumn eclipse plumage male resembles female, but with darker back. Diving duck. (46cm.)

♀

♂

♀

♂

Goldeneye Anatidae *Bucephala clangula*. **Habitat:** Breeds occasionally on lakes in Scotland; winters on lakes, reservoirs, rivers, coasts and estuaries throughout British Isles. **Notes:** Large white wing patches in flight. In eclipse plumage drake like duck. Diving duck. (46cm.)

♀

Common Scoter

♂

Common Scoter Anatidae *Melanitta nigra*. **Habitat:** A sea duck, but a few breed in upland lochs in N.W. Ireland and Scotland; mainly a passage migrant on British coasts, occasionally on reservoirs. **Notes:** Diving duck. (48cm.)

♀ winter

♂ winter

Long-tailed Duck

Long-tailed Duck Anatidae *Clangula hyemalis*. **Habitat:** Coastal waters of British Isles; rare winter visitor. **Notes:** Diving duck. White body and dark wings distinctive. (53cm.)

♂ summer

Velvet Scoter Anatidae *Melanitta fusca*. **Habitat:** Sea duck; on N. and E. coasts of Britain; rare winter visitor. **Notes:** Male black; female dark brown with two pale patches on face. (55cm.)

Velvet Scoter

Water Rail Rallidae *Rallus aquaticus*. **Habitat:** Wetland, reedbeds, water margins, ditches, sewage farms throughout British Isles; fairly common but not often seen. **Notes:** Long red bill; distinctive banded flanks. Dangling legs in flight. A skulking bird. Voice: a variety of groans, grunts and squeaks, often heard at night. (28cm.)

Moorhen Rallidae *Gallinula chloropus*. **Habitat:** Common on wetland, small lakes, ponds, slow-flowing rivers, water margins in areas with good vegetation cover throughout British Isles. **Notes:** Jerks tail when nervous. Swims with jerking head. Flight laboured with legs dangling or projecting behind tail (33cm.)

Moorhen

Coot Rallidae *Fulica atra*. **Habitat:** Common on reedy ponds, lakes and slow-flowing rivers; reservoirs and estuaries in winter; throughout British Isles. **Notes:** Large "scalloped" toes project in flight like long "tail". Patters along water before taking off. (38cm.)

Coot

Spotted Crake Rallidae *Porzana porzana*. **Habitat:** Wetland; uncommon summer visitor and passage migrant to W. Britain. **Notes:** When disturbed raises tail to display buff undertail coverts. Skulking and rarely seen. (23cm.)

Corncrake Rallidae *Crex crex*. **Habitat:** Grassland and hay meadows; breeds mainly in Scotland and Ireland, very rarely in Wales and England; rare summer visitor. **Notes:** Chestnut wings and dangling legs obvious in flight. Prefers to run and stay out of sight. Voice: a rasping, continuous "crek-crek", often heard at night. (27cm.)

Crane Gruidae *Grus grus*.
Habitat: Wetland in E. England;
very rare summer visitor.
Notes: Long-legged and long
necked with distinctive dancing
courtship display. (113cm.)

Avocet Recurvirostridae
Recurvirostra avosetta.
Habitat: Breeds on dried out
lagoons in salt marshes in
Suffolk; winters on estuaries
and salt marshes in S. and W.
England; uncommon. **Notes:**
Black and white pattern
conspicuous in flight, when legs
project beyond tail. Gait a
graceful, quick walk. Usually
solitary, except at breeding
sites. (43cm.)

Oystercatcher
Haematopodidae *Haematopus
ostralegus*. **Habitat:** Breeds on
beaches, shingle spits,
estuaries, lakes, rivers and
moors from E. Anglia north;
winters on coasts; common.
Notes: Black and white wings
and tail conspicuous in flight.
Legs orange. Flattened
orange-red bill. Wing-
beats shallow.
Usually sociable.
(43cm.)

Stone-curlew Burhinidae
Burhinus oedicnemus. **Habitat:**
Chalk grassland, sandy heaths,
wasteground, arable farmland in
S. and E. England; rare summer
visitor. **Notes:** Two whitish
wing-bars obvious in flight. Slow
wing-beats with trailing legs.
Runs furtively. Mainly active at
night and dawn. (41cm.)

Lapwing Charadriidae *Vanel[l]
vanellus*. **Habitat:** Common o
grassland, hay meadows,
farmland, moors; in winter in
water margins, mud flats,
estuaries; throughout British
Isles. **Notes:** Tail white with
black terminal band. Broad
rounded wings and leisurely,
often erratic flight.

Kentish Plover Charadriidae
Charadrius alexandrinus.
Habitat: Sandy and muddy
coasts in S.E. England; very rare
passage migrant. **Notes:**
Distinguished from other
plovers by black legs, white tail
sides, paler upper parts. (16cm.)

Ringed Plover

Little Ringed Plover
Charadriidae *Charadrius dubius*.
Habitat: Rivers, lakes (including
gravel pits), in S. and central
England; rare summer visitor.
Notes: Distinguished from
Ringed Plover by lack of white
wing-bar, flesh-coloured legs
and white line above black
forehead band. Solitary or in
pairs. (15cm.)

Ringed Plover Charadriidae
Charadrius hiaticula. **Habitat:**
Breeds on shingle, sand and
muddy shores and estuaries in
British Isles; also on lakes and
sewage farms in N. **Notes:**
Active, running with brief
pauses. Tilts to pick up food.
Flight rapid and low, white wing-
bar conspicuous. Solitary or in
small groups. (19cm.)

winter

summer

Grey Plover Charadriidae
Pluvialis squatarola. **Habitat:**
Sandy shores, estuaries,
occasionally uplands inland;
passage migrant and winter
visitor to British Isles. **Notes:**
Conspicuous black "armpits" in
flight. Has dejected, hunched
appearance on ground. Usually
in flocks. (28cm.)

summer

winter

Golden Plover Charadriidae
Pluvialis apricaria. **Habitat:**
Upland grassland and moors in
summer from S. Pennines
north; water meadows,
farmland, estuaries, shores in
winter throughout British Isles.
Notes: Undersurface of wings
white. Flight rapid, often in
flocks during winter. (28cm.)

Ruff Scolopacidae *Philomachus pugnax*. **Habitat:** Breeds in water meadows and wetland in Cambridgeshire; in winter found in water margins on lakeshores (including gravel pits), sewage farms in S.; uncommon. **Notes:** In winter distinguished from Redshank by dark tail with oval white patch on each side. Leg colour varies. (28cm.)

Ruff summer ♂

Ruff ♀

winter

Turnstone summer

Dotterel Charadriidae *Charadrius morinellus*. **Habitat:** Barren open upland and mountains above 780m in central Scottish Highlands; uncommon summer visitor. **Notes:** Winter adults are paler but retain eye-stripes and pectoral band. Often very tame. Flight rapid. (22cm.)

Turnstone Scolopacidae *Arenaria interpres*. **Habitat:** Shores and estuary mouths, around British Isles; principally a winter visitor, but non-breeding birds occur in summer in many areas. **Notes:** "Tortoiseshell" plumage replaced by dusky brown in winter. Flies reluctantly and only for short distances. Turns stones when seeking food, usually at edge of water. Usually in small groups (23cm.)

Snipe Scolopacidae *Gallinago gallinago*. **Habitat:** Wetland, water meadows, rivers throughout British Isles. **Notes:** Secretive, usually solitary. Long beak and streaked back distinctive. Zig-zag flight when flushed. White-edged tail; tail feathers produce vibrating sounds in swooping display flight. (27cm.)

Snipe

Jack Snipe Scolopacidae *Lymnocryptes minimus*. **Habitat:** Wetland and water meadows throughout British Isles; rare winter visitor. **Notes:** Distinguished from Snipe by smaller size, shorter bill and slower, more direct flight; no white on tail. (19cm.)

Woodcock Scolopacidae *Scolopax rusticola*. **Habitat:** Deciduous woodland in damp areas, wet heaths, throughout British Isles. **Notes:** Mainly crepuscular; well camouflaged and rarely seen except in flight. Distinguished from Snipe by thicker bill and more rounded wings. Flight noisy and dodging, except during slow display flight above trees. Solitary. (34cm.)

Birds

Purple Sandpiper

summer

winter

Dunlin

Little Stint

winter

summer

Knot Scolopacidae *Calidris canutus*. **Habitat:** Sandy and rocky shores and estuaries around British Isles; passage migrant and winter visitor. **Notes:** Distinguished from Dunlin and Sanderling by pale wing-bars, pale rump and tail. Often in large, compact flocks. (25cm.)

Purple Sandpiper Scolopacidae *Calidris maritima*. **Habitat:** Rocky shores, weed-covered piers and groynes; winter visitor and passage migrant to British Isles. **Notes:** Short, yellow legs give portly appearance. Narrow white wing-bars. Flight swift, direct, of short duration. Usually in small groups. (21cm.)

Little Stint Scolopacidae *Calidris minuta*. **Habitat:** Estuaries, reservoirs, lakes and sewage farms in S. and E.; scarce passage migrant. **Notes:** In winter upper parts cold grey. Flight rapid. Narrow wing-bars and grey sides to tail. Solitary, tiny wader. (13cm.)

Dunlin Scolopacidae *Calidris alpina*. **Habitat:** Breeds on grassland and moors in Scotland and N. England; elsewhere passage and winter visitor to estuaries and shores; common. **Notes:** Wheel and twist in flocks, alternately showing white undersides then darker upper parts. Prominent black belly in summer. "Hunched up" when feeding. Usually in groups, often large numbers. (18cm.)

Curlew Sandpiper

summer

winter

Curlew Sandpiper Scolopacidae *Calidris ferruginea*. **Habitat:** Estuaries and mud flats in S. Britain; passage migrant. **Notes:** Distinguished from the more common Dunlin by white rump, more elegant, upright posture, paler breast and brighter eye-stripe. (19cm.)

Sanderling Scolopacidae *Calidris alba*. **Habitat:** Sandy shores around British Isles; uncommon winter passage migrant. **Notes:** Very active bird, almost ceaseless in movements. Almost white in winter. Reluctant to take off. Wing-bars bright white. (20cm.)

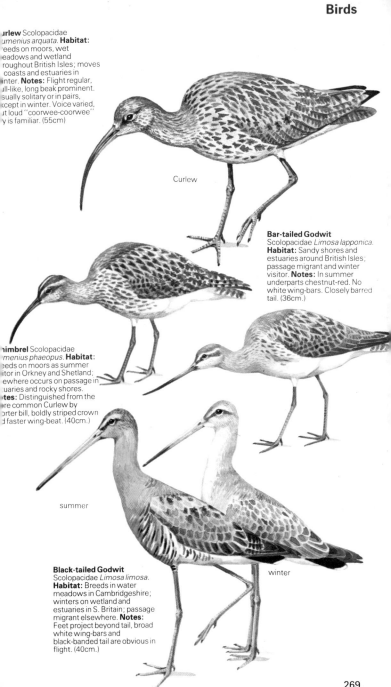

[C]urlew Scolopacidae
[Nu]menius arquata. **Habitat:**
[Br]eeds on moors, wet
[m]eadows and wetland
[th]roughout British Isles; moves
[to] coasts and estuaries in
[wi]nter. **Notes:** Flight regular,
[gu]ll-like, long beak prominent.
[U]sually solitary or in pairs,
[ex]cept in winter. Voice varied,
[bu]t loud "coorwee-coorwee"
[cr]y is familiar. (55cm)

Curlew

Bar-tailed Godwit
Scolopacidae Limosa lapponica.
Habitat: Sandy shores and
estuaries around British Isles;
passage migrant and winter
visitor. **Notes:** In summer
underparts chestnut-red. No
white wing-bars. Closely barred
tail. (36cm.)

[W]himbrel Scolopacidae
[Nu]menius phaeopus. **Habitat:**
[Br]eeds on moors as summer
[vis]itor in Orkney and Shetland;
[els]ewhere occurs on passage in
[est]uaries and rocky shores.
[No]tes: Distinguished from the
[mo]re common Curlew by
[sh]orter bill, boldly striped crown
[an]d faster wing-beat. (40cm.)

summer

Black-tailed Godwit
Scolopacidae Limosa limosa.
Habitat: Breeds in water
meadows in Cambridgeshire;
winters on wetland and
estuaries in S. Britain; passage
migrant elsewhere. **Notes:**
Feet project beyond tail, broad
white wing-bars and
black-banded tail are obvious in
flight. (40cm.)

winter

Birds

Green Sandpiper Scolopacidae *Tringa ochropus*. **Habitat:** Wetland, ponds, streams and ditches in S. England, Wales and Ireland; uncommon passage migrant and winter visitor. **Notes:** Dark upper parts, white rump and black underwings obvious in flight. Tail barred black near tip. Usually solitary. (23cm.)

Wood Sandpiper Scolopacidae *Tringa glareola*. **Habitat:** Wetland, water margins, wet woodland, sewage farms in N.E. Scotland; uncommon passage migrant. **Notes:** White rump and projecting feet obvious in flight. No wing-bars. Usually solitary. (20cm.)

Wood Sandpiper

Common Sandpiper

Common Sandpiper Scolopacidae *Actitis hypoleucos*. **Habitat:** Lakeshores and fast-flowing streams in N. and W. Britain north of mid-Wales; also in wetland and on coasts during migration; summer visitor. **Notes:** Distinctive bobbing when perched. White flash under tail in flight. (19cm.)

Redshank Scolopacidae *Tringa totanus*. **Habitat:** Breeds on water meadows, moors and wetland; winters on salt marshes and estuaries throughout British Isles; common. **Notes:** White rump and hind edge of wings conspicuous in flight. Legs bright orange. When uneasy often "bobs".(28cm.)

Spotted Redshank winter

Greenshank Scolopacidae *Tringa nebularia*. **Habitat:** Breeds on moorland lakes in N.W. Highlands of Scotland; winters on estuaries in S. Britain as uncommon passage migrant and winter visitor. **Notes:** Distinguished from Redshank by lack of wing-bar and white rump extending up lower back. Legs project beyond tail in flight. Usually solitary. (30cm.)

Spotted Redshank Scolopacidae *Tringa erythropus*. **Habitat:** Coastal lagoons, salt marsh and estuaries in S. Britain; uncommon passage migrant and winter visitor. **Notes:** Black plumage unmistakable in summer. Distinguished from Redshank by lack of wing-bar and projecting legs beyond tail in flight. (30cm.)

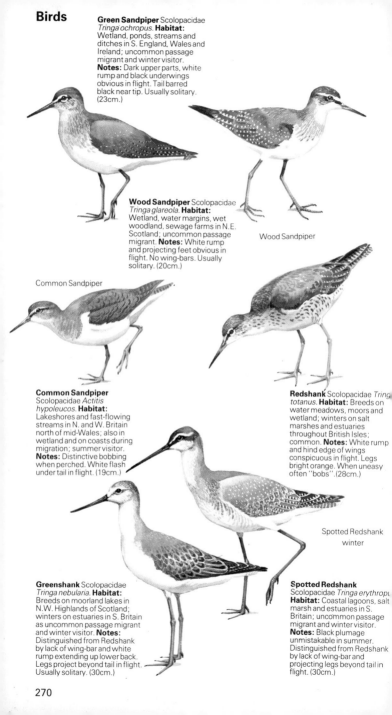

Great Skua Stercorariidae *Stercorarius skua*. **Habitat:** Open sea; breeds on moors and upland grassland on offshore islands and in Scotland; scarce passage migrant elsewhere. **Notes:** Distinguished from Arctic Skua by blunt tail, conspicuous white wing-patches and broad, rounded wings. Dashing, hawk-like flight. Could be confused with mottled brown juvenile gulls, but these are generally paler, with thicker beaks and pink legs. (58cm.)

Arctic Skua
dark phase

Arctic Skua Stercorariidae *Stercorarius parasiticus*. **Habitat:** Open sea; breeds on moors and upland grassland on offshore islands and in N. Scotland; scarce passage migrant elsewhere. **Notes:** Flight graceful and hawk-like. Pursues other sea-birds. Wings pointed with white flash at tip. Long, pointed tail projection. (45cm.)

Arctic Skua
light phase

summer ♀

winter

Grey Phalarope Scolopacidae *Phalaropus fulicarius*. **Habitat:** Coastal Britain, occasionally lakes. Passage migrant. **Notes:** Regularly swims buoyantly, looking like miniature gull. "Spins" when feeding. Takes off reluctantly and flies only short distances. (20cm)

winter

Red-necked Phalarope Scolopacidae *Phalaropus lobatus*. **Habitat:** Occasionally breeds on wetland in Scotland; elsewhere a scarce summer visitor and passage migrant, often near coasts. **Notes:** Bobs and dips beak in water, gyrating in circles; a restless, frantic behaviour. Swims, unlike most waders. In summer female much brighter coloured than male. (17cm.)

Birds

juvenile

Little Gull Laridae *Larus minutus*. **Habitat:** Coasts, wetland, reservoirs in E. England; rare winter visitor. **Notes:** Smallest European gull. Tern-like in flight, picks insects from water surface. (28cm.)

winter

Mediterranean Gull Laridae *Larus melanocephalus*. **Habitat:** Coastal; very rare summer visitor. **Notes:** In summer head black. Differs from very common Black-headed Gull in having r black on wing-tips. (38cm.)

Lesser Black-backed Gull Laridae *Larus fuscus*. **Habita** Breeds on cliffs on N. and W. coasts, islands, moors, and house roofs in coastal towns frequents rubbish tips; comm passage migrant and summe visitor. **Notes:** Grey back, yellow legs. Flight powerful, usually with much gliding. (53cm.)

and islands in British Isles, except E.; also on estuaries, lakes and inland in winter. **Notes:** Distinguished from Lesser Black-backed Gull by black back, pink legs, larger size and deeper voice. Fiercely predatory. Usually solitary or in pairs. (65cm.)

Great Black-backed Gull Laridae *Larus marinus*. **Habitat:** Breeds on cliffs on rocky coasts

juvenile

Glaucous Gull Laridae *Larus hyperboreus*. **Habitat:** Estuaries and coasts around British Isles except S. and W. England; a rare visitor. **Notes:** Large gull. Pink legs; no black on wing-tips. (63cm.).

Herring Gull Laridae *Larus argentatus*. **Habitat:** Breeds on coastal cliffs, offshore islands and house roofs in coastal towns; frequents rubbish tips, estuaries and grassland inland; very common.

Herring Gull summer

Herring Gull winter

Herring Gull juvenile

Common Gull Laridae *Larus canus*. **Habitat:** Breeds on cliffs, moors and around lochs in Scotland and Ireland, locally in England; uncommon winter visitor to coasts, wetland and upland lakes elsewhere. **Notes:** Black band on white tail. No red spot on bill. (41cm.)

Common Gull

Black-headed Gull

winter

summer

Black-headed Gull Laridae *Larus ridibundus*. **Habitat:** Breeds on cliffs, reservoirs, lakes (including gravel pits), sewage farms in British Isles; very common, especially in S.

Kittiwake

adult

juvenile

Kittiwake Laridae *Rissa tridactyla*. **Habitat:** Breeds on ledges on steep cliff faces in British Isles; summer visitor. **Notes:** Distinguished from Common Gull by all-black wing tips, black feet, dark diagonal band across wing, and dark neck bar in juvenile. Sociable. (41cm.)

Birds

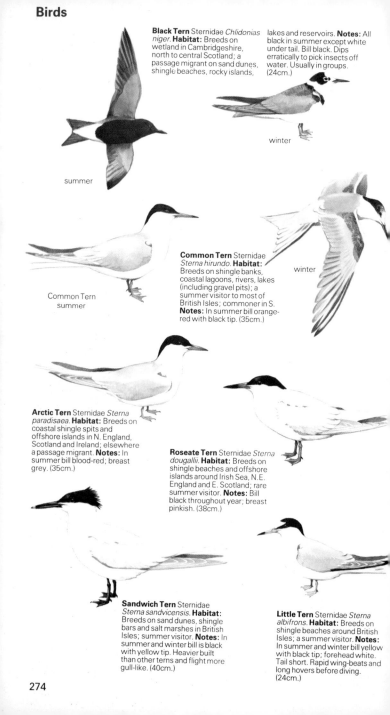

Black Tern Sternidae *Chlidonias niger.* **Habitat:** Breeds on wetland in Cambridgeshire, north to central Scotland; a passage migrant on sand dunes, shingle beaches, rocky islands, lakes and reservoirs. **Notes:** All black in summer except white under tail. Bill black. Dips erratically to pick insects off water. Usually in groups. (24cm.)

summer

winter

Common Tern Sternidae *Sterna hirundo.* **Habitat:** Breeds on shingle banks, coastal lagoons, rivers, lakes (including gravel pits); a summer visitor to most of British Isles; commoner in S. **Notes:** In summer bill orange-red with black tip. (35cm.)

Common Tern summer

winter

Arctic Tern Sternidae *Sterna paradisaea.* **Habitat:** Breeds on coastal shingle spits and offshore islands in N. England, Scotland and Ireland; elsewhere a passage migrant. **Notes:** In summer bill blood-red; breast grey. (35cm.)

Roseate Tern Sternidae *Sterna dougallii.* **Habitat:** Breeds on shingle beaches and offshore islands around Irish Sea, N.E. England and E. Scotland; rare summer visitor. **Notes:** Bill black throughout year; breast pinkish. (38cm.)

Sandwich Tern Sternidae *Sterna sandvicensis.* **Habitat:** Breeds on sand dunes, shingle bars and salt marshes in British Isles; summer visitor. **Notes:** In summer and winter bill is black with yellow tip. Heavier built than other terns and flight more gull-like. (40cm.)

Little Tern Sternidae *Sterna albifrons.* **Habitat:** Breeds on shingle beaches around British Isles; a summer visitor. **Notes:** In summer and winter bill yellow with black tip; forehead white. Tail short. Rapid wing-beats and long hovers before diving. (24cm.)

Razorbill Alcidae *Alca torda*.
Habitat: Breeds on cliffs in
British Isles; coastal waters in
winter. **Notes:** Short neck and
laterally compressed bill. Head
and back blacker than Guillemot.
Tail cocked up when swimming.
In winter throat and sides of
head white. (41cm.)

Fulmar Procellariidae *Fulmarus
glacialis*. **Habitat:** Open sea
during winter; breeds on cliffs
on coasts of Britain and Ireland;
common. **Notes:** Ungainly on
land. Wings narrower than a
gull's. Flight stiff-winged,
gliding. No black wing-tips.
(47cm.)

bridled form

summer

winter

Black Guillemot Alcidae
Cepphus grylle. **Habitat:** Rocky
coasts and cliffs; scarce
resident on W. coast of Scotland
and Ireland. **Notes:** In winter
has mottled head distinguishing
it from Guillemot's black head.
Feet and legs bright orange. On
land adopts sloping stance.
(34cm.)

Guillemot Alcidae *Uria aalge*.
Habitat: Breeds on cliff ledges
on coasts around British Isles,
with largest colonies in
Scotland; winters at sea and in
coastal waters. **Notes:** Browner
than Razorbill; white cheeks in
winter. (42cm.)

Puffin

Puffin Alcidae *Fratercula
arctica*. **Habitat:** Breeds on
inaccessible cliff tops, land slips
and remote islands, mainly on N.
and W. coasts of Britain;
summer visitor; winters at sea.
Notes: In winter bill smaller. In
flight rapid wing-beats and
dumpy outline. Perches upright
but rests horizontally. (30cm.)

Birds

Stock Dove Columbidae *Columba oenas.* **Habitat:** Woodland, parks, gardens, occasionally towns, cliffs, sand dunes throughout British Isles; in farmland and grassland in winter. **Notes:** Smaller and darker than Woodpigeon, lacking white markings. Flight rapid; grey rump and two broken black wing-bars are conspicuous. (33cm.)

Rock Dove Columbidae *Columba livia.* **Habitat:** Common on rocky coasts with caves in W. and N. Britain; as "domestic" pigeons in cities throughout British Isles. **Notes:** Feral domestic pigeons are descended from Rock Dove and have same voice. Distinguished from Stock Dove by white rump and area beneath wings, and two broad black bands across wings. (33cm.)

Turtle Dove Columbidae *Streptopelia turtur.* **Habitat:** Woodland, plantations, wooded heathland, parks, gardens and thick hedgerows in S. Britain; summer visitor and passage migrant. **Notes:** Deeply rounded tail, with white "corners" prominent in flight. Black and white patch on side of neck. Flicking wing-beats in flight. (27cm.)

Woodpigeon Columbidae *Columba palumbus.* **Habitat:** Common in woodland, parks, gardens, farmland with trees throughout British Isles. **Notes:** White neck patch with glossy green border. Broad white wing-band. "Explodes" with noisy wing claps from trees when alarmed. (41cm.)

Collared Dove Columbidae *Streptopelia decaocto.* **Habitat:** Common in trees close to human habitation in town and country and on farmland, throughout British Isles. **Notes:** Distinguished from Turtle Dove by impression of longer tail and paler body. From below, the white terminal half of black tail is diagnostic. (32cm.)

Cuckoo Cuculidae *Cuculus canorus.* **Habitat:** Woodland, moors, reedbeds and farmland throughout British Isles; summer visitor. **Notes:** Flight usually low, hurried and terminating in a long glide. Looks a little like small hawk or falcon, but has longer, pointed tail. Wings pointed. Voice a mellow "cuc-coo", female a bubbling sound. (33cm.)

Barn Owl Tytonidae *Tyto alba*.
Habitat: Grassland, farmland, churchyards and deserted buildings in British Isles. **Notes:** Eyes black. Unstreaked, white underparts. Slow flapping flight, at times wavering on very pale, rounded wings. Nocturnal, but often seen in evening. (34cm.)

Snowy Owl Strigidae *Nyctea scandiaea*. **Habitat:** Breeds on moorland in Scandinavia, occasionally in Shetland; rarely winters in Scotland. **Notes:** Male very large, white owl; female and juvenile barred with grey. Slow, gliding flight. Hunts by day. (53-65cm)

Little Owl Strigidae *Athene noctua*. **Habitat:** Grassland with scattered trees, farmland, sand dunes in England and Wales. **Notes:** Eyes bright yellow. Regularly hunts by day. Perches on telegraph poles, fence posts, etc. Flight low, rapid with deep undulations. Smallest British owl. (22cm.)

Tawny Owl Strigidae *Strix aluco*. **Habitat:** Deciduous woodland, parks, gardens, farmland in Britain; often in trees near buildings. **Notes:** Nocturnal. Eyes black. In flight large head and broad, rounded wings are prominent. Voice a familiar hooting. (38cm.)

Tengmalm's Owl Strigidae *Aegolius funereus*. **Habitat:** Coniferous forests of N. Europe; very rare visitor to N. Britain. **Notes:** Legs and feet heavily feathered. Nocturnal. (25cm.)

Short-eared Owl Strigidae *Asio flammeus*. **Habitat:** Moors, heaths, sand dunes, upland grassland in Scotland and N. England; also in S. Britain and Ireland in winter. **Notes:** Eyes yellow. Regularly hunts by day. Perches on ground adopting slanting rather than upright posture. Harrier-like flight, when pale wing-patches prominent. (38cm.)

Long-eared Owl Strigidae *Asio otus*. **Habitat:** Coniferous plantations and sometimes deciduous woodland in British Isles. **Notes:** Eyes orange. Mainly nocturnal. In flight wings and tail appear longer than Tawny Owl's. Elongated "ear" tufts. (45cm.)

Honey Buzzard Accipitridae *Pernis apivorus*. **Habitat:** Woodland; rare summer visitor to S. England. **Notes:** Juvenile has pale head and streaked under parts. Flight similar to Buzzard. (50-58cm.)

Goshawk Accipitridae *Accipiter gentilis*. **Habitat:** Rare in coniferous and mixed woodland, mainly in Wales and N. Britain. **Notes:** Female larger than male. Fast, skilful hunter. (48-60cm.)

White-tailed Eagle Accipitridae *Haliaeetus albicilla*. **Habitat:** Rocky western coasts; a very rare winter visitor, though reintroduced to Isle of Rhum. **Notes:** Juvenile has dark brown head and tail. (68-90cm.)

Golden Eagle Accipitridae *Aquila chrysaetos*. **Habitat:** Rare on barren mountains and coasts in Scotland and Lake District. **Notes:** Nape colour varies; immature bird has white rump. Broad, slotted wings. Soars and glides. Large. (75-88cm.)

Golden Eagle

Buzzard Accipitridae *Buteo buteo*. **Habitat:** Common in woodland, moorland, farmland with scattered trees, coastal districts, in Scotland, and W. England, Wales and Ulster. **Notes:** Variable plumage. Broad, rounded wings and tail. Habitually soars. (51-56cm.) **Rough-legged Buzzard** *Buteo lagopus* is similar but larger. It winters on moorland in N. and E. Britain. (50-60cm.)

Buzzard

Sparrowhawk Accipitridae *Accipiter nisus*. **Habitat:** coniferous plantations, deciduous woodland, wooded farmland, and wherever there are plenty of trees, throughout British Isles. **Notes:** Female larger than male. Juvenile resembles adult female. Wings rounded unlike falcons. Fast, dashing flight; also flaps and glides alternately. (28-38cm.)

♂

♀

Red Kite Accipitridae *Milvus milvus*. **Habitat:** Rare in upland parks and farmland with plenty of trees, in central Wales. **Notes:** Long wings with large, whitish patch and distinctive forked tail. (62cm.)

279

Marsh Harrier Accipitridae *Circus aeruginosus*. **Habitat:** Rare in wetland with extensive reedbeds in E. Anglia where sometimes breeds; elsewhere a passage migrant. **Notes:** Variable coloration. Note lack white rump. Gentle, floating flight over reeds in search of prey. (48-56cm.)

♀

Marsh Harrier

Hen Harrier Accipitridae *Circ cyaneus*. **Habitat:** Rare in upland grassland, moors, you coniferous plantations, in Scotland, N. England, N. Wale and Ireland; more widesprea on farmland and wetland in winter. **Notes:** Noticeable white rump. Female, brown, male grey. (43-51

♀

♂

Hen Harrier

♂

Montagu's Harrier

Montagu's Harrier Accipit *Circus pygargus*. **Habitat:** Wetland, moors, sand dune mainly in S.W. England; a ra passage migrant. **Notes:** Female resembles fem Hen Harrier. No white in male. Harriers hav long wings and gl briefly near gro with wings raise above back. (41 46cm.)

Osprey Pandionidae *Pandion haliaetus*. **Habitat:** Lakes, rivers, often in open woodland, and on coasts in Scotland, as summer visitor; elsewhere a

scarce passage migrant. **No** Distinctive contrasting plumage. Very long wings noticeable in flight; may hov (51-58cm.)

Hobby Falconidae *Falco subbuteo.* **Habitat:** Neutral and chalk grassland, heaths and farmland with scattered trees in S. England; rare summer visitor. **Notes:** Short tail, long wings; resembles Swift in flight. Female larger than male. (30-36cm.)

Hobby

Peregrine Falconidae *Falco peregrinus.* **Habitat:** Rare on open grassland, moors, coastal cliffs, mountains, also wetland and estuaries in winter; breeds in Scottish Highlands, W. Britain and parts of Ireland; elsewhere a winter visitor. **Notes:** Female larger than male. (38-48cm.)

Peregrine juvenile

Peregrine

Merlin Falconidae *Falco columbarius.* **Habitat:** Breeds on uplands and moors in N. Britain, central Wales, S.W. England; winters on salt marsh and fields; uncommon. **Notes:** Usually flies and perches close to ground. Nests on ground. (37-33cm.)

Merlin

Merlin

Kestrel

Kestrel Falconidae *Falco tinnunculus.* **Habitat:** Grassland, moors, open woodland, rocky coasts – almost ubiquitous throughout British Isles; especially common on motorway verges.

Notes: Female larger than male, and has brown head. Habitually hovers. (33-36cm.)

281

Birds

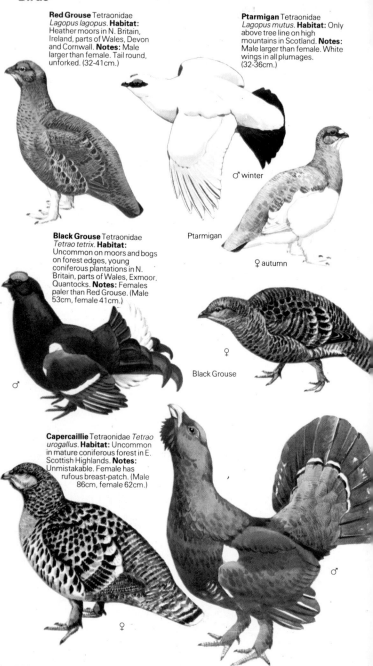

Red Grouse Tetraonidae *Lagopus lagopus*. **Habitat:** Heather moors in N. Britain, Ireland, parts of Wales, Devon and Cornwall. **Notes:** Male larger than female. Tail round, unforked. (32-41cm.)

Ptarmigan Tetraonidae *Lagopus mutus*. **Habitat:** Only above tree line on high mountains in Scotland. **Notes:** Male larger than female. White wings in all plumages. (32-36cm.)

♂ winter

Ptarmigan

♀ autumn

Black Grouse Tetraonidae *Tetrao tetrix*. **Habitat:** Uncommon on moors and bogs on forest edges, young coniferous plantations in N. Britain, parts of Wales, Exmoor, Quantocks. **Notes:** Females paler than Red Grouse. (Male 53cm, female 41cm.)

♀

Black Grouse

♂

Capercaillie Tetraonidae *Tetrao urogallus*. **Habitat:** Uncommon in mature coniferous forest in E. Scottish Highlands. **Notes:** Unmistakable. Female has rufous breast-patch. (Male 86cm, female 62cm.)

♀

♂

Hoopoe Upupidae *Upupa epops*. **Habitat:** Occasionally breeds on woodland edges in S. England; rare summer visitor. **Notes:** Unmistakable, with erectile crest; black and white wings conspicuous in undulating flight. (28cm.)

Red-legged Partridge Phasianidae *Alectoris rufa*. **Habitat:** Farmland, and chalk grassland in England. **Notes:** Prefers to run at approach of danger, but flies swiftly when flushed. Found in flocks (coveys). (34cm.)

Grey Partridge Phasianidae *Perdix perdix*. **Habitat:** Farmland, grassland and hedgerows, in most of British Isles. **Notes:** Walks in crouched attitude, squatting when alarmed. Short, rounded wings; flies low and rapidly. Found in flocks (coveys). (30cm.)

Quail Phasianidae *Coturnix coturnix*. **Habitat:** Grassland and arable farmland throughout British Isles; breeds mainly in S. England; rare summer visitor. **Notes:** Most reluctant to be flushed, especially in breeding season; prefers to hide or run from danger. (18cm.)

Grey Partridge

Quail ♂

Pheasant Phasianidae *Phasianus colchicus*. **Habitat:** Common in woodland, farmland and hedgerows throughout British Isles. **Notes:** Prefers to run for cover, otherwise noisy takeoff, rapid wing-beats and, before landing, a long glide. (65cm.)

Pheasant

♀

♂

Birds

Swift Apodidae *Apus apus.*
Habitat: Aerial, feeds over
towns, open grassland,
woodland, lakes and rivers
throughout British Isles; nests
in buildings and cliffs; common
summer visitor. **Notes:** Long,
scythe-like wings and dark
plumage distinguish it from
Swallow. Flight vigorous and
wheeling with stiffly held wings.
(17cm.)

Nightjar Caprimulgidae
Caprimulgus europaeus.
Habitat: Grassland, open
woodland, moors, heaths and
sand dunes in British Isles;
summer visitor. **Notes:**
Crepuscular. Spends day
crouched motionless along
branch or on ground. Flight light,
floating with aerobatic dashes
after flying insects. (27cm.)

Green Woodpecker Picidae
Picus viridis. **Habitat:**
Deciduous woodland, parks and
large gardens in England and
Wales. **Notes:** Flight alternate
rises with a few wing-beats then
dips with wings closed; yellow
rump prominent. Female lacks
red strip in black "moustache".
(32cm.)

Green Woodpecker

Kingfisher Alcedinidae *Alcedo
atthis.* **Habitat:** Rivers and
streams, ponds and lake
margins, throughout British
Isles, except N. Scotland.
Notes: Solitary. Flight rapid,
usually low; occasionally
hovers. Perches alertly with
nervous "bobbing" action;
dives from perch to catch fish.
(17cm.)

Great Spotted Woodpecker
Picidae *Dendrocopus major.*
Habitat: Associated with trees
in woodland, parks, gardens,
hedgerows in Britain.
Notes: Male has red nape,
juveniles red on forehead;
female no red on head. Drums
rapidly on resonant dead
branches. (23cm.)

Great Spotted
Woodpecker

Lesser Spotted Woodpecker
Picidae *Dendrocopus minor.*
Habitat: Mixed deciduous and
coniferous woodland, parks,
large gardens in England and
Wales. **Notes:** Distinguished
from Great Spotted
Woodpecker by sparrow size,
closely barred back and wings
and no red undertail. (17cm.)

Wryneck Picidae *Jynx torquilla.*
Habitat: Deciduous woodland,
parks and gardens in S.E.
England; very rare summer
visitor. **Notes:** Looks more like
passerine than woodpecker.
Hops with raised tail. (17cm.)

Black Woodpecker Picidae *Dryocopus martius*. **Habitat:** Upland coniferous forest and beech woods in N. and central Europe; not in Britain. **Notes:** Male has distinctive red crown; female a red patch on head. (45cm.)

Swallow Hirundinidae *Hirundo rustica*. **Habitat:** Open grassland, farmland, near buildings throughout British Isles; common summer visitor. **Notes:** Distinguished by long tail streamers, chestnut throat and forehead; dark blue back without rump patch. Flight graceful and aerobatic. Rarely on ground, but often flies close to it. Builds mud nests. (19cm.)

Swallow

House Martin Hirundinidae *Delichon urbica*. **Habitat:** Near human habitation in open grassland and farmland, also quarries and cliffs throughout British Isles; common summer visitor. **Notes:** Pure white underparts and rump. Short, forked tail. Builds mud nests in close colonies. (13cm.)

Sand Martin

Sand Martin Hirundinidae *Riparia riparia*. **Habitat:** Grassland near freshwater; nests in riverbanks, sand quarries and steep banks of bare soil throughout British Isles; common summer visitor.

Notes: Distinguished by brown upper parts and distinct brown chest band; no pale rump. Feeds mainly over water. Flight more fluttering and erratic than Swallow. (12cm.)

Birds

Woodlark Alaudidae *Lullula arborea*. **Habitat:** Uncommon on woodland edges, heaths and farmland in S. Britain. **Notes:** Tail short, white-tipped; eye stripes meet on nape. (15cm.)

Skylark Alaudidae *Alauda arvensis*. **Habitat:** Open areas, grassland, hay meadows, farmland, moors, sand dunes, salt marshes in British Isles. **Notes:** Tail white-edged. Flight strong and undulating. Voice is sustained bubbling trills and warblings delivered only in hovering and fluttering flight. (18cm.)

Crested Lark Alaudidae *Galerida cristata*. **Habitat:** Waste ground, sand-dunes in S.E. England; very rare passage migrant. **Notes:** Similar to Skylark but broader, more rounded with shorter tail. Crest conspicuous. (17cm.)

Shore Lark Alaudidae *Eremophila alpestris*. **Habitat:** Coasts of E. England; uncommon winter visitor. **Notes:** Summer male has two erectile tufts on head. (16cm.)

Spotted Flycatcher Muscicapidae *Muscicapa striata*. **Habitat:** Woodland edges and rides, parks and gardens throughout British Isles; summer visitor. **Notes:** Repeatedly swoops out from perch to seize flying insects then returns to perch. (14cm.)

Pied Flycatcher Muscicapidae *Ficedula hypoleuca*. **Habitat:** Deciduous and coniferous woodland, often in valleys, gardens; uncommon summer visitor; breeds in W. and N. Britain; passage migrant on E. coast and Ireland. **Notes:** In, autumn male resembles female. (13cm.)

Dunnock Prunellidae *Prunella modularis*. **Habitat:** Woodland shrub layer, scrub, hedgerows and gardens throughout British Isles. **Notes:** Skulking; rarely far from ground. Pleasant quiet song. (14.5cm.)

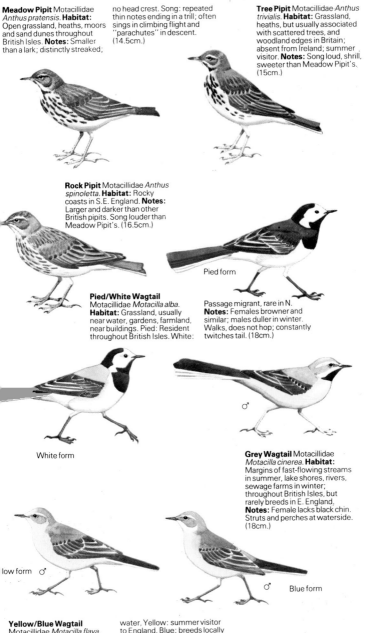

Meadow Pipit Motacillidae *Anthus pratensis*. **Habitat:** Open grassland, heaths, moors and sand dunes throughout British Isles. **Notes:** Smaller than a lark; distinctly streaked; no head crest. Song: repeated thin notes ending in a trill; often sings in climbing flight and "parachutes" in descent. (14.5cm.)

Tree Pipit Motacillidae *Anthus trivialis*. **Habitat:** Grassland, heaths, but usually associated with scattered trees, and woodland edges in Britain; absent from Ireland; summer visitor. **Notes:** Song loud, shrill, sweeter than Meadow Pipit's. (15cm.)

Rock Pipit Motacillidae *Anthus spinoletta*. **Habitat:** Rocky coasts in S.E. England. **Notes:** Larger and darker than other British pipits. Song louder than Meadow Pipit's. (16.5cm.)

Pied/White Wagtail Motacillidae *Motacilla alba*. **Habitat:** Grassland, usually near water, gardens, farmland, near buildings. Pied: Resident throughout British Isles. White: Passage migrant, rare in N. **Notes:** Females browner and similar; males duller in winter. Walks, does not hop; constantly twitches tail. (18cm.)

Pied form

White form

♂

Grey Wagtail Motacillidae *Motacilla cinerea*. **Habitat:** Margins of fast-flowing streams in summer, lake shores, rivers, sewage farms in winter; throughout British Isles, but rarely breeds in E. England. **Notes:** Female lacks black chin. Struts and perches at waterside. (18cm.)

low form ♂

♂   Blue form

Yellow/Blue Wagtail Motacillidae *Motacilla flava*. **Habitat:** Water meadows, wet grassland and farmland near water. Yellow: summer visitor to England. Blue: breeds locally in S.E. **Notes:** Yellow looks like long-tailed Canary. (16.5cm.)

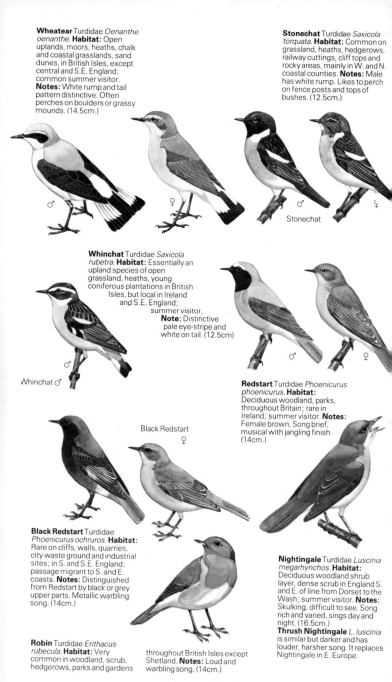

Wheatear Turdidae *Oenanthe oenanthe*. **Habitat:** Open uplands, moors, heaths, chalk and coastal grasslands, sand dunes, in British Isles, except central and S.E. England; common summer visitor. **Notes:** White rump and tail pattern distinctive. Often perches on boulders or grassy mounds. (14.5cm.)

Stonechat Turdidae *Saxicola torquata*. **Habitat:** Common on grassland, heaths, hedgerows, railway cuttings, cliff tops and rocky areas, mainly in W. and N. coastal counties. **Notes:** Male has white rump. Likes to perch on fence posts and tops of bushes. (12.5cm.)

Stonechat

Whinchat Turdidae *Saxicola rubetra*. **Habitat:** Essentially an upland species of open grassland, heaths, young coniferous plantations in British Isles, but local in Ireland and S.E. England; summer visitor. **Note:** Distinctive pale eye-stripe and white on tail. (12.5cm)

Whinchat ♂

Redstart Turdidae *Phoenicurus phoenicurus*. **Habitat:** Deciduous woodland, parks, throughout Britain; rare in Ireland; summer visitor. **Notes:** Female brown. Song brief, musical with jangling finish. (14cm.)

Black Redstart ♀

Black Redstart Turdidae *Phoenicurus ochruros*. **Habitat:** Rare on cliffs, walls, quarries, city waste ground and industrial sites; in S. and S.E. England; passage migrant to S. and E. coasts. **Notes:** Distinguished from Redstart by black or grey upper parts. Metallic warbling song. (14cm.)

Robin Turdidae *Erithacus rubecula*. **Habitat:** Very common in woodland, scrub, hedgerows, parks and gardens throughout British Isles except Shetland. **Notes:** Loud and warbling song. (14cm.)

Nightingale Turdidae *Luscinia megarhynchos*. **Habitat:** Deciduous woodland shrub layer, dense scrub in England S. and E. of line from Dorset to the Wash; summer visitor. **Notes:** Skulking, difficult to see. Song rich and varied, sings day and night. (16.5cm.)
Thrush Nightingale *L. luscinia* is similar but darker and has louder, harsher song. It replaces Nightingale in E. Europe.

Mistle Thrush Turdidae *Turdus viscivorus*. **Habitat:** Woodland, farmland, parks and gardens throughout British Isles. **Notes:** Distinguished from Song Thrush by greyer plumage, upright stance and white "corners" to tail in flight; white underwings. Flight strong and level despite frequent closure of wings. A loud, musical song. (27cm.)

Fieldfare Turdidae *Turdus pilaris*. **Habitat:** Deciduous woodland, particularly birch, fields, grassland, hedgerows and grassland throughout British Isles; common winter visitor. **Notes:** Grey head and neck; in flight prominent grey rump is distinctive. Gregarious. (26cm.)

Mistle Thrush

Fieldfare

Redwing Turdidae *Turdus iliacus*. **Habitat:** Deciduous woodland, young coniferous plantations, fields and hedgerows throughout British Isles; common winter visitor. **Notes:** Pale eye-stripe and reddish flanks and wing linings; streaked breast. Gregarious. (21cm.)

Song Thrush Turdidae *Turdus philomelos*. **Habitat:** Common in woodland, hedgerows, parks and gardens throughout British Isles. **Notes:** Small spots on buff breast; uniform brown upper parts. Flight fast and direct. Pleasant, musical song. (23cm.)

♂

♀

Blackbird Turdidae *Turdus merula*. **Habitat:** Very common in woodland, hedgerows, scrub and gardens throughout British Isles. **Notes:** Male black with yellow bill; female brown. Flight direct, tail raised and fanned when landing. Song: a series of fluty whistled phrases. (25cm.)

Birds

Ring Ouzel Turdidae *Turdus torquatus*. **Habitat:** Mountain slopes, moors, often above tree line, but also among shrubs and on coasts when on passage; in N. and W. British Isles; summer visitor. **Notes:** White gorget on breast and pale wing patch. Flight rapid; dodges behind rocks when approached. (24cm.)

Bluethroat Turdidae *Luscinia sveccia*. **Habitat:** Hedgerows and scrub in S. and E. England; rare passage migrant. **Notes:** Male has blue chin and breast bordered with black, white and red bands. Female has less blue on throat. Warbling song. (14cm.)

Icterine Warbler Sylviidae *Hippolais icterina*. **Habitat:** Woodland, gardens in S.E. England; rare passage migrant. **Notes:** Stocky, yellow and green warbler with square tail. Varied, chattering song. (13cm.)
Melodious Warbler *H. polyglotta* is similar but has more musical song. It replaces Icterine Warbler in S.W. Europe.

Savi's Warbler Sylviidae *Locustella luscinioides*. **Habitat:** Reedbeds in S.E. England; very rare summer visitor. **Notes:** White throat visible when singing. Similar to Grasshopper Warbler. (14cm.)

Cetti's Warbler Sylviidae *Cettia cetti*. **Habitat:** Rare in dense wetland vegetation in extreme S.E. England. **Notes:** unmistakable song beginning with explosive "pwit" and followed by series of staccato, fluty notes. (14cm.)

Whitethroat Sylviidae *Sylvia communis*. **Habitat:** Old grassland, scrub and hedgerows with low, thick cover throughout British Isles; summer visitor. **Notes:** Female has brown hood. Rufous patch on wings. (14cm.)

Lesser Whitethroat Sylviidae *Sylvia curruca*. **Habitat:** Old grassland, scrub and hedgerows with trees in S.E. England; local elsewhere and absent from Scotland and Ireland. **Notes:** Fast rattling song, sometimes a warble. (13.5cm.)

Dartford Warbler Sylviidae *Sylvia undata*. **Habitat:** Scrub and heaths with gorse, mainly in Hants and Dorset; resident but rare. **Notes:** Voice a scolding "tchir-r". (12.5cm.)

Willow Warbler Sylviidae *Phylloscopus trochilus*. **Habitat:** Woodland and wooded heaths, scrub, hedgerows, throughout British Isles except Shetland; common summer visitor. **Notes:** Pale legs. Sweet, descending song, ending in a flourish. (11cm.)

Chiffchaff Sylviidae *Phylloscopus collybita*. **Habitat:** Woodland, scrub, hedgerows throughout British Isles; local in N.E.; common summer visitor. **Notes:** Duller plumage than Willow Warbler. Black legs. Song: "chiff-chaff". (11cm.)

Wood Warbler Sylviidae *Phylloscopus sibilatrix*. **Habitat:** Mature deciduous woodland, particularly beech and oak, in British Isles but local in S.E., N.W. and Ireland; locally common summer visitor. **Notes:** Visible eye-stripe. Song: accelerating trill and repeated "piu". (12.5cm.)

Birds

Goldcrest Sylviidae *Regulus regulus*. **Habitat:** Mainly coniferous woodland, but also mixed and deciduous; hedgerows and gardens in winter; throughout British Isles except Shetland and Orkney; common but inconspicuous. **Notes:** Plump, fine-billed, tiny. Bright crown, double wing-bar. (9cm.)

Firecrest Sylviidae *Regulus ignicapillus*. **Habitat:** Rare in coniferous and mixed woodland, often in shrub and herb layer; scrub; breeds in S England; elsewhere passage migrant. **Notes:** Distinguishe[d] from Goldcrest by head patter[n] (9cm.)

Grasshopper Warbler Sylviidae *Locustella naevia*. **Habitat:** In thick cover in grassland, heaths, scrub, young coniferous plantations and wetland margins, throughout British Isles except N. Scotland; summer visitor. **Notes:** Rounded tail. Characteristic whirring song like winding of fishing reel. (12.5cm.)

Reed Warbler Sylviidae *Acrocephalus scirpaceus*. **Habitat:** Reedbeds in Englan[d] and Wales; local in N. and W.; summer visitor. **Notes:** Repetitive, harsh song. (12.5cm.)

Sedge Warbler Sylviidae *Acrocephalus schoenobaenus*. **Habitat:** Reedbeds, shrubs near water, water margins throughout British Isles; common summer visitor. **Notes:** Conspicuous white eye-stripe. Skulking. Distinctly grating call. (12.5cm.)

♀
Blackcap

♂

Blackcap Sylviidae *Sylvia atricapilla*. **Habitat:** Woodland shrub layer, hedgerows, large gardens throughout British Isles, except far N.; common summer visitor; occasionally overwinters. **Notes:** Rich and tuneful song. (14cm.)

Garden Warbler Sylviidae *Sylvia borin*. **Habitat:** Woodland shrub layer, heaths, scrub, parks and gardens throughout British Isles except for N.; summer visitor. Rich song, more uniform than Blackcap's. (14cm.)

Birds

Nuthatch Sittidae *Sitta europaea*. **Habitat:** Deciduous woodland, parks, gardens with trees in England and Wales. **Notes:** Climbs trees in short jerks in any direction including downwards. Tail not used as support. Hammers nuts wedged in bark. Loud, ringing call "twoit-twoit". (14cm.)

Long-tailed Tit Aegithalidae *Aegithalos caudatus*. **Habitat:** Deciduous and mixed woodland, scrub, heaths, hedgerows, throughout British Isles. **Notes:** Small black, white and pinkish bird with tail over half its length. Tail black with white edges. Northern race has pure white head and whiter underparts. (14cm.)

Treecreeper

Treecreeper Certhiidae *Certhis familiaris*. **Habitat:** Woodland, parks and gardens in Britain and Ireland; fairly common but inconspicuous. **Notes:** Climbs up trees spirally in short spurts with stiff tail pressed against bark. Extracts insects from bark with long, curved bill. Flight jerky. (13cm.)

Wren Troglodytidae *Troglodytes troglodytes*. **Habitat:** Varied, typically in scrub or shrubby woodland, parks, hedgerows and gardens throughout British Isles; common. **Notes:** Plump, tiny bird with cocked tail. Extremely active, forages among leaf litter. Flight straight with whirring wings. Voice a hard scolding "tic-tic-tic" and loud song with buzzing trill. (10cm.)

Dipper Cinclidae *Cinclus cinclus*. **Habitat:** Very characteristic of fast-flowing streams and rivers in W. and N. British Isles; rare elsewhere. **Notes:** "Bobs" on rocks in water. Wades and can feed under water. Flight rapid, usually low following streams. (18cm.)

Bearded Tit Timaliidae *Panurus biarmicus*. **Habitat:** Uncommon in water margins and reedbeds in S. and E. England. **Notes:** Also called Bearded Reedling. Tawny brown, long-tailed; males have conspicuous black "moustaches". Flight laboured on whirring wings. (17cm.)

293

Birds

Great Tit Paridae *Parus major.*
Habitat: Common in woodland, parks, scrub, gardens and hedgerows in Britain and Ireland. **Notes:** Black cap and band down centre of yellow underparts. Flight undulating and of short duration. Main call a loud, repeated "teacher, teacher". (14cm.)

Blue Tit Paridae *Parus caeruleus.* **Habitat:** Common in deciduous woodland, scrub, gardens, hedgerows in Britain and Ireland; absent from Orkney and Shetland. Often near water in winter. **Notes:** Blue cap. Yellow underparts. Flight weaker, more fluttering than Great Tit's. (12cm.)

Great Tit

Coal Tit Paridae *Parus ater.*
Habitat: Common in coniferous woodland; also deciduous woodland, parks and gardens throughout British Isles; absent from Orkney and Shetland.
Notes: Black cap with white "parting" down nape; double white wing-bars. Flight similar to Blue Tit. (12cm.)

Crested Tit Paridae *Parus cristatus.* **Habitat:** Rare in coniferous woodland, especially pine forest; occasionally in mixed and deciduous woodland, particularly in winter; mainly in E. Highlands of Scotland.
Notes: Speckled black and white crest. Seeks food on tree trunks. Less sociable than other tits. (12cm.)

Crested T

Coal Tit

Marsh Tit Paridae *Parus palustris.* **Habitat:** Deciduous woodland, scrub, hedgerows in England and Wales. **Notes:** Glossy black cap and plain brown upperparts. Nests in existing holes in trees. (12cm.)

Willow Tit Paridae *Parus montanus.* **Habitat:** Deciduous, mixed and coniferous woodland, and hedgerows, in England and Wales; especially in damp places in summer.
Notes: Matt black cap. Distinguished from Marsh Tit by pale patch in secondary wing feathers, and harsh, nasal call. (12cm.)

Great Grey Shrike Laniidae *Lanius excubitor.* **Habitat:** Grassland, scrub and hedgerows in N. and E. Britain uncommon winter visitor.
Notes: Aggressive predator. Rambling, grating song. (24cm

Red-backed Shrike Laniidae *Lanius collurio*. **Habitat:** Grassland, scrub, dry heaths, hedgerows; mainly in S.E. England; fairly rare summer visitor. **Notes:** Pointed wings, long tail. Hovers. Female all brown. (17cm.)

Red-backed Shrike

Waxwing ♀

Waxwing Bombycillidae *Bombycilla garrulus*. **Habitat:** Berry-bearing bushes in parks, gardens and hedgerows in town and country in E. Britain; occasionally further W.; winter visitor. **Notes:** Grey rump and lower back. Usually gregarious. (18cm.)

Starling Sturnidae *Sturnus vulgaris*. **Habitat:** Widespread and very common throughout British Isles. **Notes:** In summer has no speckled underparts. Voice: a repertoire of whistles and clicks woven into rambling song; imitates other birds. (21.5cm.)

Hawfinch Fringillidae *Coccothraustes coccothraustes*. **Habitat:** Mature woodland (mainly deciduous), parks, gardens; uncommon and local in England, Wales and Scotland. **Notes:** Voice an explosive "tzik". (18cm.)

Greenfinch Fringillidae *Carduelis chloris*. **Habitat:** Common on woodland edges, farmland, hedgerows, parks and gardens, throughout British Isles. **Notes:** Female browner. Voice a rapid twitter; wheezing "tswee" from male in spring; song a medley of twitters. (14.5cm.)

Goldfinch Fringillidae *Carduelis carduelis*. **Habitat:** Common in woodland edges, farmland, hedgerows, parks and gardens, throughout British Isles except N. Scotland. **Notes:** Liquid, twittering song. (12cm.)

Siskin Fringillidae *Carduelis spinus*. **Habitat:** Breeds in coniferous woodland mainly in Scotland. In winter prefers birch woodland and gardens throughout British Isles; also often seen in alder trees. **Notes:** Females greyer, no black on head. (12cm.)

295

Birds

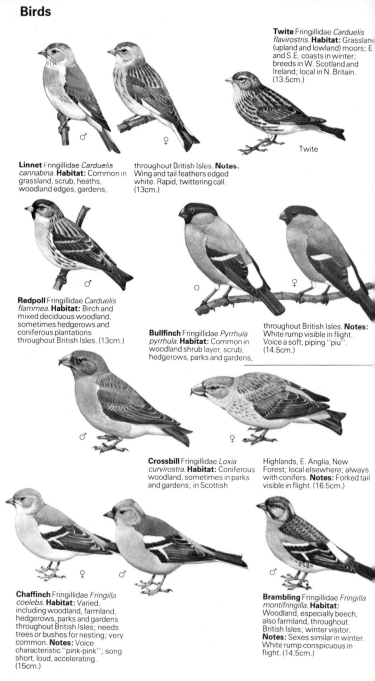

Twite Fringillidae *Carduelis flavirostris*. **Habitat:** Grassland (upland and lowland) moors; E. and S.E. coasts in winter; breeds in W. Scotland and Ireland; local in N. Britain. (13.5cm.)

Twite

Linnet Fringillidae *Carduelis cannabina*. **Habitat:** Common in grassland, scrub, heaths, woodland edges, gardens, throughout British Isles. **Notes.** Wing and tail feathers edged white. Rapid, twittering call. (13cm.)

Redpoll Fringillidae *Carduelis flammea*. **Habitat:** Birch and mixed deciduous woodland, sometimes hedgerows and coniferous plantations throughout British Isles. (13cm.)

Bullfinch Fringillidae *Pyrrhula pyrrhula*. **Habitat:** Common in woodland shrub layer, scrub, hedgerows, parks and gardens, throughout British Isles. **Notes:** White rump visible in flight. Voice a soft, piping "piu". (14.5cm.)

Crossbill Fringillidae *Loxia curvirostra*. **Habitat:** Coniferous woodland, sometimes in parks and gardens; in Scottish Highlands, E. Anglia, New Forest; local elsewhere; always with conifers. **Notes:** Forked tail visible in flight. (16.5cm.)

Chaffinch Fringillidae *Fringilla coelebs*. **Habitat:** Varied, including woodland, farmland, hedgerows, parks and gardens throughout British Isles; needs trees or bushes for nesting; very common. **Notes:** Voice characteristic "pink-pink"; song short, loud, accelerating. (15cm.)

Brambling Fringillidae *Fringilla montifringilla*. **Habitat:** Woodland, especially beech, also farmland, throughout British Isles; winter visitor. **Notes:** Sexes similar in winter. White rump conspicuous in flight. (14.5cm.)

Corn Bunting Emberizidae
Miliaria calandra. **Habitat:**
Grassland, farmland,
hedgerows, open ground in E.
Britain; local in W. and Ireland.
Notes: Song ends with sound
like jangling keys. (18cm.)

Yellowhammer Emberizidae
Emberiza citrinella. **Habitat:**
Common on farmland, in
hedgerows, scrub, woodland
margins, heaths throughout
British Isles. **Notes:** Female and
juveniles browner than male.
Song characteristic, high-
pitched, often rendered as
"little-bit-of bread-and-
no-che-eese"! (16.5cm.)

♂

Cirl Bunting Emberizidae
Emberiza cirlus. **Habitat:**
Scarce on farmland, in
hedgerows, open areas with
scrub and trees, in S. and S.W.
England. **Notes:** Female
resembles female
Yellowhammer but has
chestnut rump. Song a metallic
rattle. (16.5cm.)

♂

Reed Bunting

♀

♂

Snow Bunting Emberizidae
Plectrophenax nivalis. **Habitat:**
Mountain tops and open upland
in summer in N. Scotland (rare);
scarce on shores and grassland
near coasts around British Isles
in winter. **Notes:** Female
resembles winter male.
Summer male has black and
white plumage. Voice: a rolling
twitter. (16.5cm.)

Snow Bunting ♂

Reed Bunting Emberizidae
Emberiza schoeniclus. **Habitat:**
Locally common on wetland, in
reedbeds, wet scrub and wet
heaths, throughout British Isles.
(15cm.)

House Sparrow Passeridae
Passer domesticus. **Habitat:**
Near and in human habitation in
town and country throughout
British Isles; rarely far from

buildings; locally common.
Notes: Vocal, with variety of
cheeps, chirps and twitters.
(14.5cm.)

♀   ♂

Tree Sparrow Passeridae
Passer montanus. **Habitat:**
Woodland, parks and large
gardens throughout British
Isles, but local in W.; prefers
more open land in winter.
Notes: Sexes similar. (14cm.)

297

Golden Oriole Oriolidae *Oriolus oriolus*. **Habitat:** Deciduous woodland in S. England; rare passage migrant. **Notes:** Male bright yellow with black wings and tail; female yellow-green above, grey below. Mellow, whistled song. (24cm.)

Serin Fringillidae *Serinus serinus*. **Habitat:** Hedgerows, light woodland in S. England; rare summer visitor. **Notes:** Male has bright yellow head, dark cheeks and crown; female is duller with heavily black-streaked breast. Voice: cascading song of jingly notes and liquid twitterings. (11cm.)

Chough Corvidae *Pyrrhocorax pyrrhocorax*. **Habitat:** Uncommon on upland and coastal cliffs in parts of Ireland, Wales, Isle of Man and Inner Hebrides. **Notes:** Curved red bill and red legs. More slender than Jackdaw. Flight strong and acrobatic. Sociable. (40cm.)

Lapland Bunting Emberizidae *Calcarius lapponicus*. **Habitat:** North Sea coasts; rare winter visitor. **Notes:** Male has black head and throat, chestnut nape, yellow bill; female has very little chestnut on nape. (15cm.)

Ortolan Bunting Emberizidae *Emberiza hortulana*. **Habitat:** Hedgerows, open grassland in E. England; rare passage migrant. **Notes:** Dull pinkish-brown with greenish-grey head and throat. Song a series of buzzing but melodious notes. (16cm.)

Jay Corvidae *Garrulus glandarius*. **Habitat:** Common in woodland, parks and gardens in British Isles, except N. Scotland. **Notes:** Blue and white wing patches. Prominent white rump. Blue eyes. Flight rather jerky with rounded wings. Often in small, noisy parties. Voice a loud, harsh "skraaak". (34cm.)

Nutcracker Corvidae *Nucifraga caryocatactes*. **Habitat:** Coniferous forests in N. Britain; rare but regular visitor. **Notes:** Chocolate brown with white spots all over body. (31cm.)

Raven Corvidae *Corvus corax*.
Habitat: Scarce on coastal cliffs, mountains and moors in W. and N. British Isles. **Notes:** Big, heavy bird with massive black bill and shaggy throat feathers. Powerful often aerobatic soaring flight. When overhead, wedge-shaped tail is obvious. (64cm.)

Carrion Crow

Carrion Crow, Hooded Crow
Corvidae *Corvus corone*.
Habitat: Ubiquitous throughout British Isles. **Notes:** Heavy, black bill. Flight direct, slow and regular; rarely soars. Solitary or in pairs, except when roosting. Square tail. Voice: a croaking "kraak". (45cm.)

Rook Corvidae *Corvus frugilegus*. **Habitat:** Common on farmland with trees throughout British Isles. **Notes:** Distinguished from Carrion Crow by grey bill with bare grey skin at base. Has faster wing-beats and baggy thigh feathers. Usually gregarious. Voice: a harsh "caw". (46cm.)

Jackdaw Corvidae *Corvus monedula*. **Habitat:** Very common in open woodland, parks with old trees, cliffs, farm buildings, churchyards, houses, throughout British Isles. **Notes:** Distinguished from other crows by grey nape, ear coverts and faster wing-beats. Eyes have very prominent white iris. Gregarious. Jaunty actions in flight. Voice: a high-pitched "chak". (33cm.)

Magpie Corvidae *Pica pica*.
Habitat: Common in grassland with trees, parks, farmland, gardens in suburban and country areas, throughout British Isles. **Notes:** Pied plumage and long tail. Flight rather slow with rapid wingbeats. Often in small parties; larger gatherings in winter. Voice: a harsh chattering. (46cm.)

Mammals

Most European mammals are small, nocturnal or both. Consequently they are not often seen and are difficult to identify. The larger species (e.g. deer) can be watched, often with the aid of binoculars, and are usually fairly distinctive, though some change colour seasonally.

The smaller species pose the biggest problem. They cannot normally be identified with certainty unless they are in the hand. Most of the smaller species are shrews or rodents, for which the only definitive identification characteristics consist of details in the teeth.

Many small mammals are only ever seen dead; sometimes as trophies brought in by cats, and sometimes in owl pellets. Frequently mice, voles and shrews get trapped in discarded bottles and may be identified from their skeletal remains.

Most species may be encountered at any time of the year, even the hibernators (bats, hedgehogs, dormice) which often arouse in warm spells during the winter. The notes on habitat given beneath the illustrations are intended to be a general guide only; many mammals are very specific. Many of the carnivores (e.g. stoat, weasel, otter, polecat) have been extensively persecuted

in the past and are consequently rare or absent from large areas of otherwise suitable habitat. The larger species, particularly deer, find it difficult to disperse in Britain's fragmented and densely inhabited countryside, so tend to have a rather patchy distribution.

Many of Britain's terrestrial mammals have been introduced from abroad (e.g. grey squirrel and mink from N. America; coypu from S. America; rabbit and fallow deer from Europe) but most are now as widespread as our native species. Many species are absent from Ireland having failed to reach there before it was cut off from the mainland by rising sea levels after the last Ice Age. Most species are also naturally absent from the Scottish islands, though introductions (mostly accidental) since the Viking invasions have resulted in their having a rather random variety of small mammal species today.

Britain hosts approximately 15 species of bats, though many of them are very rare and nearly all are declining due to pesticides and habitat disturbance. This long-eared bat is seen approaching an insect prey in its woodland habitat.

Mammals

Lesser Rorqual, Little Piked
Whale Balaenopteridae
Balaenoptera acutorostrata.
Habitat: Open sea and coastal
waters all around Britain,
especially W. coast. **Notes:**
Slender in relation to length.
Blow hole inconspicuous. (Max.
10m.)

Bottle-nosed Whale Ziphiidao
Hyperoodon ampullatus.
Habitat: Open sea and coastal
waters around Britain. **Notes:**
Short snout, large bulbous head.
Young slate grey; adults black;
old males dark brown. Belly
paler. Small dorsal fin. No notch
between tail flukes. (Max. 9m)

Pilot Whale, Blackfish, Caàing
Whale Globicephalidae
Globicephala melaena.
Habitat: Open sea and coastal
waters of N. Atlantic. **Notes:**
Long, slender body; bulbous
head; low dorsal fin with deeply
curved rear edge. All black
except white throat patch. Very
long flippers. Usually occurs in
small schools. (Max. 6m.)

White-beaked Dolphin
Delphinidae *Lagenorhynchus
albirostris.* **Habitat:** Open sea
and coastal waters all around
Britain, especially in North Sea.
Notes: Short white snout; black
back; sides white with black
patches behind fins; white belly.
Fairly large black dorsal fin with
concave rear edge. Tail and
flippers black. Speckled region
behind eyes. Often leaps clear
of water. Usually in large
schools. (Max. 3m.)

Bottle-nosed Dolphin
Delphinidae *Tursiops truncatus.*
Habitat: Open sea and coastal
waters of Britain, chiefly in S.
and W. **Notes:** Occurs in
schools. Slate grey or light
brown (turns dark on stranding).
Prominent beak and dorsal fin,
which has concave rear margin.
Pale streak from beak to
blowhole. (Max 3.5m.)

Common Porpoise
Phocoenidae *Phocoena
phocoena*. **Habitat:** Open sea
and coastal waters all around
Britain. **Notes:** Smallest British
cetacean. Short and stout; head
bulbous; no beak. (Max. 1.8m.)

Common Dolphin Delphinidae
Delphinus delphis. **Habitat:**
Open sea and coastal waters of
S. and W. British Isles;
sometimes in North Sea.
Notes: Small with conspicuous
beak. (Max. 2m.)

Killer Whale, Grampus
Globicephalidae *Orcinus orca*.
Habitat: Open sea and coastal
waters of Britain. **Notes:** Black
back, white belly and patch
behind eye. Blunt head. Very tall
dorsal fin, especially in male.
Singly or in schools. (8-9m.)

Grey Seal Phocidae
Halichoerus grypus. **Habitat:**
Patchily distributed on rocky
shores, offshore islands and in
coastal waters around British
Isles. **Notes:** Colour variable.
Head large, wedge-shaped in
profile; muzzle high, flat-topped,
producing "Roman nose".
Nostrils parallel and separated
below. (Max. 3m.)

Common Seal Phocidae *Phoca
vitulina*. **Habitat:** Coastal
waters, rocky shores and
offshore islands in N.E. British
Isles. **Notes:** Difficult to
distinguish from Grey Seal in
water. Head small, rounded,
with small snout. Nostrils at V
angle, almost touching below.
(1.5-2m.)

Mammals

Hedgehog Erinaceidae *Erinaceus europaeus.* **Habitat:** Parks, gardens, hedgerows, woodland throughout mainland British Isles up to the tree line; many offshore islands. **Notes:** Hesitant gait, rolls up when disturbed, swims and climbs well. Nocturnal but active at dawn and dusk. Snorts and snuffles when hunting. Hibernates.

Pygmy Shrew Soricidae *Sorex minutus.* **Habitat:** All types of habitat where there is plenty of ground cover, including moors, throughout mainland British Isles; absent from Shetland Isles, Scilly and Channel Islands. **Notes:** Paler than common shrew. Tail as long or longer than body and rather thick. Active day and night. Very small.

Common Shrew Soricidae *Sorex araneus.* **Habitat:** Grassland, hedgerows, woodland, heaths, scrub, and occasionally moors, throughout mainland Britain and many offshore islands; absent from Ireland. **Notes:** Almost black back, pale flanks, grey belly with yellow tinge. Young are browner. Pointed nose, small eyes and ears; tail shorter than body. Active day and night.

Water Shrew Soricidae *Neomys fodiens.* **Habitat:** Grassland, including chalk, woodlands, streams, ponds, in mainland Britain; patchy in N. Scotland; absent from Ireland and many offshore islands. **Notes:** Black back, white belly; tail brown above, white below with a keel of hairs; similar long hairs on margins of feet. Active day and night. Not always associated with water.

Mole Talpidae *Talpa europaea.* **Habitat:** Grassland, woodland, country gardens, in mainland Britain; absent from Ireland and most offshore islands. **Notes:** Short black coat. Cylindrical body, large forefeet, small eyes, no external ear flaps. Lives underground and is active day and night. Avoids shallow, stony and boggy acidic soils.

Coypu Capromyidae *Myocastor coypu.* **Habitat:** Wetland in Norfolk and E. Suffolk. **Notes:** Introduced from South America. A very large rodent; shaggy brown fur on back, front fur grey. Webbed hind feet. Prominent orange incisors; squarish muzzle. Almost hairless, scaly tail.

Mammals

Grey Squirrel Sciuridae *Sciurus carolinensis*. **Habitat:** Deciduous woodland, parks, gardens and hedgerows throughout most of England and Wales, central Scotland and central Eire. **Notes:** Arboreal, diurnal, less active in winter when very silver-grey. Summer coat may be very brown.

Red Squirrel Sciuridae *Sciurus vulgaris*. **Habitat:** Woodlands, primarily coniferous, in E. Anglia, N. Wales, N. England, Scotland and Ireland; also on a few islands, including Anglesey and I.O.W. **Notes:** Arboreal with a large bushy tail. Upper parts uniform red-brown but may be paler or darker. Prominent ear tufts in winter. Diurnal.

Beaver Castoridae *Castor fiber*. **Habitat:** Rivers and lakes with wooded banks in Scandinavia; scattered in W. Europe; absent from Britain. **Notes:** Tail broad and flat. Does build dams but often lives in burrows in river banks. Largest European rodent. (1-1.4m.)

Bank Vole Cricetidae *Clethrionomys glareolus*. **Habitat:** Woodland, hedgerows, parks, gardens, garden sheds, waste ground in mainland Britain, S.W. Ireland and some offshore islands. **Notes:** Adult upper fur rich red-brown, under fur grey or cream. Young are greyer. Tail 40-60% as long as body, dark above, paler below. Ears and eyes small. (Head and body 90mm.)

Field Vole Cricetidae *Microtus agrestis*. **Habitat:** Grassland, wetland, vegetated sand dunes, grassy moors, throughout mainland Britain. Absent from Ireland and many islands. **Notes:** Rather shaggy fur, greyish brown above, pure grey below (occasionally tinged with buff). Blunt face, small ears, very short, pinkish tail. Active day and night. (Head and body 9-13cm.)
Root Vole *M. oeconomius* is very similar but larger. It replaces Field Vole in E. Europe. Absent from Britain. (Head and body 11-15cm.)
Common Pine Vole *Pitymys subterraneus* is also similar but smaller, darker, and tunnels underground more than Field Vole. It occurs in W. and central Europe but not in Britain. (Head and body 8-10cm.)

Mammals

Water Vole Cricetidae *Arvicola terrestris.* **Habitat:** Water margins, river banks, grassland, throughout mainland Britain, but local in N. Scotland and some islands; absent from Ireland. **Notes:** Rat sized but tail, ears and muzzle shorter. Fur shaggy, brown or black. Swims and dives well.

Muskrat Muridae *Ondatra zibethicus.* **Habitat:** Well-vegetated wetland and freshwater in N. Europe; formerly feral but now absent from Britain. **Notes:** North American species established as an escape from fur farms. T laterally flattened. Usually see swimming. Feet not webbed. (Head and body 30-40cm.)

Common (Brown) Rat Muridae *Rattus norvegicus.* **Habitat:** Parks, gardens, houses, farmland, rubbish tips, sewers, hedgerows, throughout mainland British Isles and many offshore islands. **Notes:** Adult fur shaggy, grey-brown above, pale grey beneath. Occasionally white or black. Young are greyer and sleeker. (Head and body 28cm, tail shorter.)

Wood Mouse, Long-tailed Field Mouse Muridae *Apodemus sylvaticus.* **Habita** Very common in woodland canopy and floor, hedgerows, farmland, grassland, gardens, rarely in houses, throughout British Isles, except a few offshore islands. **Notes:** Prominent ears and eyes, long tail. Yellowish brown back, white front often with small, isolated yellow chest patch. Juveniles greyer.

Yellow-necked Mouse Muridae *Apodemus flavicollis.* **Habitat:** Scarce in deciduous woodland canopy and floor, hedgerows, field edges, gardens in S. England and Wales; absent from Midlands and most of S.W. **Notes:** Large mouse with rich yellow-brown back, white front, large continuous yellow collar and chest patch. Juveniles greyer. Large eyes and ears, long tail.

Black Rat Muridae *Rattus rattus.* **Habitat:** Docklands and buildings associated with seaports, occasionally urban gardens. **Notes:** Colour variable; all black or brown with grey or cream belly. (Head and body 24cm long, tail usually considerably longer.)

House Mouse Muridae *Mus musculus*. **Habitat:** Houses, farmland, wasteground, hedgerows in vicinity of buildings, in Britain, Ireland and many offshore islands. **Notes** Uniform grey above, slightly lighter below. Tail about same length as head and body and rather scaly.

Harvest Mouse Muridae *Micromys minutus*. **Habitat:** Grassland, some arable farmland, hedgerows, water margins, where vegetation tall and dense, mainly south of a line from Humber to Bristol Channel; occasionally as far north as Edinburgh; absent from Ireland. **Notes:** Small, golden-yellow animal with small ears and long prehensile tail. Young lack white front of adult. Makes spherical nest 30-60cm up in vegetation.

Garden Dormouse Gliridae *Eliomys quercinus*. **Habitat:** Woodland, scrub, gardens in most of Europe, but not in Britain. **Notes:** Black markings on face, large ears and tuft of black and white hairs at tail tip distinctive. Very agile climber. Strictly nocturnal. (Head and body 10-17cm.)

Dormouse Gliridae *Muscardinus avellanarius*. **Habitat:** Rare in deciduous woodland shrub layer, coppice (particularly hazel), hedgerows, in England and Wales. **Notes:** Bushy tail, bright orange-brown back, pale buff belly and white throat. Eyes large. Juveniles greyer. Agile climber. Nests usually up in vegetation in summer, near or below ground in winter.

Fat Dormouse Gliridae *Glis glis*. **Habitat:** Deciduous and coniferous woodland canopy, house roofs, in the Chiltern hills. **Notes:** Uniform greyish brown upper fur, dark rings around eyes, whitish belly, slightly darker stripes on outside of legs. Big, bushy tail. Agile climber. (Head and body up to 17.5cm.)

Rabbit Leporidae *Oryctolagus cuniculus*. **Habitat:** Farmland, hedgerows, chalk grassland, parks and country gardens, heaths; throughout mainland British Isles up to tree line; on many offshore islands. **Notes:** Coat colour variable from white through brown to black. Mainly nocturnal but active by day if undisturbed.

Mammals

Brown Hare Leporidae *Lepus capensis.* **Habitat.** Wide, open, grassy places, especially chalk grassland, fields and arable farmland, throughout mainland Britain on low ground; a few (introduced) in Ireland, Hebrides and Shetland. **Notes:** Usually warm brown above, but black, white and sandy coloured animals occur occasionally. Underside white; ears long and black tipped; top of tail dark. Long hind legs and loping gait.

Mountain Hare Leporidae *Lepus timidus.* **Habitat:** Upland grassland and moorland in Highlands and Lowlands of Scotland, Pennines, N. Wales; also in lowland grassland in Ireland. **Notes:** Smaller than Brown Hare, with shorter ears, greyer coat, no black top to tail. Summer coat greyish brown, winter coat wholly or partly white.

Polecat Mustelidae *Mustela putoris.* **Habitat:** Farmland, woodland, wetland, river banks, sand dunes in Wales (except Anglesey and border counties). **Notes:** Distinguished from mink by lighter colour and white facial band and ear margins; from ferrets by (usually) darker colour and more restricted facial band.

Stoat Mustelidae *Mustela erminea.* **Habitat:** Grassland, wetland, woodland, moors and upland grassland, throughout British Isles, except a few islands. **Notes:** Summer coat brown above, yellowish below. Winter coat (in north) white. Tail tip always black. Active day and night.

Fox Canidae *Vulpes vulpes.*
Habitat: Woodland, farmland, sand dunes, parks and gardens in town and country, throughout mainland British Isles and on a few islands. **Notes:** Erect black-backed ears; slender muzzle; bib of throat and tail tip often white; black socks; red-brown back; grey belly.

Mink Mustelidae *Mustela vison.* **Habitat:** River banks and by water; patchily distributed throughout mainland British Isles. **Notes:** Introduced from America; dark brown, sometimes with white chin patches. May be pale brown, grey or white. Slightly bushy tail. Swims well.

Ferret Mustelidae *Mustela furo.*
Habitat: Farmland and woodland in Isle of Man, Anglesey, Renfrew, Yorkshire; occasionally elsewhere in British Isles. **Notes:** Dark form can be mistaken for Polecat, but has more white on face and throat. Albino pelage common.

Weasel Mustelidae *Mustela nivalis.* **Habitat:** Grassland, wetland, hedgerows, moors and uplands, in mainland Britain; absent from Ireland and most islands. **Notes:** Small and very fast-moving. Back rusty red to light sandy tan; underparts white, sometimes blotched with brown. Tail rather short, tip never black. Active day and night.

Mammals

Beech Marten Mustelidae *Martes foina.* **Habitat:** Deciduous woodland in S. and Central Europe. Absent from British Isles. **Notes:** Very similar to Pine Marten but has white throat patch.

Pine Marten Mustelidae *Martes martes.* **Habitat:** Upland woodlands (particularly mixed conifer and deciduous canopy and floor, also moors, in Scottish Highlands and Ireland; occasionally in N. England, Lake District and Wales. **Notes:** Long bushy tail. Rich chocolate brown with creamy orange throat patch. Juveniles lighter. Partly arboreal but hunts on ground. Active day and night.

Badger Mustelidae *Meles meles.* **Habitat:** Deciduous woodland, hedgerows, farmland, quarries, moors, rubbish tips, in mainland British Isles; also in Anglesey and I.O.W. **Notes:** White head with continuous black stripe on each side; greyish back; legs black, short and powerful; short, bushy tail.

Otter Mustelidae *Lutra lutra.* **Habitat:** Rivers and streams, coasts of Scotland (and some islands) and Ireland; rare in mainland Britain. **Notes:** Long body, short legs, flat head, small ears, prominent whiskers, long tapering tail. Webbed feet. Brown with pale throat. Swims smoothly with V-wake

Wild Cat Felidae *Felis sylvestris*. **Habitat:** Upland woodland and coniferous plantations in N. Scotland, now spreading south of Highlands. **Notes:** Larger than domestic cat. Buff or grey cross-striped with black or grey. Short, bushy tail with blunt, black tip. Heavy head, ears held horizontal; long legs.

Pony Equidae *Equus caballus*. **Habitat:** Local in upland grassland, moors, occasionally in woodland and on seashore; feral herds in New Forest, Dartmoor, Exmoor, Wales, Lake District, Northumberland, Shetland, Hebrides, W. Ireland. **Notes:** Similar to domestic stock, but tends to be small. Shaggy coat of variable colour.

Wild Boar Suidae *Sus scrofa*. **Habitat:** Deciduous woodland in most of Europe except Britain and Scandinavia. **Notes:** Male has tusks. Young are striped. Similar to domestic pig but with longer snout.

Mammals

Red Deer Cervidae *Cervus elaphus*. **Habitat:** Moors, upland woodlands and coniferous plantations, in Scotland, N.W. England and S.W. Ireland; scattered populations elsewhere in British Isles. **Notes:** Large, red-brown deer, no spots; pale rump patch including tail. Tail shorter than ear. Males usually have antlers which are shed in March/April. New antlers grown by August. Calves usually spotted.

Fallow Deer Cervidae *Dama dama*. **Habitat:** Coniferous and deciduous woodland, woodland rides, farmland, throughout most of England, parts of Wales and Ireland. **Notes:** Coat white to nearly black, commonly reddish fawn with white spots on flanks and back. Black stripe on back in summer. Winter coat paler. Tail white with black top. Antlers of male palmate. Fawns similar colour to adult summer coat.

Goat Bovidae *Capra hircus*.
Habitat: A few small feral groups on upland grassland in Scotland, N. Wales and Ireland.
Notes: Variable colour from white to dark brown. Shaggy hair. Pair of large horns.

Elk Cervidae *Alces alces*.
Habitat: Near lakes and rivers in forests in Scandinavia. **Notes:** Largest deer. Often solitary. Only males have antlers. (2.2m at shoulder.)

Roe Deer Cervidae *Capreolus capreolus*. **Habitat:** Coniferous and deciduous woodland, woodland rides, farmland, throughout most of Scotland, S. and S.W. England, parts of E. Anglia. **Notes:** A small deer. Small tail (appears tail-less). Black nose, white chin. White tail patch erected when alarmed. Back sandy or red-brown in summer, grey-brown in winter. Belly pale. Male has small, spiky antlers. Fawn has spotted coat.

Mammals

Over 15 species of bats have been recorded in Britain. Many are difficult to identify in the hand and most are impossible to identify in flight. Our bats form two distinct families – the horseshoe bats (Rhinolophidae) and 'ordinary' bats (Vespertilionidae).

Greater Horseshoe Bat
Rhinolophidae *Rhinolophus ferrumequinum*. **Habitat:** Rare in farmland and grassland in limestone areas in S. and W. England and Wales. **Notes:** Body rotund; wings broad, rounded. Fleshy spike projects between eyes. Hibernates in caves and sometimes cellars, hangs by feet with wings wrapped around body. (Wingspan 34cm.)

Lesser Horseshoe Bat
R. hipposideros is similar, but has tiny body (35mm), and wingspan of 25cm.

The vespertilionid bats have narrow, pointed wings and lack the fleshy facial elaborations seen in rhinolophids. They can all fold their wings and use them like forelegs to scramble about, and all have a narrow, pointed tragus. The largest genus is *Myotis* and its species are very difficult to differentiate; some of the more distinctive ones are shown here. Size, face colour, tail structure and tragus are critical features. (The tragus is a thin 'spear' of skin in the ear; calcar is a stiff 'spur' from the heel along trailing edge of tail membrane.)

Daubenton's Bat
Vespertilionidae *Myotis daubentonii*. **Habitat:** Parks, farmland and woodland, especially near water, throughout England, Wales and most of Scotland. **Notes:** Snub-nosed, with pinkish muzzle; ears rounded, brown, about same length as snout when folded forward. Calcar arises half way up shin; feet large. (Wingspan 22.5cm.)

Bechstein's Bat
Vespertilionidae *Myotis bechsteini*. **Habitat:** Very rare, in grassland and woodland in S.W., north to Shropshire. **Notes:** Ears very long, one and a half times length of snouth. Distinguished from long-eared bat by ears not meeting at the base.

Whiskered Bat
Vespertilionidae *Myotis mystacinus*. **Habitat:** Parks, gardens, farmland, woodland throughout England and Ireland. **Notes:** A small bat. Face dark, ears upright, pointed; feet small, calcar arises at heel. (Wingspan 22cm.)

Natterer's Bat Vespertilionidae *Myotis nattereri*. **Habitat:** Parks, gardens, farmland and grassland throughout England, Ireland and S. Scotland. **Notes:** Face brownish or red; longish snout; ears brown at tips, pink at base, extend beyond tip of snout if folded forward; tail membrane baggy; belly white. (Wingspan 28cm.)

Mouse-eared Bat
Vespertilionidae *Myotis myotis*.
Habitat: Very rare in farmland and woodland in Dorset and Sussex. **Notes:** Ears about same length as snout. Britain's biggest bat. (Wingspan 40cm; body 7cm.)

Five other genera of vespertilionids are resident in Britain. All are quite distinct, but several have two very similar species that are hard to tell apart. No attempt is made here.

Long-eared Bats
Vespertilionidae *Plecotus sp*.
Habitat: Woodland and houses throughout Britain, except N. Scotland. **Notes:** Ears as long as body, meet at their bases on top of head; snout rounded; tragus broad. Two species, difficult to distinguish. (Wingspan 25cm.)

Barbastelle Vespertilionidae *Barbastella barbastellus*.
Habitat: Rare in woodland and gardens in Wales and S. England. **Notes:** Almost black, face appears squashed. Ears broad, almost rectangular; bases meet on top of head. (Wingspan 26cm.)

Serotine Vespertilionidae *Eptesicus serotinus*. **Habitat:** Houses and woodland, mainly in S. and E. England. **Notes:** Large. Ears pointed and black; tragus narrow. Fur dark at base with paler tips giving grizzled appearance. Last section of tail projects beyond membrane. Hibernates and breeds in house roofs. (Wingspan 36.5cm.)
Northern Bat *E. nilsonii* is similar, but smaller and paler. It replaces Serotine in Scandinavia but is absent from Britain.

Noctule Vespertilionidae *Nyctalus noctula*. **Habitat:** Woodland and houses in England and Wales; replaced in Ireland by a similar species. Leisler's bat (*N. leisleri*). **Notes:** Large, long-winged bat. Fur bronze colour; ears short, rounded; tragus almost semicircular. Hibernates in house roofs and decaying trees. Flight fast, direct. (Wingspan 36cm.)

Pipistrelle Vespertilionidae *Pipistrellus sp*. **Habitat:** Houses, gardens and woodland throughout Britain, including many islands. **Notes:** Ears and tragus short and blunt. Fur brown all over. Hibernates in house roofs and decaying trees. Flight fluttery, gyrating. Britain's smallest bat. (Wingspan 21cm; body 30mm.)

319